Jonathan Hunter

Embracing Life, International Copyright © 1998
by Embracing Life Ministries
Pasadena, California

Embracing Life Series: International copyright © 1998 Embracing Life Ministries

Printed in the United States of America

Xulon Press   www.xulonpress.com

ISBN 1-60034-160-8

All rights reserved. No part of this publication may be reproduced, stored in a retrieval system or transmitted in any form by any means—for example, electronic, photocopy, recording—without the prior written permission of Embracing Life Ministries. The only exception is brief quotations in printed reviews.

Unless otherwise noted, all Scripture quotations are taken from the HOLY BIBLE, NEW INTERNATIONAL VERSION®. NIV® Copyright © 1973, 1978, 1984 by the International Bible Society. Used by permission. All rights reserved.

When quoting authors' work or the Bible, we have respected their/its particular capitalization in reference to deity.

Scripture quotations marked NASB are taken from the NEW AMERICAN STANDARD BIBLE. Copyright © 1960, 1962, 1971, 1972, 1973, 1975, 1977 by the Lockman Foundation. Used by permission.

Specified excerpts from THE SPIRIT OF THE DISCIPLINES: UNDERSTANDING HOW GOD CHANGES LIVES by Dallas Willard. Copyright © 1989 By Dallas Willard. Reprinted by permission of HarperCollins Publishers, Inc.

Specified excerpts from LIFE TOGETHER by Dietrich Bonhoeffer. English translation copyright © 1954 by Harper & Brothers, copyright renewed 1982 by Helen S. Doberstein. Reprinted by permission of HarperCollins Publishers, Inc.

Special recognition to the painter Claude Monet, 1840–1926, Giverny, France, the father of Impressionism, the visual theme used for this series.

Acknowledgements

First, this project would never have been developed if not for Andy Comiskey, the founder and director of Desert Stream Ministries. It was our "chance" meeting back in 1984 which eventually led to this publication. Our relationship over the years has borne much fruit—too bountiful to mention here. Suffice it to say that by taking me under his wing and inviting me to be a part of the Desert Stream staff, I have been the beneficiary of some of the finest ministry and godly leadership one could ever be blessed to receive.

I want to express my heartfelt gratitude to Beth Webb, my former assistant of nine years at Embracing Life, formerly ARM. Beth not only wrote chapters twelve and thirteen of *ELS*, but helped bring form and insight to all the other chapters as well. Her dedication to the ministry and the imprint she has left are, in no small part, represented here. The rest can be found in the testimonies of the many lives she touched over the years.

I also thank Brad Sargent for his contribution to Session Four and for his help in initially pulling the material together and giving it form.

Special gratitude also goes out to friend and former board member Rev. Tim Fearer for all his time and efforts copy editing *ELS*. His input was invaluable to me. So, too, were the generous contributions by Cathy Hernandez, John Bills and Jon Bogart. Their corrections and insightful comments were essential for the rewrites.

To Mike Rutland I owe thanks for the layout of the workbook—I so appreciated his enthusiasm in designing the look of it. And to Vivian Soo, Dale DeMarchi and Annette Comiskey, I offer many thanks for creating the production schedule. I'd still be dreaming about finishing *ELS* if not for them. For the new, revised edition of *ELS*, much thanks goes to Andrea Hunter, who's editing and attention to detail is greatly appreciated.

Finally, I need to acknowledge the participants in our support groups over the years who shared their pain and victories with us. Their experiences are woven into the teachings throughout *ELS*.

May Jesus Christ, the wellspring of Life, receive all the glory and honor due His name for His love and faithfulness to us all.

Embracing Life Series

Table of Contents

Session 1
Introduction to *Embracing Life Series* — 7

Session 2
Created in the image of God — 17

Session 3
Overview of an illness — 35

Session 4
Treatments and faith — 53

Session 5
Facing death and dying — 61

Session 6
Transformation and the role of the cross — 79

Session 7
Our new identity — 87

Session 8
Forgiveness, the beginning of healing — 93

Session 9
Shame, self-hatred and listening prayer — 117

Session 10
Breaking free from the spirit of death — 129

Session 11
Cultivating intimacy with Jesus — 139

Session 12
Developing a devotional life — 161

Session 13
Taking your place in the body of Christ — 181

Bibliography — 201
Embracing Life Ministry Information — 204

Introduction — Session 1

NOTES

The foundational Scripture for the *Embracing Life Series* is John 10:10 where Jesus says: "I came that they may have life, and have it to the full." Ever-increasing life in a relationship with Jesus Christ is the focus and goal of the *Embracing Life Series*. Over the next fourteen weeks it is our desire that your spirit would be refreshed and invigorated, your mind renewed, your emotions healed and your body strengthened as you encounter the living God. The material is designed to assist you and your group in that encounter. May God bless you as you pursue the full measure of life, hope and peace Jesus has in store for you.

Author's testimony & history of the series

My involvement in AIDS ministry and the writing of this series were not entirely born out of my background and medical condition. My homosexual struggles and the dynamics of my dysfunctional family (see extended testimony in the pages following chapter thirteen) certainly gave me empathy for the emotional pain of many AIDS patients I would visit over the years. However, nothing in my childhood prepared me for the physical devastation I would witness time and time again in the bodies of men, women and children dying of AIDS.

Prior to becoming a Christian, I had visited hospitals only a handful of times and most of my hospital experience was at my mother's deathbed when I was seventeen. As an adult, I went on to pursue acting as a career hoping never to darken the threshold of a hospital again. It is somewhat ironic that after my spiritual conversion I would end up spending so much time in the very facilities I vowed to permanently avoid. Such are the mysterious ways of the Lord!

Session 1 — Introduction

NOTES

In 1984, I went through the Living Waters program, Desert Stream Ministries' healing group for sexual and relational brokenness. Then, for the first time in my life, I acquired language and understanding for the sexual struggles I had experienced and the healing I so desired.

Although AIDS was already big news at the time, generalized testing was only just beginning. Having been abstinent and healthy for several years, I felt certain I was uninfected. When I did eventually get tested it came as quite a shock I was HIV positive.

Even prior to getting tested, the Lord had already given me a burden for persons with AIDS. This happened as I watched countless news stories of people vowing to beat the disease through positive thinking or a medical breakthrough. No mention of God's help was ever made. Neither seemed likely to work without the Lord's intervention. Thus, out of a sincere desire to share the transforming hope of Christ to those trapped in the hopelessness of AIDS, the beginnings of a ministry emerged.

Embracing Life was originally formed under the name AIDS Resource Ministry (ARM) in 1986. ARM began in 1985 as a small intercessory prayer group and rapidly evolved into a visitation ministry after requests came into Desert Stream's office from persons with AIDS seeking help. At that time there were no Christian support groups in the greater Los Angeles area for men and women infected with HIV. So, in 1987, a small gathering of HIV clients met in my home for what eventually would become the *Embracing Life Series*.

The *Embracing Life Series* (*ELS*) began as a bi-weekly support group focusing on the general prayer needs of the HIV positive adults who attended. Over time, recurring themes emerged; this led us to put together a series of teachings for persons with life-altering conditions. ELS used in a closed-group format offers participants a safe, reliable context in which teaching, healing prayer and heartfelt sharing can occur.

Introduction

Session 1

What subjects does ELS cover?

Over the course of fourteen weeks, *Embracing Life Series* addresses major issues in ministry to persons living with life-altering illnesses.

Several lessons do contain medical information about the treatment of AIDS, however the content of *ELS*, is not intended to be HIV-specific. Overall, the material addresses the unchanging reality of human frailty and God's life-giving power and utter dependability.

Several group leaders have asked if lessons could be extracted or adapted for their particular group, thus avoiding the necessity of having to create one from scratch. By making adjustments to the terms as needed, there is sufficient material to form a core teaching for groups dealing with various life-altering illnesses. Leaders are encouraged to adjust the material to the needs of their particular ministry. Lessons can be extracted or adapted as necessary and presented with personal creativity as well.

The topics include:

Session 1: Introduction to *Embracing Life Series*

Session 2: Created in the image of God

Session 3: Overview of an illness

Session 4: Treatments and faith

Session 5: Facing death and dying

Session 6: Transformation and the role of the cross

Session 7: Our new identity

Session 8: Forgiveness, the beginning of healing

Session 9: Shame, self-hatred and listening prayer

Session 10: Breaking free from the spirit of death

Session 11: Cultivating intimacy with Jesus

Session 12: Developing a devotional life

Session 13: Taking your place in the body of Christ

Session 14: Testimonies from the group

NOTES

Session 1 — Introduction

NOTES

What does an ELS meeting look like?

A typical schedule for a weekly meeting

Time	Activity
6:15 pm	Leader, co-leader(s) and worship leader meet to pray for the meeting.
7:00	Group begins. Short opening prayer and worship.
7:30	Worship ends with Scripture reading and/or prayer as leader(s) feel led. Announcements of upcoming events, etc. may follow.
7:45	Weekly teaching may involve questions and interaction with participants depending on chapter content and style of leader.
	Some teachings need to be split up (at leader's discretion) so that a break is available. Others can be completed in 45 minutes, concluding with prayer.
8:30	Break for refreshments.
8:40	Time for small group (gender specific) and ministry or teaching may be resumed with large group ministry at end, as indicated in bold print thoughout the series.
9:15-9:30	Evening concludes with short prayer.

We begin each meeting with a time of worship lasting about thirty minutes. We sing songs of praise and thanksgiving to God for all the healing He desires to pour upon and through us during our time together. During the worship time, worldly cares are washed away and our hearts prepared for the Lord.

At the end of our time of worship, we pray for the session, followed by the teaching, group interaction and more personal prayer ministry. Group and individual prayer must be an integral component throughout the *Embracing Life Series* for the teachings to be truly effective. This last segment can occur in small groups depending on the need and number of participants.

Introduction

Session 1

Requirements for involvement

1. Interviews are conducted with applicants before acceptance into the series.
2. A "Release from Liability Agreement" is signed by all participants to protect the host ministry. This may or may not be necessary for your group. Check with your pastoral oversight.
3. Attendance for the whole series is urged, although illnesses and emergencies naturally occur. Participants need to be informed that being absent more than three times will result in being dropped from the group (discretion advised).
4. The series involves prayers which invite the Holy Spirit to come and heal as He desires. If one is accepted and chooses to attend, respect should be given to the different denominational beliefs and expressions of each person by both the group leader and its members.

Group rules

1. Strict confidentiality should be kept by all participants concerning what is shared or prayed about in the context of the series. The leaders of the program may share information about the participants with each other only when necessary for more insight and care for the group's welfare.
2. Participants in *ELS* benefit most from learning to listen. Advice giving, lecturing, and excessive sharing can disrupt the meetings. Brevity enables everyone a chance to participate.
3. Respect for the boundaries of others (their readiness to share and disclose) must be honored. Perceived violations should be taken up with the leader privately and worked out together with the purported offender.

NOTES

Session 1   Introduction

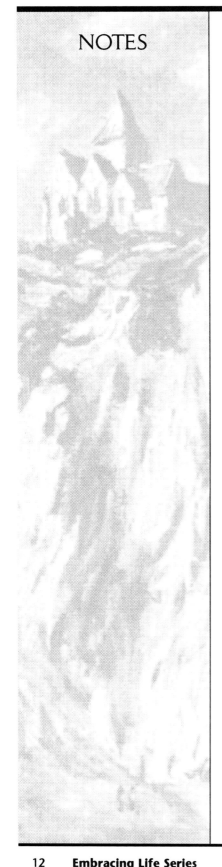

NOTES

How to use this notebook

While some people may prefer to go through the notebook material on their own, it is important to note that the series was written with a group format in mind. Hence, the exercises and prayers are more effective in that setting.

Facilitators pass out notebooks and go over them during the first part of the introductory meeting before testimonies are shared.

Participants should acquaint themselves with the next week's teaching by reading it over ahead of time. (This also applies to the supplemental reading if provided for that week.) Participants complete the reflections, questions and journaling at the end of each chapter at home after the teaching has taken place.

Leaders can and should include their own anecdotal experience in the teaching time. Bringing in other teachers to speak on the various topics can also be enriching for the group.

Leaders need to acquaint themselves ahead of time with the group questions interspersed throughout the teachings. Sometimes special preparation is needed. For example: At the end of Session Two, *all* participants take adhesive badges stating their name and condition/illness (e.g. Bob: cancer) and affix them to a cross. [Note: this necessitates that a large cross and badges are present and in place at the beginning of Session Two.]

Homework

Most chapters end with homework. Homework includes Scripture readings, supplemental readings and journaling suggestions. Because time in the group is limited it is important to do the homework and apply it practically through interaction with others in familial, social and church relationships.

Use the scriptural readings in prayer time at home. Regular, solitary time with the Lord spent in prayer, meditation and journaling are integral and vital elements necessary for one's healing and maturation in Christ.

Participants wanting guidelines for Scripture reading, prayer and journaling can refer to the supplemental reading following Session Twelve, "Developing a Devotional Life." Search out a way that works for you. *Do the homework!*

Introduction

Session 1

Testimonies at the beginning and end

In Session One, after going over the notebooks and agenda for the series, each person, including the group leaders, shares a brief, five minute testimony. Keep it short and succinct! Ask them to give their name and perhaps home church, and how they came to hear about *ELS*. Leaders may wish to give a slightly longer version.

Each person will be asked to write his or her testimony, due the fourteenth week. Much of it can be based on their answers to the weekly questions at the end of the chapter.

We ask that each member have their testimony finished and prepared to read on the last meeting date. *This is required of everyone, except the leaders.* A written testimony serves as an important witness and reminder of the healing work God has accomplished. The length can vary from one page to several depending on how the Lord leads. The participant's testimony could be used later for a presentation at church, in other group settings, or simply as a record of what the Lord has done in their life. Two versions of the author's testimony are included in the supplemental pages following this session and Session Thirteen.

Life in ever-increasing measure

Essentially, *ELS* is a healing discipleship group that promotes spiritual emotional and physical health in practical, prayerful ways. The outcome is greater intimacy with the Lord and authority over the spirit of death. However, ever-increasing life in and with Christ means risking, pressing through unfamiliar territory with Him and letting go of old familiar habits. For those of us with life-altering conditions, that poses quite a challenge. Though our medical diagnosis may seem to have limited us, we can continue growing in Christ with ever-increasing measure if we follow His lead. Gerald May writes in his book *Addiction and Grace*:

> Instead of leading to absolute quietude and serenity, true spiritual growth is characterized by increasingly deep risk taking. Growth in faith means a willingness to trust God more and more, not only in those areas of our lives where we are most successful, but also, and most significantly, at those levels where we are most vulnerable, wounded and weak. It is where our personal power seems most defeated that we are given the most profound opportunities to act in true faith. (*May*, p. 128)

NOTES

Session 1   Introduction   **Embracing Life Series**   13

Session 1 — Introduction

NOTES

My personal prayer for you is that our Lord Jesus Christ would use the contents of the *Embracing Life Series* to adjust the lens through which you presently view life. I pray you experience life and peace and hope more tangibly and powerfully—as I have—through this series.

Jesus prayed to the Father: "I have made You known to them *and will continue to make You known* in order that the love You have for me may be in them and that I myself may be in them." (John 17:26) [italics J.H.]

May His life and His love unfold within you in great measure as you seek Him diligently throughout our time together.

Readings

Testimony of Jonathan Hunter

I was involved in the gay lifestyle for ten years. However, I struggled with homosexuality from a very early age. I know now that those strong same-sex attractions I felt in my formative years were a manifestation of legitimate deep emotional needs that had gone unmet by my father. These deprivations were later acted out in erotic homosexual fantasy and behavior.

In my teens I got involved with drugs and alcohol—addictive behavior inherent in my family. Unfortunately, at the time, no one informed me of the reality and power of Jesus Christ to transform lives. The Lord remained a mere abstract principle and an outdated one at that. However, in December of 1979 a near-death experience from an accidental drug overdose forced me to acknowledge the purposelessness of my life. Miraculously, a year to the day of the overdose, I was baptized as a new believer in Christ.

Through compassionate, redemptive counsel and ministry over the years that followed, I grew in my understanding and experience of Jesus' ability to heal my sexual and emotional brokenness. This led me to share my testimony with others from the "background," notably to a friend of mine who had AIDS. Five months before he died, he accepted the Lord. Out of this experience the AIDS Resource Ministry (ARM) was begun.

In the fall of 1985, I had the HIV antibody test for the first time, convinced I would test negative. When the results came back positive I was crushed and incredulous. My naive faith assumed I was impervious to the virus. This assumption was based upon four years of sexual abstinence and change of lifestyle, plus my standing as a new creature in Christ. My new "condition" was quite an affront to my theology. My only recourse, besides giving up, was to immerse myself in community prayer and support. Very quickly I learned that without these ongoing sustaining relationships my lifeline to the Lord would be, at best, fragile against the onslaught of AIDS and its' wake of hopelessness and despair.

Time and many struggles have passed since that first HIV test. In the meantime, I have learned some indispensable imperatives in dealing with one's HIV infection. Do not do it alone. Seek out Christian community, rather than avoiding it (the latter is the enemy's objective). Support can be found. Secondly (but not in order of importance), one needs to consistently develop and nurture time with the Lord in daily prayer, meditation and study of the Word. Feed your soul with the knowledge of the Father's love for you. Always treasure in your heart that nothing, nothing can "separate us from the love of God that is in Christ Jesus our Lord."

Thirdly, though your body may continue to bear reminders of mistakes you made in the past, the Lord is not withholding healing because of them. His forgiveness is certain when we approach Him in earnestness with our confessions. Learn to receive His forgiveness in return and to get on with the process of living. Jesus said in John 10:10: "I came that they might have life and have it to the full." Take Him up on that promise and embrace life with all your heart, soul mind and strength. There is transformation and healing in that embrace.

Created in the Image of God

Session 2

He is asking us to be the chief bearers of His likeness in the world. As spirit, He remains invisible in this planet. He relies on us to give flesh to that spirit, to bear the image of God.
(*In His Image* by Dr. Paul Brand and Philip Yancey, p. 23)

Take a few minutes in the group to discuss the following questions with the leader, reading them out loud:

- When you were growing up, how comfortable were you with your physical appearance?
- What influences or circumstances in your family affected the way you felt about yourself?
- Has your condition or illness altered the way you feel about your body or affected the way you relate to others?

Our medical prognosis can profoundly alter our sense of well being. The uncertainties and stress that occur with a life-threatening illness distort our perceptions. Through the ups and downs, we need certainty and a clear, truthful vision of ourselves and the life Jesus gives us.

NOTES

Session 2 — Created in the Image of God

NOTES

Body and soul: created by God

Church tradition hasn't often provided a healthy or helpful view of the human body. Historically, the church has often preached disdain for the body because of its understanding of the "sinfulness of the flesh," or has remained silent, thus revealing an aversion to the subject. Neither ambivalence toward nor alienation from the body is in keeping with Scripture's view of our physical, created selves. We have truly suffered from false interpretations of Scripture resulting in an unhealthy separation between our spiritual and physical selves, distorting our views of both.

The concept that everything of the spirit is good and everything of the physical body, evil, ("fallen flesh") is a by-product of an ancient Greek school of thought known as *gnosticism,* a teaching that runs counter to biblical doctrine. (Gnosticism, sometimes influencing the Church in its early centuries, is the doctrine that spirit is entirely good and matter is entirely evil.) If our physical bodies were by nature and creation hopelessly wicked and evil, the Son of God would not have appeared in human flesh as Jesus of Nazareth! Psalm 139 bears witness to God's involvement in, celebration of, and commitment to us as physical beings:

> For you created my inmost being; you knit me together in my mother's womb. I praise you because I am fearfully and wonderfully made; your works are wonderful I know that full well. My frame was not hidden from you when I was made in the secret place. When I was woven together in the depths of the earth, your eyes saw my unformed body. All the days ordained for me were written in your book before one of them came to be. (Psalm 139:13-16)

We embody a marvelous, physical complexity that comes from God. But there is more.

Made in His image: God's original intent

> So God created man in his own image. In the image of God he created him; male and female he created them. (Genesis 1:27)

Foundational to a clear and truthful vision of ourselves is the biblical claim that we are created in God's image, "...God said, 'Let us make man in our image...'" (Genesis 1:26). We reflect our Maker, not only in our human character qualities and abilities, but also in our physical design by which we express those qualities and abilities.

Embracing Life Series: International Copyright © 1998 by Embracing Life Ministries. All Rights Reserved

18 **Embracing Life Series**

Created in the Image of God

Session 2

NOTES

For instance, God is creative and because we are made in God's image, we are also creative beings. We even see physical evidence of that God-given creativity in our possession of a brain that imagines, eyes that see, and hands with fingers that literally create!

God made us, body and soul, in His image. God declared His creation "very good" (Genesis 1:37). Now for the bad news.

The Fall: disfigurement created by sin

> Fallen nature is a certain manner in which the good powers deposited at the creation in our human flesh are twisted and organized against God.
> (*Spirit of the Disciplines*, Dallas Willard, p. 91)

Created humanity rebelled against God at its earliest opportunity (Genesis 3). That sinful rebellion ("the fall") had consequences. Spiritually, we were separated from God and the divine image we bear (while still remaining within us) was shattered. We suffered a spiritual death. Think of it as a wrecked car that can barely move about. It is still recognizable as a car, still reflects its creator maker by its "make," but is nevertheless designated as "totaled." Like the wrecked car, humanity suffered physical consequences when physical death entered the picture. Death became our common destination. Death's power determined the course of our lives apart from God. Our bodies now exhibit a frailness and susceptibility to all manner of death's destructive influences—life-threatening disease being the most obvious at the moment. Disease and death are results of "the fall."

Disease and death are results of "the fall"

Countless illnesses beset humanity. All around us we see ample physical evidence of the "powers...twisted and organized against God," as Willard puts it. Living with a chronic condition makes it especially difficult to appreciate the original goodness and wonder of being made in God's image.

Indeed, in the enemy's hand, our ailments can be cruel weapons that mercilessly remind us about *what* we're not: fully healed. Rather, we should continually remind ourselves of who we are now—redeemed in Christ—and that creative possibilities abound for us.

Session 2   Created in the Image of God   Embracing Life Series   19

Session 2 — Created in the Image of God

NOTES

Hope

> "Against our deep creature—sickness stands God's infinite ability to cure."
> (*Knowledge of the Holy*, A.W. Tozer, p. 47)

Though the powers of sin, sickness and death have taken humanity captive, God has provided an effective agent to break these dark powers and restore us body and soul. That restoring and healing agent is Jesus Christ and His cross.

Life is ours to embrace as God embraces us in the person of Jesus Christ. Jesus perfectly revealed God's image in His own body and soul. Jesus Christ, crucified and risen, works to restore that image in His followers. (We will say much more about this in future sessions.)

Reclaiming our identity through Christ

> …for God's temple is sacred, and you are that temple. (1 Corinthians 3:17)
> …do you not know that your body is a temple of the Holy Spirit who is in you, whom you have from God. (1 Corinthians 6:19)
> And we, who with unveiled faces all reflect the Lord's glory, are being transformed into His likeness with ever-increasing glory, which comes from the Lord, who is the Spirit. (2 Corinthians 3:18)

The Scriptures are our faithful guide into the knowledge of who we are created to be. It is in Christ and through Him that we retrieve our destinies as true "image bearers." As we grow in our spiritual understanding of God's immensely creative love for us, our entire being is affected. The Holy Spirit animates all that we are. Our bodies (hurting as they may be) are part of that transformation, too, along with our soul and spirit.

The Word of God contains the message of true life and gives us courage to live. Steeped in His love and wisdom, hope for healing can thrive in each of us. It is neither delusion nor denial to say our illness is *not* our identity. On the contrary, we identify solely with the cross and Jesus Christ's saving/healing sacrifice for us. He has removed the curse of the fall and continues to restore His Image in us daily. Thus we can choose, today, to embrace anew each and every promise of life that he has made to us in His Word.

Created in the Image of God

Session 2

In the large group, do the following activity:

- Read the list in the following pages titled "Who I am in Christ."

- Select one or two Scriptures that are particularly meaningful. After everyone has chosen a Scripture, each will, one at a time take their name badge (with their condition written on it) and attach it to the cross. After doing so, they will share the Scriptures they have chosen with the group.

- Take time to pray for each person, sealing the Scriptures they have chosen into their hearts.

SCRIPTURE READINGS
Psalm 139:1-16; 1 Corinthians 12:12-26

RECOMMENDED READINGS
Fearfully and Wonderfully Made by Dr. Paul Brand & Philip Yancey

In His Image by Dr. Paul Brand & Philip Yancey

THOUGHTS FOR JOURNALING
Write down more fully your responses and thoughts regarding the discussion questions at the beginning of the chapter and the "Who I am in Christ" list.

NOTES

Readings

Who I am in Christ

Christ in you, the hope of glory. (Colossians 1:27)

The Word of God Says:

I am:

1. God's child, for I am born again of the incorruptible seed of the word of God which liveth and abideth forever. (1 Peter 1:23)
2. Forgiven of all of my sins and washed in the blood. (Eph. 1:7; Heb. 9:14; Col. 1:14; 1 John 2:12; 1 John 1:9)
3. A new creature. (2 Cor. 5:17)
4. The temple of the Holy Spirit. (1 Cor. 6:19)
5. Delivered from the power of darkness and translated into God's kingdom. (Col. 1:13)
6. Redeemed from the curse of the law. (1 Peter 1:18-19; Gal. 3:13)
7. Blessed (Deut. 28:1-14; Gal. 3:9)
8. A saint. (Rom. 1:7; 1 Cor. 1:2; Phil. 1:1)
9. The head and not the tail. (Deut. 20.13)
10. Above only and not beneath. (Deut. 28:13)
11. Holy and without blame before him in love. (1 Peter 1:16; Eph. 1:4)
12. Elect (Col. 3:12; Rom. 8:33)
13. Established to the end. (1 Cor. 1:8)
14. Brought near by the blood of Christ. (Eph. 2:13)
15. Victorious. (Rev. 21:7)
16. Set free. (John 8:31-33)
17. Strong in the Lord. (Eph. 6:10)
18. Dead to sin. (Rom. 6:2, 11; 1 Peter 2:24)
19. More than a conqueror. (Rom. 8:37)
20. Joint heirs with Christ (Rom. 8:17)
21. Sealed with the Holy Spirit of promise. (Eph. 1:13)
22. In Christ by his doing. (1 Cor. 1:30)
23. Accepted in the beloved. (Eph. 1:6)
24. Complete in him. (Col. 2:10)
25. Crucified with Christ. (Gal. 2:20)
26. Alive with Christ. (Eph. 2:5)
27. Free from condemnation (Rom. 8:1)
28. Reconciled to God. (2 Cor. 5:18)
29. Qualified to share in his inheritance. (Col. 1:12)
30. Firmly rooted, built up, established in faith and overflowing in gratitude. (Col. 2:7)
31. Circumcised with the circumcision made without hands. (Col. 2:11)
32. A fellow citizen with the saints and of the household of God. (Eph. 2:19)
33. Built upon the foundation of the apostles and prophets, Jesus Christ himself being the Chief Cornerstone. (Eph. 2:20)
34. In the world as he is in heaven. (1 John 4:17)
35. Born of God and the evil one does not touch me. (1 John 5:18)
36. His faithful follower. (Rev. 17:14b; Eph. 5:1)
37. Overtaken with blessings. (Deut. 28:2; Eph. 1:3)
38. His disciple because I have love for others. (John 13:34-35)
39. The light of the world. (Matt. 5:14)
40. The salt of the earth. (Matt. 5:13)
41. The righteousness of God. (2 Cor. 5:21; 1 Peter 2:24)
42. A partaker of his divine nature. (2 Peter 1:4)
43. Called of God. (2 Tim. 1:9)
44. The first fruits among his creation. (James 1:18)
45. Chosen. (1 Thess. 1:4); Eph. 1:4; 1 Peter 2:9)
46. An ambassador for Christ. (2 Cor. 5:20)
47. God's workmanship created in Christ for good works. (Eph. 2:10)
48. The apple of my Father's eye. (Deut. 32:10; Ps. 17:8)
49. Healed by the stripes of Jesus. (1 Peter 2:24; Is. 53:6)
50. Being changed into his image. (2 Cor. 3:18; Phil. 1:16)
51. Raised up with Christ and seated in heavenly places. (Col. 2:12; Eph. 2:6)
52. Beloved of God. (Col. 3:12; Rom. 1:7; 1 Thess. 1:4)
53. One in Christ! Hallelujah! (John 17:21-23)

Readings

I have:

54: The mind of Christ. (Phil. 2:5; 1 Cor. 2:16)

55. Obtained an inheritance. (Eph. 1:11)

56. Access by one Spirit unto the Father. (Heb. 4:18; Eph. 2:18)

57. Overcome the world. (1 John 5:4)

58. Everlasting life and will not be condemned. (John 5:24; John 6:47)

59. The peace of God which passes understanding. (Phil. 4:7)

60. Received power; the power of the Holy Spirit; power to lay hands on the sick and see them recover; power to cast out demons; power over all the power of the enemy and nothing shall by any means hurt me. (Mark 10:17, 19; 16:17-18)

61. By and in the law of the Spirit of life in Christ Jesus. (Rom. 8:2)

I can:

62. In Christ Jesus. (Col. 2:6)

63. Do all things in Christ. (Phil. 4:13)

64. Do even greater works than Christ Jesus. (John 14:12)

I possess:

65. The greater one in me because greater is he who is in me than he who is in the world. (1 John 4:4)

I press:

66. Toward the mark for the prize of the high calling of God. (Phil. 3:14)

I:

67. Always triumph in Christ. (2 Cor. 2:14)

My life:

68. Shows forth his praise. (1 Peter 2:9)

69. Is hidden with Christ in God. (Col. 3:3)

Readings

From

"In His Image"

Dr. Paul Brand & Philip Yancey

Ch. 3: Restoration

> Adam himself lies now scattered on the whole surface of the earth. Formerly concentrated in one place, he has fallen; having been broken to pieces, as it were, he has filled the universe with his debris. However, God's mercy has gathered together from everywhere his fragments and by fusing them in the fire of his charity, has reconstituted their broken unity.
>
> St. Augustine, *City of God*

> The Christian ideal changed and reversed everything so that, as the gospel puts it, "That which was exalted among men has become an abomination in the sight of God." The ideal is no longer the greatness of Pharaoh or of a Roman emperor, not the beauty of a Greek nor the wealth of Phoenicia, but humility, purity, compassion, love. The hero is no longer Dives, but Lazarus the beggar; not Mary Magdalene in the day of her beauty, but the day of her repentance; not those who acquire wealth, but those who have abandoned it; not those who dwell in palaces, but those who dwell in catacombs and huts; not those who rule over others, but those who acknowledge no authority but God's.
>
> Leo Tolstoy, *What Is Art*

I am standing in the sublime Sistine Chapel. Most tourists have left, twilight approaches, and the light has rippened to a golden hue. My neck ached slightly from supporting my head at odd angles, and I wonder fleetingly how Michelangelo felt after a day of working on these ceiling murals.

My eyes keep drifting back to the pivotal scene which shows God imparting life to man. The image of God stands for all that gives worth and dignity to individual men and women, and nothing could better display that indwelling power than the paintings that surround me. And yet even as I stare at the creation scene something troubles me. Michelangelo succeeded wonderfully at depicting human duality and the drama of creation. But he clearly failed, as all artists must, at portraying God Himself. Michelangelo's God is not spirit, but a God made in the image of man.

Six centuries before Christ, the Greek philosopher Xenophanes observed that "If oxen and horses and lions had hands or could draw with hands and create works of art like those made by men, horses would draw pictures of gods like horses, and oxen of gods like oxen. Aethiopians have gods with snub noses and black hair; Thracians have gods with grey eyes and red hair." Michelangelo's God has the shape and texture of humanity—even a sloping Roman nose just like Adam's. The artist portrayed the likeness between God and man literally and physically, not spiritually. In fact, if you took Adam's face in the painting, aged it around the eyes, and crowned it with flowing white locks and a beard, you would have Michelangelo's depiction of God the Father.

How can an artist possibly represent a God who is spirit? And if we cannot see Him, how can we contemplate His image? Our vocabulary, superb and precise when describing the material world, falls silent before the inner processes of spirit. The very word "spirit" in many languages means nothing more than breath or wind. But the entire Old Testament insists upon the central truth that God is spirit and that no physical image can capture His essence.

The second of the Ten Commandments forbids drawing a picture or making a sculptured image intended to represent God. Whenever the Jews tried, God viewed it as profanation. After living in a country where graven images and idols abound, I can well understand the prohibition.

Hinduism has over a thousand different images, and I could hardly walk a block in an Indian town without seeing an idol or representation. As I watched the effects of

Readings

those images on the average Indian, I observed two common results. For most, the images trivialize the gods. The gods lose any aura of sacredness and mystery and become rather like mascots or good luck charms. A taxi driver mounts a goddess statue on his taxicab and offers flowers and incense as a prayer for safety. For other Indians, the gods may become grotesque symbols that evoke an attitude of fear and bondage. Calcutta's violent goddess Kali, for example, has a fiery tongue and wears a garland of bloody heads around her waist. Hindus may worship a snake, a rat, a phallic symbol, even a goddess of smallpox; such images crowd the ornate temples.

Wisely, the Bible warns us against reducing the image of God to the level of physical matter; such an image too easily limits our concept of His real nature. We may begin to think of Him as a bearded old man in the sky, like the figure in Michelangelo's painting. Being a spirit, present everywhere, God can have no confining shape. "To whom, then, will you compare God?" asks Isaiah. "What image will you compare him to?" (40:18).*

We have, therefore, a God who cannot be captured in a visible image. But what does God look like? How can I find Him? Where is His image? Somehow the essence of God entered the bodies of the first created humans, and they bore His image on this planet. For a time the two natures, the physical nature of organs and blood and bone and a spiritual nature allowing direct communion with God, fit together in harmony. Sadly, that condition failed to last.

An event recorded in Genesis 3 disrupted the harmony between the two natures. Adam's and Eve's rebellion forever marred the image of God they carried, and at that moment a huge gulf fissured open, destroying the unity between God and mankind. Now when we gaze on human beings we find lurking among them the likes of Genghis Khan, Josef Stalin, and Adolf Hitler. And, yes, dramatic evidence of the broken image spills out of every one of us. Individual human beings can no longer express adequately a likeness to God; history proves darkly our unlikeness to Him.

It is not enough for us to mirror forth the residue of spirit and worth inside each person. We need something greater, far greater, to know what God is like. We need a new image, a new demonstration of God's likeness on our planet.

Christians believe we got such an image in the person of Jesus Christ, the Second Adam, whose coming proved so revolutionary that it became the exact center of a new religion. God the spirit agreed to become a man and incarnate His spirit. Inside a body of skin and bone and blood, the divine lived in matter as a microcosm, like the sun in a drop of water. In G. K. Chesterton's succinct phrase, "God who had been only a circumference was seen as a center."

* See Isaiah 44 for a speech from God that gives a forceful and yet witty summary of the foolishness of making idols.

> Copyright ©1984
> by Paul Brand & Philip Yancey, pp 34-37.
> Used by permission of
> Zondervan Publishing House.

Readings

From:

"Fearfully & Wonderfully Made"

Dr. Paul Brand & Philip Yancey

Ch. 3: Diversity

> We often think that when we have completed our study on one, we know all about two, because "two is one and one." We forget that we have still to make a study of "and."
> (Sir Arthur Eddington)

More than amoebae and bats skulk in my medical laboratory. One drawer contains neatly filed specimens of an array of cells from the human body. Separated from the body, lifeless, stained with dyes and mounted in epoxy, they hardly express the churn of living cells at work inside me at this moment. But if I parade them under the microscope, certain impression about the body take shape.

I am first struck by their variety. Chemically my cells are almost alike, but visually and functionally they are as different as the animals in a zoo. Red blood cells, discs resembling Lifesaver candies, voyage through my blood loaded with oxygen to feed the other cells. Muscle cells, which absorb so much of that nourishment, are sleek and supple, full of coiled energy. Cartilage cells with shiny black nuclei look like bunches of black-eyed peas glued tightly together for strength. Fat cells seem lazy and leaden, like bulging white plastic garbage bags jammed together.

Bone cells live in rigid structures that exude strength. Cut in cross section, bones resemble tree rings, overlapping strength with strength, offering impliability and sturdiness. In contrast, skin cells form undulating patterns of softness and texture that rise and dip, giving shape and beauty to our bodies. They curve and jut at unpredictable angles so that every person's fingerprint—not to mention his or her face—is unique.

The aristocrats of the cellular world are the sex cells and nerve cells. A woman's contribution, the egg, is one of the largest cells in the human body, its ovoid shape just visible to the unaided eye. It seems fitting that all the other cells in the body should derive from this elegant and primordial structure. In great contrast to the egg's quiet repose, the male's tiny sperm cells are furiously flagellating tadpoles with distended heads and skinny tails. They scramble for position as if competitively aware that only one of billions will gain the honor of fertilization.

The king of cells, the one I have devoted much of my life to studying, is the nerve cell. It has an aura of wisdom and complexity about it. Spider-like, it branches out and unites the body with a computer network of dazzling sophistication. Its axons, "wires" carrying distant messages to and from the human brain, can reach a yard in length.

I never tire of viewing these varied specimens or thumbing through books which render cells. Individually they seem puny and oddly designed, but I know these invisible parts cooperate to lavish me with the phenomenon of life. Every second my smooth muscle cells modulate the width of my blood vessels, gently push matter through my intestines, open and close the plumbing in my kidneys. When things are going well—my heart contracting rhythmically, my brain humming with knowledge, my lymph laving tired cells—I rarely give these cells a passing thought.

But I believe these cells in my body can also teach me about larger organisms: families, groups, communities, villages, nations—and especially about one specific community of people that is likened to a body more than thirty times in the New Testament. I speak of the Body of Christ, that network of people scattered across the planet who have little in common other than their membership in the group that follows Jesus Christ.

My body employs a bewildering zoo of cells, none of which individually resembles the larger body. Just so, Christ's Body comprises an unlikely assortment of humans. Unlikely is precisely the right word, for we are decidedly unlike one another and the One we follow. From whose design come these comical human shapes which so faintly reflect the ideals of the Body as a whole?

Novelist Frederick Buechner playfully described the motley crew God selected in Bible times to accomplish His work:

"Who could have predicted that God would choose not Esau, the honest and reliable, but Jacob, the trickster

Readings

and heel, that he would put the finger on Noah, who hit the bottle, or on Moses, who was trying to beat the rap in Midian for braining a man in Egypt and said if it weren't for the honor of the thing he'd just as soon let Aaron go back and face the music, or on the prophets, who were a ragged lot, mad as hatters most of them…?

"And of course, there is the comedy, the unforeseeableness, of the election itself. Of all the peoples he could have chosen to be his holy people, he chose the Jews, who as somebody has said are just like everybody else only more so—more religious than anybody when they were religious and when they were secular, being secular as if they'd invented it. And the comedy of the covenant—God saying 'I will be your God and you shall be my people' (Exodus 6:7) to a people who before the words had stopped ringing in their ears were dancing around the golden calf like aborigines and carrying on with every agricultural deity and fertility god that came down the pike."

The exception seems to be the rule. The first humans God created went out and did the only thing God asked them not to do. The man he chose to head a new nation known as "God's people" tried to pawn off his wife on an unsuspecting Pharaoh. And the wife herself, when told at the ripe old age of ninety-one that God was ready to deliver the son He had promised her, broke into rasping laughter in the face of God. Rahab, a harlot, became revered for her great faith. And Solomon, the wisest man who ever lived, went out of his way to break every proverb he so astutely composed.

Even after Jesus came the pattern continued. The two disciples who did most to spread the word after His departure, John and Peter, where the two He had rebuked most often for petty squabbling and muddleheadedness. And the apostle Paul, who wrote more books than any other Bible writer, was selected for the task while kicking up dust whirls from town to town sniffing out Christians to torture. Jesus had nerve, entrusting the high-minded ideals of love and unity and fellowship to this group. No wonder cynics have looked at the church and sighed, "If that group of people is supposed to represent God, I'll quickly vote against Him." Or as Nietzsche expressed it, "His disciples will have to look more saved if I am to believe in their savior."

Yet our study of the Body of Christ must allow for this impossible dream, for all we are is a collection of people as diverse as the cells in the human body. I think of the churches I have known: Is there another institution in town with such a mosaic assortment of unlikes? Young radicals, uniformed in jeans, share the pews with Republican bankers in three-piece suits. Bored teenagers tune out the sermon even as their eager grandparents turn up their hearing aids. Some members gather as methodically as a school of fish, then quickly break apart to return to their jobs and homes. Others want close communities and migrate together like social amoebae.

I could easily cluck my tongue at the absurdity of the whole enterprise, seemingly doomed to fail. Jesus prayed that we "may be one" as He and God the Father are one (John 17:11). How can any organism composed of such diversity attain even a semblance of unity?

As the doubts rumble inside me, a sober and quieting voice replies, "You have not chosen Me. I have chosen you." The chuckle at Christ's Body is caught in my throat like cotton. For if anything is to be believed about the collection of people who follow Him, it is that we were called by Him. The word church, ekklêsia, means "the called-out ones." Our crew of comedians from central casting is the group God wants.

During my life as a missionary surgeon in India and now as a member of the tiny chapel on the grounds of the Carville leprosy hospital, I have seen my share of unlikely seekers after God. And I must admit that most of my worship in the last thirty years has not taken place among people who have shared my tastes in music, speech, or even thought. But over those years I have been profoundly—and humbly—impressed that I find God in the faces of my fellow worshippers by sharing with people who are shockingly different from each other and from me.

C. S. Lewis recounts that when he first started going to church he disliked the hymns, which he considered to be fifth-rate poems set to sixth-rate music. But as he continued, he said, "I realized that the hymns (which were just sixth-rate music) were, nevertheless, being sung with devotion and benefit by an old saint in elastic-side boots in the opposite pew, and then you realize that you aren't fit to clean those boots. It gets you out of your solitary conceit."

A color on a canvas can be beautiful in itself. However, the artist excels not by slathering one color across the canvas but by positioning it between contrasting or complementary hues. The original color then derives richness and depth from its milieu of unlike colors.

The basis for our unity within Christ's Body begins not with our similarity but with our diversity.

It seems safe to assume that God enjoys variety, and not just at the cellular level. He didn't stop with a thousand insect species; he conjured up three hundred thousand

Readings

species of beetles and weevils alone. In his famous speech in the Book of Job, God pointed with pride to such oddities of creation as the mountain goat, the wild ass, the ostrich, and the lightning bolt. He lavished color, design, and texture on the world, giving us Pygmies and Watusis, blond Scandinavians and swarthy Italians, big-boned Russians and petite Japanese.

People, created in His image, have continued the process of individualization, grouping themselves according to distinct cultures. Consider the continent of Asia for a crazy salad. In China women wear long pants and men wear gowns. In tropical Asia people drink hot tea and munch on blistering peppers to keep cool. Japanese fry ice cream. Indonesian men dance in public with other men to demonstrate that they are not homosexual. Westerners smile at the common Asian custom of marriages arranged by parents; Asians gasp at our entrusting such a decision to vague romantic love. Balinese men squat to urinate and women stand. Many Asians begin a meal with a sweet and finish it with a soup. And when the British introduced the violin to India a century ago, men started playing it while sitting on the floor, holding it between the shoulder and the sole of the foot. Why not?

Whenever I travel overseas, I am struck anew by the world's incredible diversity, and the churches overseas are now beginning to show that cultural self-expression. For too long they were bound up in Western ways (as the early church had been bound in Jewish ways) so that hymns, dress, architecture, and church names were the same around the world. Now indigenous churches are bursting out with their own spontaneous expressions of worship to God. I must guard against picturing the Body of Christ as composed only of American or British cells; it is far grander and more luxuriant than that.

I grew up in a denomination called the Strict and Particular Baptists, from which I learned faith and love for God and the Bible. Unfortunately, I also was taught how crucially better we were than every other church. We were not even allowed to have communion with other Baptist denominations. My great-grandparents, Huguenots, had escaped Catholic persecution in France, and as children we were taught that nuns and priest were akin to the devil. My Christian growth since those days has required some abrupt adjustments.

I have learned that when God looks upon His Body, spread like an archipelago throughout the world, He sees the whole thing. And I think He, understanding the cultural backgrounds and true intent of the worshippers, likes the variety He sees.

Blacks in Murphy, North Carolina, shout their praises to God. Believers in Austria intone them, accompanied by magnificent organs and illuminated by stained glass. Some Africans dance their praise to God, following the beat of a skilled drummer. Sedate Japanese Christians express their gratitude by creating objects of beauty. Indians point their hands upward, palms together, in the *namaste* greeting of respect, that has its origin in the Hindu concept, "I worship the God I see in you," but gains new meaning as Christians use it to recognize the image of God in others.

The Body of Christ, like our own bodies, is composed of individual, unlike cells that are knit together to form one Body. He is the whole thing, and the joy of the Body increases as individual cells realize they can be diverse without becoming isolated outposts.

Ch. 4: Worth

Whereas American mothers preserve, often in bronze, their children's first shoes—celebrating freedom and independence—a Japanese mother carefully preserves a small part of her child's umbilical cord—celebrating dependence and loyalty.
(Stephen Franklin)

As a boy growing up in India, I idolized my missionary father who responded to every human need he encountered. Only once did I see him hesitate to help—when I was seven, and three strange men trudged up the dirt path to our mountain home.

At first glance these three seemed like hundreds of other strangers who streamed to our home for medical treatment. Each was dressed in a breechcloth and turban, with a blanket draped over one shoulder. But as they approached, I noticed differences: a mottled quality to their skin, thick, swollen foreheads and ears, and strips of blood-stained cloth bandaging their feet. As they came closer, I noticed they also lacked fingers and one had no toes—his limbs ended in rounded stumps.

My mother's reaction differed from her normal gracious hospitality. Her face took on a pale, tense appearance. "Run and get papa," she whispered to me. "Take your sister, and both of you stay in the house!"

My sister obeyed perfectly, but after calling my father I scrambled on hands and knees to a nearby vantage

Readings

point. Something sinister was happening, and I didn't want to miss it. My heart pounded violently as I saw the same look of uncertainty, almost fear, pass across my father's face. He stood by the three nervously, awkwardly, as if he didn't know what to do. I had never seen my father like that.

The three men prostrated themselves on the ground, a common Indian action that my father disliked. "I am not God—He is the One you should worship," he would usually say, and lift the Indians to their feet. But not this time. He stood still. Finally, in a weak voice he said, "There's not much we can do. I'm sorry. But wait where you are; don't move. I'll do what I can."

He ran to the dispensary while the men squatted on the ground. Soon he returned with a roll of bandages, a can of salve, and a pair of surgical gloves he was struggling to put on. This was most unusual—how could he treat them wearing gloves?

Father washed the strangers' feet, applied ointment to their sores, and bandaged them. Strangely, they did not wince or cry out as he touched their sores.

While father bandaged the men, mother had been arranging a selection of fruit in a wicker basket. They took the fruit but left the basket, and they disappeared over the ridge I went to pick it up.

"No!" mother insisted. "Don't touch it! And don't go near that place where they sat." Silently I watched father take the basket and burn it, then scrub his hands with hot water and soap. Then mother bathed my sister and me, though we had had no direct contact with the visitors.

That incident was my first exposure to leprosy, the oldest recorded disease and probably the most dreaded disease throughout history. Although I might have recoiled from the suggestion as a boy of seven, I eventually felt called to spend my life working among leprosy patients. For the past thirty years I have been with them almost daily, forming many intimate and lasting friendships among these courageous people. During that time, many exaggerated fears and prejudices about leprosy have crumbled, at least in the medical profession. Partly because of effective drugs, leprosy is now viewed as a controllable, barely contagious disease.

However, in most parts of the world less than a quarter of leprosy patients are actually under any form of treatment. Thus, to many it is still a disease that can cause severe lesions, blindness, and loss of hands and feet. How does leprosy produce such terrible effects?

As I studied leprosy patients in India, several findings pushed me toward a rather simple theory: could it be that the horrible results of the disease came about because leprosy patients had lost the sense of pain? The disease was not at all like a flesh-devouring fungus; rather, it attacked mainly a single type of cell, the nerve cell. After years of testing and observation, I felt sure that the theory was sound.

The gradual loss of the sense of pain leads to misuse of those body parts most dependent on pain's protection. A person uses a hammer with a splintery handle, does not feel the pain, and an infection flares up. Another steps off a curb, spraining an ankle, and, oblivious, keeps walking. Another loses use of the nerve the triggers the eyelid to blink every few seconds for lubricating moisture; the eye dries out, and the person becomes blind.

The millions of cells in a hand or foot, or the living and alert rod and cone cells in the eye, can be rendered useless because of the breakdown of just a few nerve cells. Such is the tragedy of leprosy.

A similar pattern can be found in other diseases. In sickle cell anemia or leukemia the malfunction of a single type of cell can quickly destroy a person. Or, if the cells that keep kidney filters in repair fail, a person may soon die of toxic poisoning.

This fact of the body—the worth of each of its parts—is graphically revealed by a disease such as leprosy. The failure of one type of cell can bring on tragic consequences. One who studies the vast quantity of cells and their startling diversity can come away with a sense that each cell is easily expendable and of little consequence. But the same body that impresses us with specialization and diversity also affirms that *each* of its many members is valuable and often essential for survival.

Interestingly, the worth of each member is also the aspect most often stressed in biblical imagery of the Body of Christ (see Rom. 12:5, 1 Cor. 12, and Eph. 4:16). Listen to the mischievous way in which Paul expresses himself in 1 Corinthians: "Those parts of the body that seem to be weaker are indispensable, and the parts that we think are less honorable we treat with special honor. And the parts that are unpresentable are treated with special modesty, while our presentable parts need no special treatment. But God has combined the members of the body and has given greater honor to the parts that lacked it, so that there should be no division in the body, but that its parts should have equal concern for each other. If one part suffers, every part suffers with it; if one part is honored, every part rejoices with it" (vv. 22-26).

Paul's point is clear: Christ chose each member to

Readings

make a unique contribution to His Body. Without that contribution, the Body could malfunction severely. Paul underscores that the less visible members (I think of organs like the pancreas, kidney, liver, and spleen) are perhaps the most valuable of all. Although I seldom feel consciously grateful for them, they perform daily functions that keep me alive.

I must keep coming back to the image of the body, because in our Western societies the worth of persons is determined by how much society is willing to pay for their services. Airplane pilots, for example, must endure rigorous education and testing procedures before they can fly for commercial airlines. They are then rewarded with luxurious lifestyles and societal respect. Within the corporate world, visible symbols such as office furnishings, bonuses, and salaries announce the worth of any given employee. As a person climbs, he or she will collect a sequence of important-sounding titles (the U.S. government issues a book cataloging ten thousand of them).

In the military, the chain of command defines a person's worth. One salutes superior officers, gives orders to those of lower rank, and one's uniform and stripes alert everyone to his or her relative status. In civil service status is reflected in an individual's "GS grade," a numerical label.

Our culture is shot through with rating systems, beginning from the first grades of school when children receive marks defining relative performance. That, combined with factors such as physical appearance, popularity, and athletic prowess, may well determine how valuable people perceive themselves to be.

Living in such a society, my vision gets clouded. I begin viewing janitors as having less human worth than jet pilots. When that happens, I must turn back to the lesson from the body, which Paul draws against just such a background of incurable competition and value ranking. In human society, a janitor has little status because he is so replaceable. Thus, we pay the janitor less and tend to look down on him. But the body's division of labor is not based on status; status is, in fact, immaterial to the task being performed. The body's janitors are indispensable. If you doubt that, talk with someone who must go in for kidney dialysis twice a week.

The Bible directs harsh words to those who show favoritism. James spelled out a situation we can all identify with: "Suppose a man comes into your meeting wearing a gold ring and fine clothes, and a poor man in shabby clothes also comes in. If you show special attention to the man wearing fine clothes and say, 'Here's a good seat for you,' but say to the poor man, 'You stand there,' or, 'Sit on the floor by my feet,' have you not discriminated among yourselves and become judges with evil thoughts?" He concludes, "If you show favoritism, you sin and are convicted by the law as lawbreakers. For whoever keeps the whole law and yet stumbles at just one point is guilty of breaking all of it" (James 2:2-4, 9-10).

Paul states the same truth positively, "Here there is no Greek or Jew, circumcised or uncircumcised, barbarian, Scythian, slave or free, but Christ is all, and is in all" (Col. 3:11).

In our rating-conscious society that ranks everything from baseball teams to "the best chili in New York," an attitude of relative worth can easily seep into the church of Christ. But the design of the group of people who follow Jesus should not resemble a military machine or a corporate structure. The church Jesus founded is more like a family in which the son retarded from birth has as much worth as his brother the Rhodes scholar. It is like the body, composed of cells most striking in their diversity but most effective in their mutuality.

God requires only one thing of His "cells": that each person be loyal to the Head. If each cell accepts the needs of the whole Body as the purpose of its life, then the Body will live in health. It is a brilliant stroke, the only pure egalitarianism I observe in all of society. He has endowed every person in the Body with the same capacity to respond to Him. In Christ's Body a teacher of three-year-olds has the same value as a bishop, and that teacher's work may be just as significant. A widow's dollar can equal a millionaire's annuity. Shyness, beauty, eloquence, race, sophistication—none of these matter, only loyalty to the Head, and through the Head to each other.

Our little church at Carville includes one devout Christian named Lou, a Hawaiian by birth, who is marked with visible deformities caused by leprosy. With eyebrows and eyelashes missing, his face has a naked, unbalanced appearance, and paralyzed eyelids cause tears to overflow as if he is crying. He has became almost totally blind because of the failure of a few nerve cells on the surface of his eyes.

Lou struggles constantly with his growing sense of isolation from the world. His sense of touch has faded now, and that, combined with his near-blindness, makes him afraid and withdrawn. He most fears that his sense of hearing may also leave him, for Lou's main love in life is music. He can contribute only one "gift" to our church,

Readings

other than his physical presence: singing hymns to God while he accompanies himself on an autoharp. Our therapists designed a glove that permits Lou to continue playing his autoharp without damaging his insensitive hand.

But here is the truth about the Body of Christ: not one person in Carville contributes more to the spiritual life of our church than Lou playing his autoharp. He has as much impact on us as does any member there by offering as praise to God the limited, frail tribute of his music. When Lou leaves, he will create a void in our church that no one else can fill—not even a professional harpist with nimble fingers and a degree from Julliard School of Music. Everyone in the church knows that Lou is a vital, contributing member, as important as any other member—and that is the secret of Christ's Body. If each of us can learn to glory in the fact that we matter little except in relation to the Body, and if each will acknowledge the worth in every other member, then perhaps the cells of Christ's Body will begin acting as He intended.

Ch. 5: Unity

> We cannot live for ourselves alone. Our lives are connected by a thousand invisible threads, and along these sympathetic fibers, our actions run as causes and return to us as results. (Herman Melville)

The biologist takes from an incubator an egg containing a fully developed young chicken. Just fourteen days ago this egg was a single cell (the largest single cell in the world is an unfertilized ostrich egg). Now it is a mass of hundreds of millions of cells, a whirlpool of migrating protoplasm hurriedly dividing and arranging itself to prepare for life outside. The biologist cracks that shell and sacrifices the chick.

Though the embryo is now dead, some of its cells live on. Word travels fast through the body, but it may be days before the far outposts surrender. From the tiny heart the biologist extracts a few muscle cells and drops them in saline solution. Under the microscope the individual cells appear as lone, spindly cylinders, crisscrossed like sections of railroad track. Their destiny is to throb, and they persist even in the anarchic world apart from the body. Each cell beats out an incessant rhythm—pitiful and useless palpitations when isolated from the chick. But if properly nourished, these lonely cells can be kept alive.

Unlinked by a pacemaker, the cells beat irregularly, spasmodically, each tapping out a rhythm approximate to the 350 beats a minute normal to a chick. But as the observer watches, over a period of hours an astonishing phenomenon occurs. Instead of five independent heart cells contracting at their own pace, first two, then three, and then all the cells pulse in unison. There are no longer five beats, but one. How is this sense of rhythm communicated in the saline, and why?

Some species of fireflies act similarly. A wanderer discovers a cluster of them in a jungle clearing, flickering haphazardly. As he watches, one by one the fireflies fall into sync until soon he sees not dozens of twinkling lights but one light, switched on and off, with fifty branch locations. The heart cells and the fireflies sense an innate rightness about playing the same note at the same time, even when no conductor is present.

Cooperation, a curious phenomenon of cells outside the body, is the essential regimen of life inside. There, every heart cell obeys in tempo or the animal dies. Each cell is flooded with communication about the rest of the body. How does the roaming white cell in the bat's wing know which cells to attack as invaders and which to welcome as friends? No one knows, but the body's cells have a nearly infallible sense of *belonging*.

All living matter is basically alike; a single atom differentiates animal blood from plant chlorophyll. Yet the body senses infinitesimal differences with an unfailing scent; it knows its hundred trillion cells by name. The first heart transplant recipients died, not because their new hearts failed, but because their bodies would not be fooled. Though the new heart cells looked in every respect like the old ones and beat at the correct rhythm, *they did not belong*. Nature's code of membership had been broken. The body screams "Foreigner!" at imported cells and mobilizes to destroy them. This conundrum of the immune reaction keeps organ transplant science in its kindergarten phase.

To complicate the process of identity, the composite of Paul Brand today—bone cells, fat cells, blood cells, muscle cells—differs entirely from my components ten years ago. All cells have been replaced by new cells (except for nerve cells and brain cells, which are never replaced). Thus, my body is more like a fountain than a sculpture: maintaining its shape, but constantly being renewed. Somehow my body knows the new cells belong, and they are welcomed.

What moves cells to work together? What ushers in the higher specialized functions of movement, sight, and

Readings

consciousness through the coordination of a hundred trillion cells?

The secret to membership lies locked away inside each cell nucleus, chemically coiled in a strand of DNA. Once the egg and sperm share their inheritance, the DNA chemical ladder splits down the center of every gene much as the teeth of a zipper pull apart. DNA re-forms itself each time the cell divides: 2, 4, 8, 16, 32 cells, each with the identical DNA. Along the way cells specialize, but each carries the entire instruction book of one hundred thousand genes. DNA is estimated to contain instructions that, if written out, would fill a thousand six-hundred-page books. A nerve cell may operate according to instructions from volume four and a kidney cell from volume twenty-five, but both carry the whole compendium.* It provides each cell's sealed credential of membership in the body. Every cell possesses a genetic code so complete that the entire body could be reassembled from information in any one of the body's cells, which forms the basis for speculation about cloning.

The Designer of DNA went on to challenge the human race to a new and higher purpose: membership in His own Body. And that membership begins with a stuff-exchange, analogous to an infusion of DNA, for each new cell in the Body. The community called Christ's Body differs from every other human group. Unlike a social or political body, membership in it entails something as radical as a new coded imprint inside each cell. In reality, I become genetically like Christ Himself because I belong to His Body.

The more I ponder the implications of this analogy, the more it illuminates for me a spiritual truth which the Bible states often but in puzzling terms:

"Do you not realize that Christ Jesus is in you?" "I have been crucified with Christ and I no longer live, but Christ lives in me"- Paul. And, "I am in my Father, and you are in me, and I am in you." "I am the vine; you are the branches" - Jesus (2 Cor. 13:5; Gal. 2:20; John 14:20; John 15:5).

I can only fathom the concept of being visited by the living Christ by considering its parallel in the physical world: the mystery of life in which DNA passes on an infallible identity to each new cell. Christ has infused us with spiritual life that is just as real as natural life. I may sometimes doubt my new identity or perhaps feel like my old self, but the Bible statements are unequivocal. "Whoever believes in the Son has eternal life," said Jesus, "but whoever rejects the Son will not see life" (John 3:36). The difference between a person joined to Christ and one joined to Him is as striking as the difference between a dead tissue and my organic body. DNA has organized chemicals and minerals to form a living, growing body, all of whose parts possess its unique corporate identity. In a parallel way, God uses the materials and genes of natural man, splitting them apart and recombining them with His own spiritual life.

Jesus made the interchange possible: the Virgin Birth assumes that His DNA was fully God and fully human joined in one. And now, through union with Him, I can carry within me the literal presence of God.

This unfathomable idea of an actual identity exchange is implicit in conversion. Jesus described the process in terms His hearers could understand. To Nicodemus He called it being "born again" or "born from above," indicating that spiritual life requires an identity change as drastic as a person's first entrance into the world.

As a result of this stuff-exchange, we carry within us not just the image of, or the philosophy of, or faith in, but the actual substance of God. One staggering consequence credits us with the spiritual genes of Christ: as we stand before God, we are judged on the basis of Christ's perfection, not our unworthiness. "If anyone is in Christ, he is a new creation; the old is gone, the new has come!...God made him who had no sin to be sin for us, so that in him we might become the righteousness of God (2 Cor. 5:17, 21). Elsewhere, Paul underscored, "Your life is now hidden with Christ in God" (Col. 3:3). We are "in Him" and He is "in us."

Just as the complete identity code of my body inheres in each individual cell, so also the reality of God permeates every cell in His Body, linking us members with a true, organic bond. I sense that bond when I meet strangers in India or Africa or California who share my loyalty to the Head; instantly we become brothers and sisters, fellow cells in Christ's Body. I share the ecstasy of community in a universal Body that includes every man and woman in whom God resides.

Along with the incredible benefits of our identity transfer come some sobering responsibilities. When we act in the world, we quite literally subject God to that activity. Paul applied the body analogy to impress upon promiscuous Corinthians the full extent of their new identity. "You are members of Christ's Body," he warned. "Shall I then take the members of Christ and unite them with a prostitute? Never! Do you not know that he who unites himself with a prostitute is one with her in body?"

Session 2　　　　　　　　　　　　　　　　　　　　　　　　　　　　　　　　Embracing Life Series　　33

Readings

And are not your own; you were bought at a price. Therefore honor God with your body" (1 Cor. 6:15-16, 19-20).

I cannot imagine a more sobering argument against sin. Paul appeals not to a guilt-inducing "God is watching you" argument, but to a mature realization that we literally incarnate God in the world. It is indeed a heavy burden.

The process of joining Christ's Body may at first seem like a renunciation. I no longer have full independence. Ironically, however, renouncing my old value system—in which I had to compete with other people on the basis of power, wealth, and talent—and committing myself to Christ, the Head, abruptly frees me. My sense of competition fades. No longer do I have to bristle against life, seizing ways to prove myself. In my new identity my ideal has become to live my life in such a way that people around me recognize Jesus Christ and His love, not my own set of distinctive qualities. My worth and acceptance are enveloped in Him. I have found this process of renunciation and commitment to be healthy, relaxing, and wholly good.

* The DNA is so narrow and compacted that all the genes in all my body's cells would fit into an ice cube; yet if the DNA were unwound and joined together end to end, the strand could stretch from the earth to the sun and back more than four hundred times.

> Copyright 1980
> by Paul Brand & Philip Yancey, pp35-48.
> Used by permission of
> Zondervan Publishing House.

Overview of an illness

Session 3

NOTES

This session is, ultimately, about how the things of the natural speak of the invisible. The Apostle Paul writes in Romans 1:20: "God's invisible qualities...have been clearly seen, being understood from what has been made..." We could say that consequences of the fall, e.g. sickness and disease, are poignant symbols of another sort—the affects of an enemy bent on marring the image of God in humanity.

The overview we're studying is of HIV/AIDS—from infection to full-blown illness. As we'll see, there are fascinating physical/spiritual comparisons that can be derived from how it works. Analogies can be made between the lethal, operative methods of HIV in destroying one's immune system and the enfeebling effects of sin, both personally and corporately in the Body of Christ. In both cases, the prescription for hope comes from Jesus Christ, the Great Physician.

It is not unusual for one living with a life-altering illness to be less than informed of how it works. When HIV/AIDS first appeared, it baffled medical scientists. Now, many years later, it still takes a lot of homework to stay abreast of all its complications. Nevertheless, God is not bewildered, nor confounded by the nature of disease. In fact, He is thoroughly knowledgeable of everything that transpires in the physical realm. His wise Spirit is able to guide us through the medical thicket of confusion into understanding—no matter how confounding our condition.

Session 3

Overview of an illness

NOTES

Some years ago, early on in the AIDS epidemic, I prayed to the Lord for understanding of how HIV worked. Descriptions from doctors and scientific studies at the time were terribly confusing...especially for us patients. Not being a medical student, myself, most of the terminology was totally foreign to me. All I wanted was a modicum of understanding, not a degree. I needed divine intervention. He was true to His word: *"If any of you lacks wisdom, he should ask God, who gives generously to all without finding fault, and it will be given to him"* (Jas.1:5).

The word-picture analogy for HIV/AIDS that He gave me proved to be simple and easy to grasp. Doctors and nurses have since confirmed its effectiveness in explaining (in layman's terms) a complicated illness. It's a reliable template for understanding the processes of infection/progression of HIV in the human body as well as the activity of sin's infection/progression in the believer.

Take time before and after reviewing the following material, to ask the Lord for greater understanding and revelation of your condition, including its spiritual counterpart.

A word/picture analogy

Picture an outpost or fortress at night with watchmen posted at its gates. Every watchman's responsibility is to guard that fortress from any forced or unwelcome entry.

To get past the watchman into the interior, a clever intruder has to disguise and present himself in such a way as to convince the watchman that he is friend, not foe. If successful, this wolf in sheep's clothing will prove fatal both for watchman and the inhabitants beyond the gate.

When the watchmen are quietly and systematically disposed of, the unsuspecting populace within and its dormant troops will become perilously vulnerable to attack from without.

Meanwhile, outside the gates, invading troops await, poised to overrun the city. They'll soon march right through the gates, unannounced, unopposed, overtaking the fortress and all its defenses.

The invasion

Your physical body is just such a fortress and white blood cells (T-cells or CD4 cells), are its watchmen. CD4's station themselves around vulnerable openings (cuts or breaks in the skin) which antigens (germs, bacteria, virus etc.) use to enter the blood system.

Overview of an illness

Session 3

CD4's are supposed to signal the rest of the immune (defense) system that a foreigner has entered. When signalled, complementary CD8 "killer" cells should come to the rescue and attack the foreign invader.

How it gets in

1. HIV enters one's body through cuts or breaks—gateways/openings in the skin, on the body, in the mouth, vagina and anal lining.
2. Fluids containing the virus must enter the blood system. Infected cells are found only in fluids contaminated with blood: semen, vaginal fluids, urine, feces and saliva, all with varying concentrations.
3. HIV infection occurs during sexual activity, when sharing needles, during blood transfusions, or from an infected mother to infant before, during or after birth or from accidental exposure.

The deception

Like the intruder in the word-picture mentioned before, HIV comes clothed in deceptive garb. The AIDS virus has a protective protein coating with markers that match the markers found on the human white blood cells it seeks to take over. HIV deceives its new host and attaches to the cell. Once the virus attaches and is incorporated into the nucleus of the host cell, the CD4's ability to warn the rest of the body's defense system of the invasion is rendered ineffective.

The infiltration

HIV, similar to other viruses, needs a host cell.

1. HIV invades various cells in the bloodstream: the vital CD4 white blood cells and macrophages.
2. HIV bonds with the CD4 and subsequently unloads its viral genetic material directly into the nucleus of the human host cell.
3. While most viruses and human cells have genetic material coded in DNA, HIV's is in RNA. Through a process known as reverse transcriptase the RNA is converted into its host's DNA, thus making bonding complete, literally converting the CD4 cells into viral factories.

NOTES

Session 3

Overview of an illness

NOTES

Replication

In time the "occupied" human cell will manufacture more HIV.

1 Using the storehouse of materials in the host cell, new HIV particles eventually form. They can burst or bud out of the host cell, traveling through the blood system seeking to take over other CD4 cells.

2 The virus' destructive path renders a crucial part of the body's defense system ineffectual.

3 The end result is a crippled compromised immunity, leaving the body vulnerable to diseases that a healthy and vital immune system could easily fight off.

Note: People don't die directly from HIV itself; they die from diseases that overrun a body with an HIV-depressed immune system.

Picturing the subdued immune system

HIV infection can produce a highly compromised immune system, thus hastening death. The condition of someone with AIDS is so devastating it has been likened to tying an individual's hands behind thim, chaining their feet, strapping a large bag of sand on their back, throwing them into the ocean and telling them to swim! Like the drowning person, the impared immune system of those with AIDS is overwhelmed by the onslaught of debilitating diseases.

Stages of HIV

Historically, AIDS has been the catch-all word frequently misapplied to all stages of the disease, from initial HIV infection to the illnesses associated with fully developed AIDS.

Many medical professionals describe the different stages as:

1 **HIV infection:** when a person's bloodstream is exposed to HIV.

2 **HIV positive:** when the infected person's immune system develops detectable antibodies to help fight off HIV.

3 **HIV disease:** the stage at which one is infected and the virus has taken hold in the body. HIV disease is diagnosed with a CD4 count of 200 and below. That stage includes fully developed AIDS, when serious "opportunistic infections" attack the weakened body.

Embracing Life Series: International Copyright © 1998 by Embracing Life Ministries. All Rights Reserved

Overview of an illness

Session 3

Testing for infection

Testing for the presence of HIV runs the following course:

1. Testing for the presence of HIV antibodies in the body, i.e. antibodies produced in response to the presence of the virus.
2. Testing for the evidence of viral activity in the body.

Testing for antibodies: The name of the initial HIV antibody test is called ELISA. This is an overly-sensitive test so as not to miss any infected persons. It is the initial test administered. If the ELISA test is positive, the Western Blot is given to confirm the results.

Viral load tests track trends in viral replication in blood plasma which, along with the other indicators, enable doctor and patient to anticipate what rate of progression—if any—the virus is making. This test has become the most crucial for determining viral activity and treatment. Ongoing CD4 monitoring is usually done with this test to determine prior damage to the immune system.

Some of the diseases associated with HIV disease or fully developed AIDS are the following:

1. **Parasitic infections:** Pneumocystis carinii pneumonia (PCP), toxoplasmosis, cryptosporidium
2. **Cancers:** Kaposi's Sarcoma (KS), lymphoma
3. **Viral:** Cytomegalovirus (CMV), herpes, shingles
4. **Fungal infections:** Candiasis
5. **Tuberculousis and related infections:** Mycobacterium avium complex (MAC)
6. **Wasting syndrome** (unexplained dramatic weight loss)

Since 1987, a diagnosis of any one of these diseases would have meant a diagnosis of AIDS. However, since that time, new diseases, those diseases particular to women have been added to the list. In 1993 a criterion for a diagnosis with AIDS was established: a positive HIV test result combined with a CD4 count of less than 200 (the normal range being 800-1,000).

NOTES

Session 3 — Overview of an illness

NOTES

Treatment/cure

At the time of this writing no cure for AIDS or vaccine to prevent HIV infection has been developed. However successes of new drug combination therapies offer much help. With access to these drugs, many expect HIV infection to become a chronic condition rather than a terminal one. In our next chapter we will be discussing decision-making in the treatment process, and the questions of faith that it provokes.

> Father, we thank You for creating our bodies. We marvel at the magnificent complexity of our makeup. We are so grateful that Your Spirit has come to reside in us and that You are able to restore in us what fallen nature has compromised and destroyed. Apart from You and the wisdom You give us we can not cure ourselves. Lord, continue to minister truth and healing to our bodies that we might live free from the judgements of the fall.

SCRIPTURE READINGS

1 Corinthians 12:18; 1 Corinthians 12:26-27; Psalm 103; Proverbs 4:20-22

THOUGHTS FOR JOURNALING

The picture of the "watchmen cells" was the result of praying to the Lord for a simple explanation of HIV. If the nature of your illness does not correspond to the immune system analogy given at the beginning of this chapter, ask the Lord to give you a metaphor that would more easily explain it.

If you have your own pictures that would be helpful to others in explaining HIV infection write them down.

Readings

HIV GLOSSARY

A

ACTG: AIDS Clinical Trials Group. The ACTG is comprised of 59 U.S. medical centers that evaluate treatments for HIV and HIV-associated illnesses. The ACTG studies are sponsored by the National Institute of Allergy and Infectious Diseases (NIADID), a division of the National Institute of health (NIH).

Active Immunization: immunization produced by the body's own immune system in response to foreign antigens. It generally results in antibody reproduction, and also may initiate a protective cellular immune response. Vaccination is an example of active immunization.

Acute: rapid in onset; severe, possibly life-threatening; opposite of chronic

Acyclovir (Zovirax): an anti-viral drug used in the treatment of herpes simplex virus-1 and 2, herpes zoster (shingles) and sometimes for acute varicella-zoster virus (chickenpox). When used in combination with AZT, acyclovir appears to prolong survival among people with AIDS.

Adjuvant: a substance incorporated into or injected simultaneously with a vaccine, which acts to potentiate the immune system's response; any substance that enhances the effectiveness of another drug or substance.

Adoptive immune transfer: refers to the use of a graft of immune tissue from a healthy donor to build a replacement immune system in an individual whose immune system has been damaged or destroyed. Bone marrow transfer (BMT) is an example of immune system transfer.

Aerosolized pentamadine: a drug used as a preventative treatment for *Pneumocystis carinni pneumonia* (PCP). It is administered as a fine spray and inhaled.

Albumin: a simple protein found in the tissues and fluids. Serum albumin is albumin in the clear liquid portion of the blood or serum.

Allogenic: refers to a graft or transfer from a non-genetically identical but HLA matched (protein marker-matched) individual.

Alternative therapy/medicine: refers to non-standard, non-allopathic therapies, e.g. Chinese herbs and acupuncture.

Ambulatory: able to walk and move about without assistance; not confined to bed.

Amebiasis: infection with pathogenic amebas (a type of protozoan).

Amino acid: the basic structural unit of proteins, the unique sequences of which are specified by genes. There are 20 different known types of amino acids.

Anabolic steroids: hormonal substances that promote the synthesis of proteins and the building of muscle mass.

Anabolism: refers to the cellular synthesis of organic molecules and/or the building of proteins in the body.

Anemia: a condition marked by an abnormally low number of red blood cells or by a decreased concentration of hemoglobin, resulting in a reduction of the supply of oxygen to the cells and tissues; often accompanied by fatigue and weakness.

Anergy: lack of an immune response to the presence of a foreign substance (antigen). This may indicate the inability of the immune system to mount a normal allergic response.

Angiogenesis: the growth of new blood vessels.

Angular chelitis: inflammation and fissures radiating from the corners of the mouth due to nutritional deficiencies, atopic dermatitis.

Anorexia: the lack or loss of appetite for food.

Antibiotic: a natural or synthetic substance that destroys or inhibits the growth of microorganisms, especially bacteria.

Antibody: an immunoglobulin (protein) secreted by immune system plasma cells which have evolved from B-cells. Antibody production occurs in response to the presence of an antagonistic, usually foreign substance (antigen) in the body. Specific antibodies bind to and either neutralize or destroy specific antigens. The antigen/antibody reaction forms the basis of non-cellular immunity.

Antigen: any substance that antagonizes or stimulates the immune system to produce antibodies. Antigens are often foreign substances such as bacteria or viruses that invade the body.

Antigenemia: the presence of detectable amounts of antigens in the blood.

Antihistamine: a compound that counteracts histamine, a cytokine that is released by basophils and mast cells in response to exposure to a foreign antigen; commonly used for treating allergic reactions

Session 3   Embracing Life Series   41

Readings

and nasal congestion and for blocking stomach acid secretion.

Antioxidant: a substance that inhibits oxidation or reactions promoted by oxygen or peroxides. Antioxidants can bind with and neutralize free radicals.

Antisense: a complement piece of DNA or RNA that recognizes another piece of DNA or RNA. By binding to its complement, antisense molecules can prevent DNA/RNA from being used in the synthesis of a new virus.

Antiretrovirals: agents used to suppress the activity of retroviruses such as HIV.

Aphthous ulcers: small, often painful shallow lesions on the mucous membranes lining the mouth; also known as "canker sores."

Assay: a test used to detect the presence and concentration of a drug, substance or microorganism in the blood or other body fluids or tissues.

Aspergillosis: an infection of the lung and sinuses caused by *Aspergillus*, a fungus. Aspergillosis can spread through the blood to other organs. Symptoms include fever, chills, difficulty breathing and coughing up blood. If the infection reaches the brain it may cause dementia or other neurologic problems.

Asymptomatic: a state of not feeling or showing outward symptoms or signs of disease, despite the presence of a disease causing agent.

Atrophy: to waste away, or a condition of wasting; usually refers to the loss of muscle tissue.

Autologous: refers to a transplant or transfusion in which the donor and recipient are the same individual, for example a transfusion of blood that was previously removed from the recipient and stored.

B

Bacillus, bacilli: a group of gram-positive, rod-shaped bacteria typically found in the soil.

Bacterimia: the presence of bacteria in the blood; sepsis.

bacteria: simple, single-celled microorganisms that can cause disease in humans and animals.

Bactrim: one of the brand names for trimethoprim-sulfamethoaxole (TMP-SMX), the preferred treatment for PCP. Septra is another brand name for this drug.

Basic fibroblast growth factor (bFGF): a chemical that promotes angiogenesis, which is essential for the development of Kaposi's sarcoma and other neoplasms.

Basophil: a type of white blood cell that releases chemicals in allergic reactions; basophils that leave the blood stream become mast cells in tissues.

B complex: a group of several water-soluble vitamins that includes B (thiamin), pantothenic acid and folic acid.

bDNA (branched DNA assay): a DNA test for detecting and measuring HIV RNA in the blood plasma of people with HIV. bDNA testing can be used to monitor the effectiveness of anti-HIV drugs and to gauge HIV disease progression.

Beta-2 microglobulin: a protein found in the blood. Elevated blood levels of this protein are associated with immune activation, replication of HIV and progression of HIV disease.

Beta carotene: a form of carotene, precursor to vitamin A, a red-orange pigment found in plants and plant-eating animals, and also found in dark green and dark yellow fruits and vegetables. Beta carotene is an antioxidant and may have beneficial effects on the immune system.

Biliary system: pertaining to the bile, bile ducts or gallbladder.

Biohazard: a hazard to people or their environment caused by a biological agent or condition.

Blood brain barrier: a barrier between the blood and the brain that selectively permits or prohibits substances from passing from the bloodstream to the brain. Many drugs will not cross this barrier and therefore cannot be used to treat infections of the brain.

Bone marrow: the soft, spongy tissue interior of the bones that is responsible for producing cells in the blood, including red and white blood cells and platelets.

Bone marrow transfer (BMT): a graft of the bone marrow from one individual to another to reconstitute the recipients damaged immune system.

Bronchoscopy: a procedure for diagnostic inspection with flexible fiber optics of the trachea, bronchi and lungs.

Bulimia: an eating disorder characterized by binge eating, followed by forced purging by means of self-induced vomiting or use of laxatives.

Readings

C

Calcium: a metallic element essential for bone maintenance and proper neural and muscular function. Found in dairy products and other food.

Cachexia: a condition characterized by general ill-health and malnutrition.

Candidiasis: a disease caused by the yeast like fungus, *Candida albicans*. Cadidiasis can affect the skin, nails and mucous membranes throughout the body including the mouth, throat, vagina, intestines and lungs.

Carbohydrate: an organic molecule that is composed mainly of carbon, hydrogen and oxygen atoms and which constitutes a major class of animal foods.

Caries: decay or destruction of parts of the tooth; "cavities".

CD4 cell: a critically important type of immune system white blood cell (also known as the T-helper or T4 cell) that helps the body fight infection. CD4 cells release cytokines that coordinate the activity of a broad range of immune cells, including B cells, which produce antibodies. HIV invades these cells and weakens and destroys them. Physicians regularly monitor CD4 cell counts in HIV-infected individuals as an indication of the progression of HIV disease; severe immunosupression is correlated with T-helper counts below 200 cells/mm^3.

Cellulitis: an inflammation of subcutaneous connective tissue; infection is caused by bacteria and treated with antibiotics.

Chemoprophylaxis: the use of chemical agents for disease prevention.

Chemotherapy: the use of drugs of other chemical agents in the treatment of a disease.

Chronic: referring to a process, such as a disease process, that occurs slowly and persists over a long period of time; opposite of acute.

Cimetidine (Tagamet): a drug developed to treat peptic (stomach) ulcers by stopping the secretion of stomach acid. Cimetidine is under study for treatment of HIV disease.

Clarithrmycin (Biaxin): an antibiotic approved in oral form for the treatment of common bacterial infections in non-immunocompromised patients and, in combination with at least one other drug for the treatment of disseminated MAC; also under study for treatment of toxoplasmosis. High doses may cause abdominal pain.

CMI multitest (cell-mediated immunity multitest): a test that uses a variety of antigens to assess immune competence.

Coccidiomycosis: a fungal disease acquired by inhalation of dust particles containing *Cociodes immitis* spores that can cause lesions to develop in the upper respiratory tract and lungs; sometimes disseminates to visceral organs, bones, skin and other tissues. Symptoms include cough and wasting. The infection may be benign and self-limited or virulent and severe.

Coenzyme Q: a substance that aids in the oxidation of food within cells to create energy.

Cofactor: a substance, microorganism or environmental factor that activates or enhances the action of another entity such as a disease-causing agent.

Cohort: a group of individuals in a study who share a statistical factor.

Colony stimulating factor (CSF): proteins responsible for controlling the production of white blood cells. Types include granulocyte colony stimulating factor (Neupogen) and granuloctye machrophage-colony stimulating factor (Sargramostim) which are to alleviate neutrophenia (low neutrophil count) caused by drugs such as AZT and gancliclovir.

Commensal organisms: organisms that live in the body without causing disease.

Corticosteroids: any number of steroid substances obtained from the cortex of the adrenal gland or manufactured synthetically. Corticosteroids are immunosuppresive and people with HIV should be cautious about taking them for longer than a few weeks.

CPCRA: Community Programs for Clinical Research on AIDS. A community-based clinical trials network sponsored by NIAID with units in 15 cities. CPCRA studies focus on new treatments for opportunistic infections, particularly in underserved populations.

Cross-reactive: refers to an antigen that provokes a response from antibodies that originally developed to another, primary antigen.

Cryptococcus: yeast-like fungus that can cause cryptococcal meningitis, a life-threatening disease that affects the central nervous system.

Readings

Cryptosporidiosis: a disease caused by the parasite Cryptosporidium parvum, which is found in the intestines of animals. The parasite is transmitted to humans by direct contact with the feces of an infected animal, by ingestion of contaminated food or water or by oral-anal sexual contact (rimming). The parasite grows in the intestines and bile ducts and causes severe chronic diarrhea and weight loss. In immunocompromised individuals cryptosporidiosis may be life-threatening.

Culture: the growth of microorganisms or living tissue in the laboratory in solutions that promote their growth.

Cytokine: a chemical messenger protein released by certain white blood cells including macrophages, monocytes and lymphocytes. Cytokine facilitates communication between immune cells and between immune cells and the rest of the body.

Cytomegalovirus (CMV): a virus in the herpes family. CMV infection can occur without causing symptoms. In people with advanced HIV disease, CMV may reactivate to cause serious illness, including blindness, pneumonia, colitis, nerve inflammation and/or death.

Cytotoxic T-lymphocyte (CTL; CD8 cell): a white blood cell in the immune system that targets and kills cells infected with viruses, bacteria, parasites and other microorganisms.

Cytotoxicity: the quality of being capable of producing a specific toxic action against cells.

D

Diapsone: the common name for an antibiotic drug used in the treatment and prophylaxis of PCP and other diseases.

Dehydroepiandrosterone (DHEA): a hormone produced by the adrenal cortex and testes, a weak androgen steroid.

Delayed-type hypersensitivity: cell-mediated immune response that produces a cellular infiltrate and edema, redness and induration (hardness) between 48 and 72 hours after exposure to an antigen.

Dementia: chronic loss of mental capacity with organic origins that affects a person's ability to function in a social or occupational setting. Dementia involves the progressive deterioration of thinking, behavior and motor skills. AIDS-related dementia may be caused by HIV or by other infections.

Dermatologist: a physician who specializes in treating diseases of the skin.

Dermatome: the linear or stripe-shaped distribution of nerve sensation of the skin.

Dietician: a person specializing in dietetics, the study of nutrition and the use of special diets for prophylaxis and treatment of disease.

Disseminated: spread, distributed or occurring throughout the body.

DNA: deoxyribonucleic acid. Found in the nucleus of a cell as a double-stranded chemical chain that stores and transmits genetic information in living cells. The particular sequence of the four unique nucleotide chemical building blocks of a DNA chain forms the genetic code of a cell.

Dorsal: pertaining to the back.

Down-regulation: reduction of the rate at which a process occurs, a substance is released, etc.

Dronabinol (Marinol): a drug used to reduce nausea and vomiting caused by chemotherapy in cancer patients and for use as an appetite stimulant in people with HIV-related wasting syndrome. Dronabinol is derived from THC, the active ingredient in marijuana.

Droplet nuclei: airborne particles that transmit infection, especially tuberculosis.

Dysregulation: refers to interruption of our interference with normal process(es).

E

Edema: swelling caused by an abnormal accumulation of fluid in body tissues.

Efficacy: effectiveness, efficiency, the ability to achieve a desired result.

Encephalitis: a life-threatening inflammation of the brain.

Encepalopathy: any disease of the brain.

Endocrine gland: a ductless gland that regulates bodily functions via the secretion of hormones into the bloodstream. The endocrine glands into the hypothalamus, pitituary gland, thyroid, adrenal glands and gonads.

Engraftment: transfer of tissue or organs from one individual to another; transplant

Enteric: pertaining to the intestines.

Envelope: the outer covering of a virus. The HIV envelope contains two protein units called gp120 and gp41; gp120 is the part of HIV that attaches itself to the surface protein of CD4 cells.

Readings

Enzyme-linked immunosorbent assay (ELISA): a laboratory blood test used to detect the presence of HIV and other antibodies.

Eosinophil: a white blood cell whose granules readily absorb a red stain called eosin; eosinphils play roles in allergic reactions and the elimination of parasites.

EPA: Environmental Protection Agency; the federal agency charged with implementing and enforcing environmental regulations and controlling pollutants and toxins in the environment.

Epidemiology: the study of the frequency, distribution and behavior of a disease in a defined population.

Epithelium: the thin layer of cells that covers the internal and external surfaces of the body, including body cavities, ducts and vessels.

Epstein-Barr virus (EBV): a virus of the herpes family. EBV infection is common and usually symptomatic in childhood, may cause infectious mononucleosis in young adults and may be severe in immunocompromised individuals. EBV is associated with lymphomas in persons with HIV disease.

Erythematous: relating to an inflammatory redness of the skin.

Erythocyte: a mature red blood cell (RBC) that contains the molecule hemoglobin. The main function of the RBC is to transport oxygen and carbon dioxide between the lungs and the tissues.

Erythropoietin (EPO, Procrit, epogen): a natural growth factor that stimulates the production of red blood cells. A genetically engineered form of EPO is used for the treatment of severe anemia.

Esophageal: pertaining to esophagus, the tube between the oral cavity and the stomach.

Estrogen: "female sex hormone" any natural or synthetic substance that exerts biological affects characteristic of hormones such as estradiol, a hormone formed by the ovaries, placenta and testes. Estrogen stimulates secondary sexual characteristics in females.

F

Folic acid: a B complex vitamin important for red blood cell production.

Food and Drug Administration(FDA): the federal government agency responsible for regulating the development and usage of prescription drugs.

Free radical: a molecule that contains unpaired electron(s); they are highly reactive and can cause cellular damage.

Fulminant: referring to a condition that is severe and/or aggressive.

Fungus: a class of microbes that includes yeast, molds and mushrooms.

G

Gamma Hydroxy Butyrate (GHB): a precursor and breakdown product of the neurotransmitter gamma aminobutyric acid (GABA). GHB has been used as an veterinary, recreational and bodybuilding drug. It has some growth hormone stimulating as well as hallucinogenic and nervous system depressant properties. Side effects include seizures and coma.

Gamma interferon (immune interferon, actimmune): a cytokine associated with cell-mediated immune responses.

Gastrointestinal: relating to the stomach and intestines.

Gene: the biological unit of heredity; genes contain the genetic or hereditary information encoded by DNA, and are located at a unique position in a sequence of genes in the cell's nucleus. Genes determine many aspects of human physiology.

Gene therapy: procedures that treat disease at the molecular level. Examples include altering the DNA of a pathogen to make it less harmful or adding genes to cells to produces missing essential enzymes.

Genotype: the specific genetic makeup or "blueprint" of an individual.

Germicide: an agent that is toxic or destructive to germs or microorganisms.

Giardiasis: a common infection with the protozoa *Giardia*, which is spread via contaminated food and water and by fecal-oral contact. *Giardia* infects the intestines and produces nausea cramping and diarrhea.

Gingivitis: inflammation of the gingvia, the gums of the mouth; gum disease.

Glucocorticoid: a steroid-like substance capable of influencing metabolism and exerting an anti-inflammatory effect, eg. cortisol.

Glutathione: an oxidation reduction agent needed for cellular production of energy. There have been reports of depressed levels of glutathione in HIV positive individuals, and reports of glutathione-related suppression of HIV *in vitro*.

Readings

Glycoprotein: refers to a small unit made of a sugar and a protein molecule, often a part of the cell's membrane.

Gonad: an organ that produces sex cells (sperm and ova); a testis or ovary.

Gonadotropin: a hormone that acts on the gonads to promote their growth and function.

Gonnorhea: a sexually transmitted disease which involves urethitis (inflammation of the urethra) and inflammation of the genital and/or other mucous membranes; untreated gonnorhea may spread to the upper genital tract of other internal organs. Caused by the bacteria *Neisseria gonnorhea*.

GP-120: a protein on the outer shell or envelope, of HIV. GP-120 is the portion of HIV that binds to a helper T-cell's surface portion, CD4. The "120" refers to its molecular weight.

GP-160: glycoprotein molecular weight 160, a protein on the outer shell of HIV that enables it to enter human cells; cleaved into the gp120 and gp41 portions of the HIV envelope.

Granuloma: an inflammatory lesion containing phagocytes.

H

Hairy Leukoplakia: a condition believed to be caused by the Epstein-Barr virus, a herpes virus. Symptoms include small, white, hair-like projections on the side of the tongue. It is seen almost exclusively in people who are HIV positive.

Hematologic: relating to the study of blood.

Hematopoiesis: the process by which blood cells are produced in the marrow.

Hemoglobin: the red, iron-based protein of red blood cells which transports oxygen from the lungs to tissues throughout the body.

Hepatitis: an inflammation of the liver that may be caused by viruses or toxic agents.

Hepatitis A (infectious hepatitis): an inflammatory disease of the liver with a short incubation period; can be spread by fecal-oral and/or household contact. Disease may be mild to severe and often produces jaundice (yellowing of the skin and whites of the eyes).

Hepatitis B (serum hepatitis): a viral liver disease that can be acute or chronic and even life-threatening, particularly in people with poor immune resistance. Like HIV, the hepatitis B virus can be transmitted by sexual contact, contaminated needles, contaminated blood or blood products or perinatal transmission, but unlike HIV, it is transmissible through close, casual contact.

Herpes simplex virus 1 (HSV-1): a virus that can cause painful blisters usually occurring on the lips ("fever blisters" or "cold sores") or in the mouth or around the eyes. The symptomatic disease stage occurs at unpredictable intervals or weeks, months, or years. The latent (inactive) virus can reactivate due to emotional stress, physical trauma, other infections or suppressions of the immune system. HSV-1 responds well to treatment with acyclovir.

Herpes simplex virus 2 (HSV-2): a virus closely related to HSV-1 that causes similar lesions. However, HSV-2 is usually transmitted sexually, and its lesions are generally in the anogenital area. HSV may become disseminated in people with the HIV disease.

Herpes zoster (shingles): a skin condition characterized by painful blisters in a linear distribution on one side of the body, which generally dry up and scab leaving minor scarring. Shingles is caused by a reactivation of a previous infection with the varicella-zoster virus (VZV) which causes chicken pox, usually in childhood. Shingles may be a symptom of HIV disease progression and may recur in people with poor immunity.

Histocompatibility: immunologic identity or similarity sufficient to allow a successful transgenic graft. Implies that the donor and recipient have the same histocompatibility genes.

Histoplasmosis: a disease caused by a fungal infection acquired from inhaling spores (present in soil or dust) of the fungus *Histoplasma capsulatum*. The disease is most often found in the lungs, where it produces a tuberculosis-like lung inflammation, but may also become disseminated. The disease may become life-threatening in individuals with suppressed immune systems.

HIV-2: human immunodeficiency virus type-2. A virus similar to HIV that is found primarily among West Africans.

HIV Ig: antibodies that are made in response to HIV infection. An engineered form made by Abbot has been clinically tested in children with HIV.

Hormone: an active regulatory chemical messenger substance formed in one part of the body and carried in the blood to another part of the body, where it coordinates cellular functions. Many hormones are produced by endocrine glands.

46   **Embracing Life Series**   Session 3

Readings

Human chorionic gonadotropin (HCG): a hormone secreted during pregnancy that maintains the fetus during early development. It has been shown to suppress the development of Kaposi's sarcoma cells *in vitro*, alpha-HCG refers to the alpha chain of HCG.

Human growth hormone (HGH): a peptide hormone secreted by the anterior pituitary gland in the brain. HGH enhances body growth by stimulating carbohydrate and protein metabolism.

Human leukocyte antigens (HLA): protein markers used to test tissues for immunologic similarity or histocompatibility. Also the genetic locus that codes for an individual's specific major histocompatibility complex (MHC) pattern.

Human pappilomavirus (HPV): a member of the papova family of viruses, HPV caused warts may appear as flat or nipple like protrusions. Certain strains of HPV have been associated with cervical and anal cancer.

Humoral: pertaining to body fluids, primarily serum and lymph; those aspects of the immune responses that are associated with circulating antibodies.

Humoral immunity: the immunity that is mediated by B cells and involves production of antibodies. Humoral immunity is associated with th production of cytokines interleukin-4 and interleukin-10.

Huntington's disease: a complex neurologic disease, thought to be hereditary, that causes dementia and loss of control of movement.

Hyperkeratosis: a skin condition characterized by thickening and hardening of the skin.

Hypergonadism: underproduction of hormones by ovaries or testes, e.g. a low testosterone level.

Hypothalamic-pitituiary-gonadal axis: a feedback loop between glands that regulates hormone levels. The hypothalamus produces hormones that control secretion of hormones by the pitituary gland, which in turn regulates the activity of the gonads.

Hypothalamus: a gland in the brain that controls and integrates the automatic nervous system and regulates the production of hormones by endocrine glands.

I

Idiopathic: denoting a disease or condition of unknown cause.

IgA: a type of immunoglobulin (antibody) that is secreted by and acts upon the linings of the openings of the body, e.g., the gastro intestinal and genitourinary tracts.

IgC: the most common type of immunoglobulin (antibody) which provides the bulk of specific immunity against antigens.

Immunity: the natural or acquired resistance to a specific disease. Immunity may be partial or complete, long–lasting or temporary.

Immunocompromised: pertaining to reduced function of the body's immune system.

Immunoendocrinology: a hybrid branch of medicine combining the study of the immune system (immunology) and the study of the endocrine glands and their hormones and effects (endocrinology).

Immunoflorescence: a rapid, inexpensive test that uses a dye to identify cells and invading organisms. The test can differentiate between various disease causing organisms, e.g., varicella-zoster virus from herpes–simplex virus.

Immunogen: an antigenic substance that stimulates an immune response.

Immunogenicity: having the properties of an antigen.

Immunoglobulin: proteins that acts as antibodies to help the body fight off disease by combining with a neutralizing or destroying specific antigens. There are 5 classes: IgC, IgA, IgD, IgM, and IgE.

Immunomodulating therapy: a immunotherapy that attempts to reconstruct or enhance a damaged immune system. Examples in experimentation for AIDS include passive hyperimmune therapy, and CD8 cell line expansion.

Immunomodulator: a substance capable of modifying 1 or more functions of the immune system.

Immunosupression: reduced function of 1 or more components of the body's immune system. HIV infection causes immunosupression and other immune dysfunctions.

Induration: a hardening of soft tissue caused by infiltration of macrophages and other white blood cells at the site of injection of an antigen. Induration indicates that an immune response is being mounted by the body.

Intercurrent: occurring at the same time.

Interleukin: a chemical hormone messenger secreted by and affecting many different cells in the immune system.

Session 3   Embracing Life Series   47

Readings

Interleukin-1 (IL-1): a natural cytokine released by monocytes, macrophages, T-cells and other immune cells that fight infection.

Interleukin-2 (IL-2): a cytokine that is produced by both T-helper and suppressor lymphocytes. IL-2 increases the expression of natural killer and other cytotoxic cells. IL-2 is associated with a cell-mediated or TH-1 immune response. A recombinant version of IL-2 is under study as a treatment for HIV disease.

Interleukin-4 (IL-4): a cytokine released by lymphocytes that enhances the humoral response, increasing antibody production.

Interleukin-6 (IL-6): a cytokine whose production affects many different cells in the immune system.

Interleukin-10 (IL-10): a cytokine released by lymphocytes that enhances the humoral response, increasing antibody production.

Interleukin-12 (IL-12): a cytokine that induces the production of natural killer and other cytotoxic immune cells. IL-12 is a associated with a cell-mediated or TH-1 immune response. A recombinant IL-12 is under study as a treatment for HIV disease.

Intramuscular: within the substance of a muscle. Intramuscular drugs are injected directly into the muscle.

Intravenous (IV): within or into a vein. Intravenous drugs are injected directly into the veins.

In vitro: Latin for "in glass"; refers to studies done in the laboratory.

In vivo: Latin for "in the body of a living organism"; refers to studies done using human and animal subjects.

Irradiation: exposure to x-rays or other radiation. Irradiation may be used to kill pathogens or as a treatment for neoplastic disease.

Isolate: a specific strain of a particular microbe (i.e., strains of HIV-1).

Isoniazid (INH): an orally administered drug used in the prevention and/or treatment (with other drugs) of active tuberculosis.

Isosporiasis: a disease caused by the parasite *Isopora belli*, an occyst-forming microorganism usually found in tropical climates. Infection in humans are usually mild, but *Isopora* can cause diarrhea and weight loss in immunocompromised persons.

IVIG: broad-spectrum intravenous immunoglobulins used to treat immunodeficient states in which the body does not produces enough of its own antibodies. Recombinant and pooled immunoglobulins from blood donors have been used to help people with HIV-disease, especially children, resist bacterial infections.

K

Kaposi's sarcoma (KS): an abnormal growth in the walls of blood or lymph vessels visible through the skin and/or mucous membranes. KS typically appears as pink to purple lesions on the surface of the skin, but it can also occur internally. KS occurs more commonly among gay and bisexual men with HIV-disease than among HIV-infected heterosexual men and women. The cause of KS is unknown but is likely multifactorial.

L

Lactobaccilus acidophilus: bacteria that makes up part of the normal flora of the human intestine, mouth and vagina. Some types of yogurt contain acidophilus and may help restore normal bacteria balance after antibiotic treatment.

Latent: refers to a state in which a pathogenic organism is present but not actively replicating or causing illness.

L-carnitine: a chemical substance that stimulates fatty acid oxidation and synthesis.

Lean body mass: muscle tissue

Legionellosis (Legionnairre's disease): an upper-respiratory tract infection caused by *Legionella* bacteria, which are widely distributed in nature and may be spread via contaminated water supplies such as the cooling systems of large buildings. The infection is often acquired in a hospital.

Lesion: an abnormal change in tissue caused by disease or injury.

Liposome (lipid vesicle): a spherical particle of lipid molecules suspended in an aqueous or water-like medium inside a tissue or a cell; a spherical particle of fat or oil (lipid) suspended inside a cell or in the bloodstream.

Listeriosis: an infection caused by *Listeria monocytogenes*, an aerobic rod-shaped bacteria that may be present in meat, poultry and raw or unpasteurized milk or milk products, particularly certain types of cheese. Listeriosis is most often manifested in adults as meningitis or as an infection of pregnant women

Readings

and their new-borns. May cause a mild flu-like illness or more serious symptoms in immunocompromised persons.

Lymph node: a small immune system organ located throughout the body along lymph-carrying vessels, with concentration in the neck, groin and armpits. Lymph nodes store lymphocytes and are the sites of antigen presentation and immune activation.

Lymphoma: any of a group of malignant diseases originating in the lymph nodes.

Lymphoproliferative: producing lymphoid cells.

M

MAC: a disease caused by a bacterium found in the soil. In PWA, it can spread through the bloodstream to infect lymph nodes, bone marrow, liver, spleen, spinal fluid, lungs and intestinal tract. Symptoms of MAC include a prolonged wasting, fever, fatigue and enlarged spleen. Rifabutin is FDA-approved for the prevention of MAC in HIV positive individuals with fewer than 100 T-helper cells. Clarthromycin (Biaxin) is FDA-approved for the treatment of active MAC, but is generally used in combination with other drugs.

Major histocompatibility complex (MHC): refers to cell surface proteins vital to "self" and determine whether a graft will be accepted or rejected; they are requested for antigen presentation. There are 2 classes of MHC molecules, MHC-1 and MHC-II, which are present on immune system cells.

Malabsorption: a decreased intestinal absorption resulting in loss of appetite, muscle pain and weight loss. Due to damage the tissues and cells lining the intestinal tract have lost their ability to properly transfer nutrients.

Malignant: used to describe cells or tumors growing in an uncontrolled fashion, either spreading to other sites through the bloodstream or invading nearby normal tissues. By definition, cancers are always malignant and the term "malignancy" implies a cancer.

Malnourished: supplied with less than the minimum amount of nutrients essential for sound health and growth.

Malnutrition: faulty nutrition resulting from poor diet, undereating or abnormal absorption of nutrients from the gastrointestinal tract.

Mantoux test: refers to the *M.tuberculosis* skin test invented by French physician, Charles Mantoux; also known as the PPD test.

Mast cell: a basophil (type of immune system white blood cell) that has left a blood vessel and entered into a tissue. Mast cells release histamine and herapin in allergic reactions (as do basophils within the blood vessels).

Megestrol acetate (Megace): an appetite stimulant FDA-approved for the treatment of HIV-related wasting syndrome.

Megadose: a much greater than normal dose, especially of vitamins, in amounts 10 times or more than the Recommended Daily Allowance.

Megakaryocyte (Thromboblast): a large mutilobed cell in the bone marrow that gives rise to platelets.

Meningitis: a disease that causes inflammation of the meninges, the membrane casings that cover the brain and spinal cord.

Metabolism: the process of building the body's molecular structures (proteins) from nutrients and of breaking them down for energy production and excretion.

mRNA: messenger RNA; pieces of riblonucleic acid that carry the genetic code information from DNA, leading to the building of new proteins.

Mutation: a change in the character of a gene that is perpetuated in subsequent cell divisions.

Mycosis: a disease caused by fungus.

N

NDA: New Drug Application. After completing Phase III clinical trials a drug sponsor may file an NDA with the FDA. If the NDA is approved by the FDA, the drug may be marketed by the manufacturer.

Neoplasm: a tissue that grows more rapidly than normal; a tumor or growth; cancer. A neoplasm that doesn't spread to other tissues is described as benign. A neoplasm that has the potential to spread (metastasize) to other tissue is termed malignant and is commonly called cancer.

Neutrophil: the most common type of white blood cell. Neutrophils release chemicals involved in inflammation and are the immune system's primary defense against bacterial infections. The normal range of neutrophils is from 3,000 to 7,000.

Nevirapine: an experimental anti-HIV drug; a non-nucleoside HIV reverse transcriptase inhibitor.

Nf-kB: a regulatory protein that binds to certain genes that code for IL-2 and HIV, increasing their activity.

Readings

Nucleoside analog: a class of synthetic compounds that mimic the building blocks of DNA. Some of these compounds, like AZT, ddc and ddI, suppress replication of HIV by interfering with the production of the reverse transcriptase enzyme, thereby causing premature termination of the DNA chain.

Nutrient: any item of food that nourishes or promotes growth and metabolism.

Nutrition: the process involved in taking in and metabolizing food material by living plants and animals.

Off-label: use of a FDA-approved drug for an indication other than for which the drug was approved.

Oncologist: a physician who specializes in the study of cancers or tumors.

Opportunistic disease or infection (OI): an illness caused by a microorganism that does not cause disease in people with a normal immune system. If the immune system becomes weak, such a microorganism may cause serious or even life-threatening diseases.

Orthopedic: relating the branch of medicine that deals with preserving and restoring function of the musculoskeletal system using physical or surgical methods.

P

p24 antigen: the core protein fragment of HIV. The p24 antigen test measures this fragment in the bloodstream. A positive result for the p24 antigen suggests HIV replication, and may mean the individual has a higher chance of developing AIDS in the future.

p24 antibody test: a test that measures the amount of antibodies in the blood against the p24 antigen.

Pancreatitis: inflammation of the pancreas; symptoms may include intense abdominal pain, nausea, vomiting, constipation and possibly jaundice; pancreatitis can be life-threatening. The anti-HIV drugs, ddI and, more rarely, ddC may cause pancreatitis in some individuals.

Parasite: an organism that lives on or in the host and derives nourishment from it. Some cause inflammation, but others cause infection and destroy tissue. Human parasites include fungi, yeast, bacteria, protozoa, worms and viruses.

Pathogen: any disease causing agent.

Perinatal: concerning the period around the time of birth.

Periodontal disease: a disease of the gums and bone supporting the teeth.

Peripheral neuropathy: a disorder of the nerves, usually involving the hands or feet and sometimes the legs, arms and face. Symptoms may include numbness, a tingling or burning sensation, sharp pain, weakness, partial paralysis and abnormal reflexes.

Phagocyte: a type of carrier white blood cell that "scavenges" bacteria, foreign particles and other cells.

Phase I trial: the first step in human testing of a drug. Designed to evaluate drug toxicity at different dose levels in a small number of volunteers.

Phase II trial: the second step in the evaluation of a drug in humans. Phase II studies are designed to evaluate drug effectiveness and involve more study participants than Phase I studies. Phase II studies proceed only if 1 or more Phase I studies have shown the drug's toxicity level to be acceptable within a given dose range.

Phase III trial: the expansion of Phase II trials up to 3,000 volunteers; designed to support information gathered in Phases I and II; Phase III trials also compare the drug being tested to other agents or to a placebo, either alone or in a combination.

Placebo: an inert, inactive substance. In placebo-controlled studies, a placebo is given to one group of individuals, while the drug being tested is given to another group. The results obtained in the two groups are then compared. Used to avoid bias from researchers, health providers, patients.

Plasma: the fluid that carries blood cells and nutritive substances throughout the body, removes metabolic waste products from the body organs, and is a medium for chemical communications between different parts of the body.

Pneumocystis Carinii Pneumonia: a life-threatening type of pneumonia thought to be caused by a protozoan.

Prophylaxis: a treatment that helps to prevent a disease or condition before it occurs, also known as primary prophylaxis.

Protease: a type of enzyme whose production is necessary for HIV to replicate.

Protease inhibitor: an agent that blocks the action of the protease enzyme that prevents HIV replication.

Readings

R

REV: an HIV regulatory protein important for the production of new virus particles.

RNA: a ribonucleic acid. A single-stranded nucleic acid involved in the transcription of genetic information from DNA. RNA controls the synthesis of protein in all living cells and can take the place of DNA in some viruses, including HIV.

S

Sensory neuropathy: damage or necrosis of nerves serving the sensory organs resulting in numbness, tingling or pain in the extremities.

Seroconversion: the time in which the person's antibody status changes from negative to positive.

Serum: the clear, fluid, non-cellular portion of the blood.

Sputum: mucus or other matter ejected from the throat by coughing or spitting.

Steroid: any of numerous substances that include sterals, certain hormones, D vitamins and some carconagenic substances. Steroid drugs are often used to reduce inflammation in the body.

Standard treatment: a drug or combination of drugs explicitly approved by the FDA for treating the disease or condition in question.

Symptomatic: displaying perceptible, subjective changes in the body or its functions that indicate disease.

Subcutaneous: beneath the skin, but not into deeper muscle tissue.

Synergistic: the action of two or more drugs that, when taken together, have an effect greater than the total effect of the individual drugs.

Systemic: affecting the whole body.

T

Testosterone: a steroid hormone produced by the testes, testosterone is the major male sex hormone; essential for spermatogenesis and the growth and development of reproductive organs and secondary sex characteristics of males. Testosterone supplementation is sometimes used as an experimental treatment for HIV-related wasting.

Thalidomide (synovir): a sedative drug with mutation causing effects. Thalidomide is under investigation for treatment of ulcers and other conditions in persons with HIV disease.

3TC (Lamivudine): a nucleoside analog with anti-HIV and anti-hepatitis B activity. Possible side effects includes hair loss.

Toxoplasmosis: an opportunistic infection caused by the microscopic parasite Toxoplasma gondii, found in undercooked meat and cat feces.

Thrush: lesions caused by the fungus *candida* that appear as white plaques in the mouth especially on the tongue and palate.

TB (Tuberculosis): an infectious disease caused by Mycobacterium tuberculosis that typically affects the lungs but may occur in other organs.

V

Viral load: the number of viral particles (usually HIV) in a sample of blood plasma. It is measured by PCR and bDNA tests.

Vitamin: an organic substance that acts as a coenzyme and/or regulator of metabolic processes. Most vitamins are present in natural foods or supplements; some vitamins are produced within the body.

W

Wasting syndrome: a condition characterized by atrophy of lean body mass and involuntary weight loss of at least 10 percent of normal body waste.

Weight-gain supplements: high-calorie, nutrient-rich foods or drinks used to increase body weight; often recommended for individuals with wasting syndrome.

Western blot: a laboratory test of blood for specific antibodies; more accurate than the ELISA test, the Western blot is used as a confirmatory test if an HIV ELISA test is positive.

Treatments and faith

Session 4

NOTES

This week's session will give group members an opportunity to discuss the physical, emotional and spiritual changes they have gone through during the treatment of their condition. As with the previous session, the example used will be HIV/AIDS and the various approaches used for its treatment. HIV/AIDS is highlighted because of the broad range of familiar illnesses, infections and treatments associated with it.

Living with a life-altering illness necessitates monitoring one's health; we share responsibility with our doctors in that process. Our participation is simply exercising good stewardship over the temple God has given us. However, for those with chronic conditions, the medical options and problems that present themselves can be ongoing and daunting. The choices to be made for treatment are often "quality of life" issues that, for Christians, call one's faith and belief in divine healing into question. Few opportunities in the church exist to openly discuss with others the interplay of medicine and faith. That makes this session all the more important.

When going over the categories of treatment that follow, allow ample time for group members to share about their decision-making process and the role their faith bears upon it. Respect should be given to each person in the group as they share their unique experience. Please keep in mind this is not a time for advice-giving from others.

Session 4 — Treatments and faith

NOTES

Treatments

There are four key categories of treatment options for treating HIV/AIDS as well as most other life-altering conditions.

1. Standard drug treatments
2. Immune system modulators/stimulators
3. Nutritional approaches
4. Co-factor reduction

Standard drug treatments

Treatments in this category are the "mainstream" approaches. They use drugs that have been clinically tested and approved by the FDA (Food and Drug Administration).

Examples: These include the antivirals, protease inhibitors, and complementary drugs (e.g. bactrim, acyclovir) that address the infections and diseases associated with HIV/AIDS disease.

Immune modulators and stimulators

This group includes those drugs or natural herb compounds that work to repair and/or rebuild the body's immune system. For HIV/AIDS that would mean replenishing the white blood cells.

Examples: The protease inhibitors appear to cause the numbers of CD4 cells to increase. Steroids, gamma globulin (rich in antibodies), and various antioxidants and minerals reportedly act to protect and boost the number of cells, too.

Nutritional approaches

These include herbs, vitamins and other natural food substances that benefit the body. Their claims include enhanced immuno-activity and/or reduced toxic side-effects of anti-viral drug treatments.

Examples: Phyto (plant) chemicals, blue-green algae (reportedly increases energy and CD4 count), vitamin C therapy, and oxygen therapy.

Treatments and faith

Session 4

Co-factor reduction

Co-factors are any agents (chemical, genetic, germs, or nutrients), behaviors, or habits that place stress on the immune system and thus precipitate disease.

These are co-factors: Substance abuse/dependency on ingested, injected and inhaled drugs; certain sexual activity and addictions that increase the risk of sexually transmitted diseases (STD's); poor hygiene habits; insufficient rest and sleep; certain unrelated health problems; smog; genetic makeup; germ exposure; additional strains of HIV; other viruses, bacteria and protozoa which deplete the immune system cells; damaging foods and ingredients (e.g., artificial ingredients).

Co-factor reduction involves refraining from high-risk behavior which leads to re-infection of HIV strains and other STD's; abstinence from chemicals and substances which lower immune efficiency; reducing stressors with exercise and a proper diet.

Life decisions

Though the long term side-effects of newly discovered medications remain to be seen, they have enabled many to recover their health and live longer. The welcome health benefits of medical science notwithstanding, the discovery of new treatments present important moral/ethical questions as well.

Reflect and consider the following questions (discussion in larger group is optional):

- What should be done for those who can't afford the latest procedures/medications or get access to them due to geographical locale?
- Should the Church advocate for them? Who should foot the bill?
- Does everyone have a *right* to healthcare and to what extent?

NOTES

Session 4

Treatments and faith

NOTES

Prayer

> If any of you lacks wisdom, he should ask God, who gives generously to all without finding fault, and it will be given to him. (James 1:5)

More and more we read about the "discovery" of prayer as a viable supplement to the process of healing. Studies have measured the effects of praying for people, and the results are substantial. Patients tend to heal faster and live longer. All this should come as no surprise to the Christian who prays.

Prayer was not included in the category of "alternative treatments" because for the Christian, prayer is intended to be more than supplemental; it is a way of life. Because we are God's creation, He invites us to look to Him for sustenance and guidance in all areas of our lives. This includes the well being of our physical body the temple of His Holy Spirit.

Sometimes, however, its difficult to discern the counsel of God in the midst of counsel from others. One may feel unduly pressured by doctors to take certain pharmaceuticals and by friends who offer their favorite remedies. One can be overwhelmed by conflicting advice and the insecurity of wondering what God's perfect will is. What we really need is the peace of God to be at the center of all our decisions. He will give us that peace if we seek Him for it.

Take time now to discuss the following questions:

- Have you experienced the "peace of God" in your treatment decisions?
- Do you have any reports of healing from prayer to share with the group?
- In closing this week's lesson, pray for the healing presence of God to touch the lives of everyone. Ask for His wisdom to guide the group members in all the important decisions they have to make with regard to their health.

Treatments and faith

Session 4

SCRIPTURE READINGS
Proverbs 4:20-22; Psalm 90; Philippians 4:7

THOUGHTS FOR JOURNALING

Should you embrace the medical approach (which can involve some very toxic drugs), following the regimen diligently is necessary for a successful outcome; and a half-hearted, sloppy effort will only do more harm than good when it comes to the efficacy of the treatment.

If you are having difficulty deciding, list the pros and cons of taking it in your journal and pray over your list.

Ask the Lord to give you His peace with regard to your decision, whichever way it goes. Fully embrace the choice you make; God will honor it.

NOTES

Readings

"Making Meds Easier to Take"

Marcy Fenton, M.S., R.D., & Jefferey Bowman

If you are experiencing headaches, loss of appetite, diarrhea or other reactions to medications for more than a few days, you should contact your doctor and discuss your regimen. With many of the protease inhibitors, adverse side-effects fade once your system becomes accustomed to the medication, usually within a few weeks.

Do not change your dosage on any of the anti-HIV medications without the approval of your doctor. Although some physicians will prescribe a low dose, working up to a higher dose in order to minimize side-effects, this needs to be supervised. Taking a lower dose of medication may cause you to become resistant.

The following are suggestions to help cope with the possible nutritional problems that can occur. Experiment, and find what works best for you.

diarrhea

- Follow a low–lactose, low–fat diet. Eliminate milk or substitute it with "LactAid" or "Dairy Ease."
- Drink plenty of clear liquids, such as cranberry juice and chicken broth.
- Avoid gas-forming foods like fried foods, carbonated beverages, cabbage, broccoli, peppers and cucumbers.
- Eat foods at room temperature, avoiding very hot (temperature-wise) foods.
- Avoid caffeine (cola, coffee, chocolate).
- Wash foods, hands, and food preparation services thoroughly—wash, wash, wash.

nausea and vomiting

- Keep kitchen and entire living area well ventilated. Give yourself some fresh air.
- Drink plenty of fluids, including fresh water, herbal teas, clear broths.
- Eat low-fat foods, such as skinless baked chicken and baked potatoes, rather than fried.
- Try soft, non-spicy foods, such as egg noodles and cottage cheese.
- Eat small, frequent meals throughout the day.
- Try dry, salty foods, such as saltine crackers.
- Avoid highly sweetened foods, such as candy and syrups.
- Supplement with high calorie liquid drinks between meals.
- Eat at a relaxed pace and be sure to take deep breaths.

mouth pain / dry mouth

- Eat soft, semi-soft or pureed foods.
- Avoid acidic and spicy foods.
- Eat foods at room temperature.
- Use a straw to bypass painful area.
- Rinse mouth frequently with medicated wash.
- Dip hard foods into a beverage or soup to soften.
- Try Popsicles before eating to numb mouth.

fever

Remember, your caloric and fluid needs are increased when you have a fever.

- As much as possible, eat a high calorie, high protein diet.
- Increase fluid intake, drink fluids with calories, such as juices, fruit drinks or sports drinks instead of plain water or diet drinks.
- Eat foods with a high fluid content, like fruit ices, gelatin, soups, sherbet, grapes, watermelon.

Session 4   Embracing Life Series   59

Readings

altered taste

- Good oral hygiene is critical—rinse your mouth before eating. Avoid greasy, fried foods, chocolate, coffee, tea.
- Make sure your multiple-vitamin supplement contains zinc and vitamin A. Check with your doctor about supplementation.
- Add fresh herbs, spices and condiments to foods.
- Marinate meats and poultry. Remember: Do not use raw meat juices after cooking. Use a separate marinade if you wish to add it over cooked meat.
- If red meat tastes bitter, try high protein foods that are more bland, like fish or chicken.
- Sour candies, peppermints, added fruits or fruit juices can help.

In addition to dealing with medicinal side-effects, it is important to always optimize your nutritional potential. Be sure that the foods you eat are working for you and that you are not depleting your own nutritional resources with "poor" choices. Choose foods that are high in protein, calories, vitamins and minerals.

- Eliminate or cut back on caffeine. Caffeine acts as a diuretic, causing a loss of water and minerals. It can also act as an appetite suppressor—not a good idea at this stage of the game. You want your appetite hearty! It can worsen diarrhea and increase malabsorption of calories and nutrients.
- Minimize weight loss. Eat small, nutritious meals five to six times a day. Keep convenient, high calorie, high protein snacks on hand at all times. If you are having trouble eating, drink liquids 30 minutes before or after solid foods. Supplement with high calorie protein shakes.
- Eliminate or decrease alcohol consumption. Alcohol contributes to a decrease in absorption of many nutrients with an increased risk for deficiencies of Vitamins A, D, E, B complex, glucose, certain amino acids, zinc, magnesium and calcium.
- Ensure maximum absorption of medications. Take all medications as directed. Take medications two hours before or after taking antacids or supplements containing calcium, magnesium, iron or aluminum.

- Develop a daily regimen and stick to it. If you develop a daily routine, then remember to eat five or six meals, when to take medications and supplements and how to decrease side-effects will become much easier. Use a Daily Food and Medication Schedule (available in the HIV Resource Center or call (213) 993-1612) to keep track and keep you on schedule. Try a few well-known tricks, including:
  - Post-It notes on bathroom mirrors, in your car, on your calendar.
  - Tape your schedule to your refrigerator door.
  - Use a pill box which has several compartments, including those for time of day, day of week, etc.
  - Try a pillbox equipped with a timer which you can set to go off when you are due to take your medicine. You can also use a watch with a timer.
  - Ask around. Others may have some tricks that will work for you. And share yours with others!

Remember, you deserve help to maintain your nutritional health. Ask your doctor for a referral to a registered dietitian experienced and sensitive in HIV nutrition issues. Medical treatment without nutrition intervention seems as useless as nutrition without treatment.

Used by author permission.
AIDS Project LA.
"APLA Positive Living," Sept., 1996

Session 5
Facing death and dying

> What is God saying in this calamity? It is a reminder that life in this world is frail and uncertain. We cannot boast of tomorrow. It is therefore vital that we sort out our relationship with God here and now. Then we are ready for anything. *"Teach us to number our days,"* prayed the psalmist *"that we may get a heart of wisdom. (Psalm 90:12)* (*Fear No Evil* by David Watson, p.130)

At one time, HIV/AIDS was universally referred to as a terminal disease; a cold, demoralizing term for those who had it, leaving little room for hope.

New medical discoveries have changed that prognosis, although the subjects of death and dying are likely to stay close associates for some time. Of course, everyone is terminal—we are all going to die one day. Nevertheless, those living with a life-altering condition are forced to think about physical death sooner and more often than anyone would like.

We've been given an opportunity with our situation to confront our feelings about death and dying now, avoiding an emotional collision later on. We can exchange our fears for peace and assurance. The question is: Are we willing to face the situation head on? Debra Jarvis writes in her booklet, *HIV Positive: Living with AIDS:*

> Death takes a lot of energy. You have to work hard at not thinking about death. Every time you have your blood drawn, swallow a pill, look in the mirror, you have to face death. Think how much energy it takes to deny it!

NOTES

Session 5

Facing death and dying

NOTES

But how can we face death and go on with our lives? Doesn't accepting death mean that we have given up living? Absolutely not! Is a good book or film any less enjoyable because we know it is going to end?

It is the same way with life—for all of us. Because, whether we have AIDS or not, we are all going to die…Talking about death and trying to understand death can take the fear out of it. If we turn on a light in a dark room, suddenly all the shadows disappear.
(*HIV Positive: Living with AIDS*, Debra Jarvis, p. 38-39)

Jesus Christ is the one person who can turn on the light of truth regarding death and dying. Jesus himself walked right into the jaws of death, experienced it, and then conquered it. He walked out of his own grave. As we consider our own mortality, Jesus who is Lord, illuminates the way before us. His identification with our mortal experience is totally and wholly redemptive:

Since the children have flesh and blood, he too shared in their humanity so that by his death he might destroy him who holds the power of death—that is, the devil—and free those who all their lives were held in slavery by their fear of death. (Hebrews 2:14-15)

The mystery and fears surrounding death are not totally eliminated from our lives when we become Christians, but their power over us is defeated and put in proper perspective under the Lordship of Jesus Christ. Our Advocate in life thus enables us to walk *through* the "valley of the shadow of death."

An exercise

The exercise on the following page may be your first occasion to consider how you might cope with news of impending death. The questions may be relevant to your present condition.

As with all the group exercises it is important that everyone participate. Keep in mind, there is no wrong answer! The leader should read the situation and questions aloud, allowing time between questions for everyone to jot down their answers. When everyone has completed the exercise go over each question, having everyone share their answers.

62 **Embracing Life Series**

Facing death and dying   Session 5

Facing death and dying

Session 5

NOTES

Imagine that you are at your doctor's office. You are there to get lab results for tests done to identify abnormal activity going on in your body of late. As you sit across from the doctor, studying his face, you sense the results are not good. After going over each lab report, he calmly informs you that the situation is very serious, indeed. For what you have, there is no cure. Furthermore, life expectancy for your type of illness is usually a year—from early detection to death. Your doctor answers what questions he can and then goes over future treatment and care possibilities. He lets you know he will be there for you and do all he medically can to keep you healthy and comfortable. Having heard all you can for right now, you leave his office to begin processing this news.

Consider what has just been read. Miraculous healing intervention from the Lord notwithstanding, answer the following questions as honestly as you can:

- What are you feeling? How will you tell your family this news?

- How do you think your family will react?

- How will you spend your next birthday, and other holidays, knowing they may be your last? How might your plans for these celebrations be different than in the past?

- Consider how you best like to spend your leisure time. What impact might your illness have on those activities?

- Who will take care of you?

- How will this impact the people in your family and your relationships with them?

- What impact will this have on your life goals? What are your priorities now? What do you most want to do?

(This exercise was adapted with permission from a Personal Exercise written by Pam Grant.)

Session 5   Facing death and dying

Embracing Life Series   63

Session 5 — Facing death and dying

NOTES

Embracing hope

> Do not be afraid. I am the First and the Last. I am the Living One; I was dead, and behold I am alive for ever and ever! And I hold the keys to death and Hades. (Revelation 1:18)

It is the assurance of God's Word that enables all Christians to face the dying experience with hope. Hope in everlasting life with Christ is the context in which we can discuss what we really feel about death and dying. Make the following Scriptures a personal prayer to the Lord.

> For I am convinced that neither death nor life, neither angels nor demons, neither the present nor the future, nor any powers, neither height nor depth, nor anything else in all creation, will be able to separate us from the love of God that is in Christ Jesus our Lord. (Romans 8:38-39)

> He will wipe away every tear from [our] eyes. There will be no more death or mourning or crying or pain, for the old order of things has passed away. (Revelation 21:4)

> ... And so we will be with the Lord forever. [Let us] therefore encourage each other with these words. (1 Thessalonians 4:17-18)

> ... Be strong and courageous ... The Lord himself goes before you and will be with you; he will never leave you nor forsake you. Do not be afraid; do not be discouraged. (Deuteronomy 31:7-8)

In closing, consider the following quote by David Watson who wrote as he faced his own imminent death:

> In one sense, the Christian is not preparing for death. Essentially he is preparing for life, abundant life in all its fullness. The world, with its fleeting pleasures, is not the final reality, with heaven as a shadowy and suspect unknown. The best and purest joys on earth are only a shadow of the reality that God has prepared for us in Christ. Eternal life begins as soon as we receive Christ as our Saviour. We can start enjoying it now, in increasing measure, and should be preparing, not for death, but for the consummation of that perfect quality of life when we are completely in God's presence for ever. (*Fear No Evil,* by David Watson, p. 167)

Facing death and dying

Session 5

SCRIPTURE READINGS

Romans 8:38; 1 Corinthians 15:26, 53-58.

Revelation 1:18; 21:1-5; Psalm 116.

Hebrews 2:14-15.

RECOMMENDED READINGS

Fear No Evil by David Watson

When God Doesn't Make Sense by Dr. James Dobson

THOUGHTS FOR JOURNALING

Write down your reflections about your own answers to the exercise and then your reaction to the answers of other group members.

Were there any surprises?

If you have participated in a similar exercise in the past, do you notice any changes in your answers?

Consider leading your family or friends through this exercise.

NOTES

Readings

From

"Fear No Evil"

David Watson

Ch. 18: What is God saying to me?

During the last few months I have felt extremely vulnerable. Unexplained aches and pains all too easily appear sinister. For the last three months, for example, I have had increasing backache—a common complaint but something I have never known in my life. Has the cancer gone round to my spine? What exactly is going on? Both my doctor and specialist say that in their opinion it is purely muscular and postural. But the pain continues, especially when I am standing (as I often am), and I wonder why? Why *now*? It is an easy temptation to fear the worst.

Then the tumor in my liver, which for the first time I could feel a few weeks ago, began to harden and became sore—so sore, in fact, that I could sleep only in one position. Again, what was going on? In one difficult week recently, my specialist thought that the tumor in the liver was definitely growing, but three days later my surgeon was sure that it was *not* growing—if anything slightly smaller and softer.

During this period we had special times of prayer for my healing. They were always extremely helpful. The sore, hard lump is no longer sore (and much softer), but the pains in my back seem to get worse—for whatever reason.

Walking by faith is rather like walking on a tightrope: at times it is exhilarating, but it requires only the slightest knock to make me feel insecure and anxious. In the last week or so I have been bothered more by asthma, which probably indicates an increased level of stress. I have also not been sleeping so well as before.

I mention all this, not to wallow in self-pity (I *still* believe that God is healing me) but to emphasize that the question 'why suffering?' is far from theoretical. I am profoundly aware that many millions in the world are suffering much more acutely than I am, yet the pains and vulnerability are still there.

For those who believe in a good God, the dilemma is so acute, that Rabbi Kushner concludes that God cannot be all powerful after all. Using the analogy of quantum physics where it seems that certain events happen in the universe at random, Kushner believes that there is 'randomness in the universe . . . Why do we have to insist on everything being reasonable? Why can't we let the universe have a few rough edges?'[1] According to Kushner, God is not in control of everything, although he is on our side whenever bad luck dominates. Evil sometimes finally prevails and is not always overcome by good. Kushner claims that God does not have the whole world in his hands, and therefore is not responsible for malformed children, for natural disasters, or fatal diseases. These simply lie outside his jurisdiction.

It is a neat theory, and it saves us from the unacceptable conclusion of blaming God for all the evil in the world. However, If God is not in ultimate control, he cannot truly be God. If there is no final justice, no eventual triumph of good over evil, God is not the God who has revealed himself in the Bible and in the person of Jesus Christ. If there is some whimsical evil force greater than God, making God finite and limited, we live a futile existence in a meaningless world—as the atheist maintains. If God is not God of all, he is not God at all. There is little hope for any of us, apart from resigning ourselves to a fortuitous mortality in a universe ruled by chance. We cannot ultimately be sure of anything except being at the mercy of unleashed and unpredictable evil.

However, the ringing conviction of the Scriptures is that *the Lord reigns!* Even in the one supreme case of truly innocent suffering, the crucifixion of Jesus, God knew what he was doing. He had not lost control. As Simon Peter declared, all the rulers put together could do only what God had planned to take place (Acts 4:27f:). At the time no one could see why such excruciating suffering should destroy the only sinless man that had ever lived, the Son of God himself. Later the disciples saw it as clearly as could be. 'Christ died for our sins once for all,' wrote Peter. 'He the just suffered for the unjust, to bring us to God' (1 Peter 3:18, *New English Bible*). There on the cross Christ bore the penalty for our sin once for all, so that we might be reconciled to God.

Readings

Nevertheless, although Christians down the ages have seen in Christ's sufferings the salvation of the world, what can we say about the myriads of others whose sufferings and death have never had any special significance, or none that we could discern?

James Mitchell in *The god I want* once wrote angrily: 'The value of a god must be open to test. No god is worth preserving unless he is of some practical use in curing all the ills which plague humanity—all the disease and pain and starvation, the little children born crippled or spastic or mentally defective: a creator god would be answerable to *us* for these things at the day of judgment—if he dared to turn up.' Here is the bitter anger that many feel towards God when faced with senseless and hopeless suffering.

Interestingly enough we find many expressions of anger against God in the Psalms. The psalmist often reveals the deepest hurts of his heart, whether they are godly or not.

> Why dost thou stand far off, O Lord?
>
> Why dost thou hide thyself in times of trouble? (Psalm 10:1)
>
> My God, my God, why hast thou forsaken me?
>
> Why art thou so far from helping me, from the words of my groaning? O my God, I cry by day, but thou dost not answer; and by night, but find no rest. (Psalm 22:1f)
>
> My tears have been my food day and night, While men say to me continually, 'Where is your God?' (Psalm 42:3)

Here are some cries taken almost at random from the Psalms. Similar quotations are numerous. It is worth mentioning that when we feel angry, bitter, helpless or in despair, it is good to be honest with God about our feelings. In fact, it is much better expressing our anguish *to* God than talking resentfully *about* God to others. God can take on anger. Indeed he did take our anger and all our other sins when his Son died on the cross for us. He wants us to be honest with him and not to put on a pious mask when we approach him.

At the same time, the psalmist in Psalm 73, having complained bitterly about his continuous suffering, comes humbly to realize that his attitude toward God was all wrong:

> When my thoughts were bitter and my feelings were hurt, I was as stupid as an animal; I did not understand you...What else have I in heaven but you? Since I have you, what else could I want on earth? My mind and my body may grow weak, but God is my strength; He is all I ever need ...
>
> (v.v. 21-26, Good News Bible)

Behind much anger about suffering is our human arrogance which assumes that God must somehow justify his existence and explain his actions before we are prepared to consider the possibility of believing in him.

Sometimes I am asked, 'Is God relevant to me?' But that is not the crucial question at all. A much more vital issue is this: 'Am I relevant to God?' The astonishing answer is that each of us is incredibly relevant to an infinite God of love who is with us in all our afflictions and wants to deliver us from negative reactions to those afflictions.

In our natural self-centeredness we tend to think that we are at the center of the universe, and that God (if he exists at all) is there simply to meet our needs. We regard him as a servant whom we call in from time to time to clear up the mess we are in—a mess often of our own doing. But we are not at the center of the universe. God is. And God is not our servant. He is our Lord. The question is not 'Why should I bother with God?' but 'Why should God bother with me?' That is a much harder question to answer. There is no reason why God should bother with me at all, since I have so often turned my back on him. But he does. For God is love. Sometimes it is only through suffering that our self-importance is broken. We need humbly to realize our own smallness and sinfulness in contrast to God's greatness and holiness.

Franklin D. Roosevelt, when President of the United States of America, used to have a little ritual with the naturalist William Beebe. After dinner together, the two men would go outside and look up into the night-sky. They would find the lower left-hand corner of the great square of Pegasus. One of them would then recite these words: 'That is the spiral galaxy of Andromeda. It is as large as our Milky Way. It is one of a hundred million galaxies. It is

Readings

750,000 light years away. It consists of a hundred billion suns, each one larger than our sun.' They would then pause for a few moments, and Roosevelt would finally say, 'Now I think we feel small enough! Let's go to bed!' Although man has great dignity, being made in the image of God, he must also appreciate his smallness and his natural inability to grasp more than a tiny fraction of total reality.

This was the substance of God's answer to Job. In four great chapters God gently challenged Job as to how much he understood about God and his ways of working. Humbly at the end of it all, Job realized that he knew virtually nothing, and his demand to fathom all the answers to his suffering was both foolish and unreasonable. 'I have uttered what I did not understand,' he said. 'I despise myself, and repent in dust and ashes.' Then God began to bless him once again.

Some will not find this satisfactory. Together with our suffering, they will say, do we also have to be browbeaten by God into submission? Is that the moral of the story? We should not think of it like that. If we have any conception of the greatness of God we should refrain from pressing the question *Why?* however understandable that might be. On many thousands of issues we simply do not and cannot know. Why does God allow the birth of severely handicapped children? I don't know. Why are some individuals plagued with tragedies for much of their lives, whilst others suffer hardly at all? I don't know. Why is there seeming injustice on every side? I don't know. The questions are endless if we ask why? Instead we should ask the question *What?* 'What are you saying to me, God? What are you doing in my life? What response do you want me to make?' With that question we can expect an answer.

It is my conviction that God is always trying to speak to us in his love, even when his word is hard to accept. 'Man shall not live by bread alone,' said Jesus, 'but by every word that proceeds from the mouth of God.' This was a quotation from the Old Testament which Jesus used when being tempted by his adversary in the wilderness. More important than anything is knowing God's will and doing it. It is far more important than having intellectual answers to all our philosophical questions about God and man, suffering and pain. Life anyway is short and uncertain, but God's word endures for ever. However, our lives are often so full of other things that we find it impossible to hear or discern what God is saying to us. Our ears are deaf, our minds dull and our wills stubborn. We do not hear God speak, or if we do, we fail to respond.

It is sometimes only through suffering that we begin to listen to God. Our natural pride and self-confidence have been stripped painfully away, and we become aware, perhaps for the first time, of our own personal needs. We may even begin to ask God for help instead of protesting about our condition or insisting on explanations. I have met several people who do not profess any commitment to Christ who still pray when facing suffering.

During the ministry of Jesus on earth, a tower fell in Siloam and killed eighteen innocent people. 'Why did God allow it?' was the immediate question pressed by those around him. We may have exactly the same question when we hear of accidents, earthquakes and disasters every day in the news. Jesus replied, not by answering the vexed question of suffering nor by giving a satisfactory solution to this particular tragedy. As perfect Man, accepting our human limitations, Jesus may not even have known the reason why. Instead he came back to the practical challenge of God's word: 'I tell you...unless you repent you will all likewise perish' (Luke 13:1-5). It may sound a little bleak, but Jesus was far more concerned with a person's eternal well being than merely satisfying an intellectual curiosity. Here he was dealing not with the question of Why? but with the question What? What is God saying in this calamity? It is a reminder that life in this world is frail and uncertain. We cannot boast of tomorrow. It is therefore vital that we sort out our relationship with God here and now. Then we are ready for anything. 'Teach us to number our days,' prayed the psalmist 'that we may get a heart of wisdom' (Psalm 90:12).

Through the unexpected diagnosis of cancer I was forced to consider carefully my priorities in life and to make some necessary adjustments. I still do not know why God allowed it, nor does it bother me. But I am beginning to hear what God is saying, and this has been enormously helpful to me. As I turn to the Bible, I find passages coming alive for me, perhaps more than ever before. As I praise God or listen to

---

Session 5   Embracing Life Series   69

Readings

worship cassettes, my vision of the greatness and love of God is being continually reinforced. I am content to trust myself to a loving God whose control is ultimate and whose wisdom transcends my own feeble understanding.

C. S. Lewis once put it graphically like this: 'God is the only comfort, he is also the supreme terror: the thing we most need and the thing we most want to hide from. He is our only ally, and we have made ourselves his enemies. Some people talk as if meeting the gaze of Absolute Goodness would be fun. They need to think again!' God is so concerned that we should know his love that he will sometimes speak to us in severe terms if we will not listen to him in any other way. The suffering may be ours, or that of someone else whom we know and love. Whatever it is, we should think carefully about what God is trying to say to us. C.S. Lewis elsewhere emphasizes that it is a poor thing if we turn to God only in suffering, *only* because there is nothing better to be had. 'It is hardly complimentary to God that we should choose him as an alternative to hell; yet even this he accepts. The creature's illusions of self-sufficiency must, for the creature's sake, be shattered.'[2] Humbly we need to learn that because God is love, there is the awful possibility of neglecting and forfeiting his love, and at the same time he offers us the unspeakable joy of knowing that love in our own experience, perhaps especially in the midst of suffering.

Joni (pronounced Johnny) Eareckson, as an athletic young girl of seventeen broke her neck when diving into the sea and has been totally paralyzed from the neck down ever since. She suffered considerably during her lengthy periods in hospital, and even as a deeply committed Christian found herself asking, often with anger and frustration, the question Why? A wise friend said this to her: 'You don't have to know why God let you be hurt. The fact is, God knows—and that's all that counts. Just trust him to work things out for good, eventually, if not right away.'

'What do you mean?' asked Joni.

'Would you be any happier if you did know why God wants you paralyzed? I doubt it. So don't get worked up trying to find meaning to the accident.'[3]

If we insist on pursuing the question Why? we shall only increase our sense of frustration and perhaps bitterness. We only add to our injury and block the way for God's love to reach us.

Michael Quoist has expressed it well in one of his *Prayers of Life*.[4] He imagined God speaking to him:

> Son I am here.
> I haven't left you,
> How weak is your faith!
> You are too proud.
> You still rely on yourself . . .
> You must surrender yourself to me.
> You must realize that you are neither big enough or strong enough.
> You must let yourself be guided like a child.
> My little child.
> Come, give me your hand, and do not fear.
> If there is mud, I will carry you in my arms.
> But you must be very very little,
> For the Father carries only little children.

It is in this quiet, restful, child-like trust in the Father of love that will enable us to experience his peace, even in the very worst of storms.

Ch. 21: The Present Moment

Eleven months have passed since the cancer in my body was first detected—eleven months of the limited life I am expected to have left, the original sentence being about one year. The medical prognosis is still the same, and the latest scan showed a further increase in the tumor. The future officially is bleak, and I am getting used to people looking at me as a dying man under sentence of death. Nothing is certain. I'm not out of the wood yet. Everything is a matter of faith.

That is why I have written the book at this stage. I am not looking back at a painful episode in the past; the difficulties are still with me. I am not writing from a position of comparative safety; I am at present in the thick of it, with humanly speaking no answers, no certainties, no proof of healing—nothing except a somewhat daunting unknown. And yet in

Readings

reality, my position is not fundamentally different from that of anyone else. No one knows what the future holds. Our lives are full of ifs and buts and supposings. Nothing is sure apart from death. Whether we like it or not, everyone has to live by faith. The *object* of faith is naturally of absolute importance, and may vary considerably. Some will trust in God, others in money, luck, prosperity, health, medicine, philosophy or wishful thinking. But no one can escape the risk of faith when it comes to the greatest issues of life and death.

The opposite to faith is fear, and I have found that there is a constant running battle between the two. In one sense, fear is faith in what you do not want to happen. Job once said, 'The thing I fear comes upon me, and what I dread befalls me' (3:25). There is a powerful truth in that statement. When we are afraid of something, we almost pre-condition it to happen. Our fears, however unfounded and irrational they may be, can trigger the fulfillment of those fears.

Fear has been described as the greatest threat to health in our generation, simply because fear is so widespread. Fear is a great deceiver and destroyer. It robs our minds of peace; it distorts our understanding; it magnifies our problems; it breaks our relationships; it ruins our health; it goads us into foolish, impulsive and sometimes violent action; it paralyses our thinking, trusting and loving.

Repeatedly Jesus had to rebuke his disciples for their fears and lack of faith: 'Why are you afraid? Have you no faith?' (Mark 4:40). The context of that particular challenge is interesting. The disciples were in a boat, caught in a violent storm on the Sea of Galilee; and even though some of them were tough and experienced fishermen, they were scared stiff. So they woke Jesus, who was asleep in the boat: 'Teacher, do you not care if we perish?' It seemed to them that he did not care, since he was sleeping peacefully in the tempest. At once Jesus rebuked the wind and the waves, and there was a great calm. But Jesus was clearly disappointed that his disciples had not yet learned to trust God in the midst of their difficulties. '*Why* are you afraid?'

God never promises to protect us from problems, only to help us in them. If we leave God out of the picture, those difficulties might so strip away our sense of security that we feel vulnerable, anxious and afraid. On the other hand, those same difficulties could drive us back to God and so strengthen our faith. We might feel just as vulnerable, but we *have* to trust God because there is really no alternative; and then we discover that God is with us in the dark as in the light, in pain as in joy. When I was going through a traumatic time in my life, a friend of mine said, 'You cannot trust God too much.'

What we may not realize is how much we are trapped by our own thoughts and words. If we fill our minds with negative ideas, we may plunge into self-pity, despondency or fear. Even our bodies may react negatively with disease. The more we reflect on our hurts, the more we shall be bound by bitterness and prone to physical afflictions, such as arthritis. If we fail in some task and dwell upon that failure, we may get angry with ourselves (and no doubt angry with others also), and this could precipitate deep depression—depression is often a matter of suppressed anger. The more we think about our fears, or express them to others, the more gripped by anxiety we shall become, to the point of crippling phobias.

I have had to watch all this carefully over the last eleven months. When I've had a difficult day or week, I sometimes find myself saying, especially in the middle of the night, 'I've got cancer, it's spreading and I'm dying. How am I going to tell the children?' At times like these I sweat a bit. But when I am more awake I realize that negative thoughts only accelerate the disease and could lead to an early death. How then should I control my thoughts? Should I say instead, 'I'm fit and well and there's nothing wrong with me at all?' That would be a positive remark and possibly beneficial; but it is not an honest statement and has no substance apart from wishful thinking. It might be called 'faith', but it's a dangerous faith without any solid foundation. That is the weakness of those who teach 'the power of positive thinking'. Without any doubt positive thinking is far better than negative, but the question remains: what are the grounds for such definite thoughts? What is the basis of such faith?

As a Christian I am called to rest my faith firmly on God and on the promises of God's word. Jesus said that this was the solid rock on which the house of my life would stand firm against even the fiercest storms. Constantly Jesus endorsed the authority of

Readings

God's word: he knew it, taught it, lived by it, and corrected his opponents by bringing them back to the truth of it: 'You are wrong, because you know neither the Scriptures nor the power of God' (Matthew 22:29). Here too was the basis of faith for the apostles and the early Church: they knew that God was faithful and that his word could not be broken. Convinced of the ultimate reality of this, they went through fire and water, torture and martyrdom, because they knew that nothing at all could ever separate them from the love of God in Christ Jesus (see Romans 8:28-39 and Hebrews 11).

This has also been the faith that has sustained countless Christians down the centuries, many of whom have suffered acutely for their commitment to Christ. Martin Niemöller was incarcerated in a Nazi concentration camp for many years, but was allowed the Bible as his one possession. He wrote: 'The Bible: what did this book mean to me during the long and weary years of solitary confinement and then for the last four years at Dachau cell-building? The word of God was simply everything to me—comfort and strength, guidance and hope, master of my days and companion of my nights, the bread which kept me from starvation, and the water of life which refreshed my soul. And even more, "solitary confinement" ceased to be solitary.' This is the constant experience of those who have dared to take God at his word, despite all the odds against them.

In order to maintain a positive faith and not give way to negative fears, I have found it important to go on thanking God for the truth of his word and for the power of his Spirit at work within me. When I am asked (as I often am), 'How are you?' I reply truthfully, 'I'm feeling fine, and I believe that God is continuing to heal me. But I should be grateful for your prayers.' That is where my faith stands. From God's word I do not doubt he wants to heal me, and there have also been personal assurances of this healing through the remarks of many Christians from all over the world. Of course I realize that logically speaking we may all be wrong. But my faith is neither groundless nor mindless. I have good reason for believing that God *is* healing me, and I shall go on trusting him and praising him whatever I may be feeling like. I cannot honestly say 'I *have* been healed' because there is no medical evidence to support that at present. A few Christians have written (rather unhelpfully) rebuking me for my lack of faith in not accepting that healing is now an accomplished fact. However, I can only be honest with where I am; and since my faith is in a God who is not limited by the scientific worldview I believe that God *is* healing me, and I am accepting many engagements for the next year or two without thinking too much about the 'risk' entailed. From a Christian perspective, that seems to be both a reasonable and a responsible position of faith.

Nevertheless, I am aware of the spiritual battle involved. I was temporarily thrown when a close Christian friend of mine asked if I was booking a reserve speaker for my various engagements. I knew he was deeply concerned to remove all extra pressures from me, but his question still disturbed me. There is admittedly a fine dividing line between faith and foolishness, but how could I genuinely believe in God's healing if I were at the same time booking an alternative speaker in case I were ill?

At the end of September I went with my team to the beautiful Bernese Oberland in Switzerland to lead a week's conference for Christian pastors and workers. It proved a wonderful week. In spite of everything having to be translated into German (which none of our team spoke), the sense of God's presence and the joy of Christian fellowship was almost breathtaking. There were pastors from Eastern Germany and Poland too, which added to the quality of the week. As a special bonus we had an afternoon cruising down Lake Thun, a day in Bern (surely the most beautiful capital in the world), and another day up the mountains overlooking the Eiger and Jungfrau. Ironically, all previous English speakers invited to this annual conference had canceled, sometimes at the last moment. I was the only one who actually made it, even though no one was entirely certain about this until we arrived! I am glad to say that no alternative speaker had been booked on this occasion!

In October I found myself speaking at a number of special lunches, dinners, services and festivals where there were excellent numbers and an unusual degree of interest, no doubt partly due to my illness. My autobiography *You Are My God*, published on October 3rd, had record sales, running into its fifth

Readings

printing by the end of that month! Also I had more interviews on radio and for the press than I had known during several years put together. I thought again of that prophetic word given before my operation that my future ministry would increase rather than decrease.

'What if you are not healed?' I am sometimes asked. Although it does not help to dwell on that question too much, I realize that it is a perfectly fair one; and that is where the Christian hope for the future is so enormously important. Of course I cannot *know* that I shall have ten to twenty years more to live. I cannot *know* that I have even one. But that is also true of every one of us. With all our planning for the future, we need to live a day at a time and enjoy each day as a gift from God. 'This is the day which the Lord has made; let us rejoice and be glad in it' (Psalm 118:24). Some Christians speak of the *sacrament of the present moment*: we need to live, not just a day at a time, but moment by moment, seeking to do God's will for each moment of our life. That alone is the way in which we can know the fullness of God's joy and peace.

'What about those who are praying for you, if you are not healed? Will not their faith be severely shaken, if they are so convinced that you will be well?' Once again, that is a reasonable question. My answer is that it's God's responsibility! God is so much bigger than our mistakes. Indeed our relationship with him deepens only when we work through disappointments, confusion, bewilderment and, at times, despair. I cannot let the thought of 'disappointing those who are praying for me' become a negative pressure in my life. I am delighted that so many *are* praying for me, and I believe that their prayers are being answered. If I am wrong, God is well able to handle that one. He has had plenty of experience!

In the Bible, one shining example of faith is Abraham who left his homeland in obedience to God, and who trusted God's promise of a son even when he was 100 years old and his wife ninety. The apostle Paul made this comment about Abraham: 'No distrust made him waver concerning the promise of God, but he grew strong in his faith as he gave glory to God, fully convinced that God was able to do what he had promised' (Romans 4:20f). The tense of the Greek verb suggests that as Abraham *went on* giving glory to God (i.e. praising God), his faith became strong and the miracle happened.

This is the way in which we encourage our faith. Basing our trust on the assurance of God's word and faithfulness, we continue to praise God for the truth of his word until it is fulfilled. In Hebrews 11, the great chapter on faith, the writer acknowledges that sometimes faith is not rewarded this side of heaven. But whatever the size of the problem, the length of the battle, or the outcome of our faith, we are called to trust in God and to keep our eyes on Jesus.

That, after all, is the ultimate purpose of our life. 'Eternal life', said Jesus when praying, 'means knowing you, the only true God, and knowing Jesus Christ whom you sent' (John 17:3, *Good News Bible*). Nothing is more important than our relationship with God, both for this life and for the next.

A doctor complained recently, 'Our patients expect us to make them immortal!' Many cling tenaciously to this life because they fear there is nothing more to come. Today's preoccupation with youth and youthfulness demonstrates the same deep-seated anxiety about the future, especially that last enemy death, of which cancer seems the most frightening symbol.

One day we stand to lose everything of this world, and no one knows when that day will come. Once we have lost our lives to God, however, we belong eternally to him; and in Christ we have all that is ultimately important. If we spend our time worrying about ourselves, we have missed the whole point of our existence. C. S. Lewis expressed it like this: 'Look for yourself, and in the long run you will find only hatred, loneliness, despair, rage, ruin and decay. But look for Christ and you will find him, and with him everything else thrown in.'[5] That is the only security that ultimately makes sense.

God offers no promise to shield us from the evil of this fallen world. There is no immunity guaranteed from sickness, pain, sorrow or death. What he does pledge is his never-failing presence for those who have found him in Christ. Nothing can destroy that. Always he is with us. And, in the long run, that is all we need to know.

Readings

[1] *When Bad Things Happen to Good People,* by Harold Kushner

[2] *The Problem of Pain,* by C.S. Lewis.

[3] *Joni* by Joni Eareckson, Pickering and Inglis, 1976.

[4] Published by Gill and Macmillan Limited, 1963.

[5] *Mere Christianity,* Fountain Books, 1952.

Copyright 1984 by Anne Watson, pp124-132, 152-159. Used by permission of Harold Shaw Publishers, Wheaton, IL 60189.

Readings

"At war in peace"

Jonathan Hunter

Just a few months ago, three friends of ours with HIV became very ill at the same time and needed hospitalization. When informed of their circumstances, I called a night of intercession in order to inquire of the Lord. When our intercession began, it was fueled by anxious expectations of words foreshadowing miraculous healing. Our restlessness finally gave way to His sovereign purpose for our gathering. As our emotionally-charged prayer quieted down, the Lord began to speak to us in pictures and words.

I was given a powerful, vivid vision. It was of a city—great, wide and flat stretching to the sea. Off in the distance, an ominous, black wall of smoke, perhaps a thousand feet high, was moving toward me across the city. At its base, shooting upwards, were deep, red flames of devastating ferocity. The destructive force decimated everything in its path. In the foreground I could make out a steady stream of angels descending and ascending to heaven; they carried with them limp bodies of men and women that I knew must be persons who had died from AIDS. It was significant that they were being taken before the approaching holocaust but for reasons I could only guess. Was this to be the fate of our friends? What disturbing future was coming that they could not endure? Everyone at our meeting was struck by the intensity of the vision. A scriptural confirmation was given by another—Isaiah 57:1-2:

> The righteous perish and no one ponders it in his heart; devout men are taken away and no one understands that the righteous are taken to be spared from evil. Those who walk uprightly enter into peace. They find rest as they lie in death.

What ensued was a profound peace in the room—an awe and reverence for the Sovereign God of the universe. I could hear Him speaking to me: "Do you know what you are asking for when you seek a second chance at life for these people?!" I thought about my own rescue from the precipice of death back in 1979 when I had an accidental drug overdose and a "near-death" experience. Why had I survived? And then to go on to test positive and not get sick! In those powerful moments, pregnant with His Spirit, He spoke again: "My son, you cannot know the entirety of My ways but you can know My peace. Receive this gift and pray for others to know the same. It is from that peace that My life ushers forth." As we quietly rested, we were enveloped by the train of His glory which seemed to flow down from the throne room itself into our meeting place. Philippians 4:6-7 came to mind:

> The Lord is near. Don't be anxious about anything but in everything by prayer and petition, with thanksgiving present your requests to God, and the peace which transcends all understanding will guard your hearts and minds in Christ Jesus.

Immovable, we sat there, eyes open, looking to each other, shaking our heads in wonderment over the Lord's goodness to us. Finally, with thanksgiving to God, our meeting disbanded and each of us went home.

Since that time I have had time to ponder over that special occasion. All three, Sheila, Tom and Chuck have died. The vision and Scripture from Isaiah had been prophetic. Their deaths, however, have not emasculated our prayers for healing. It's just that now we seek a discipleship in Jesus that brings forth life out of true peace. Granted, our ultimate peace is in heaven, but more can be had on earth. In the case of our friends, peace was ephemeral. Much as each one loved Jesus Christ, there were arresting circumstances in their lives—unhealed memories and relational conflicts that constantly militated against the life-affirming peace that the Lord wanted them to know.

To find a godly peace, we cross a battlefield just to reach the place where we can hear His voice saying: "Be still and know that I am God." However, there are countless opportunities afforded us which can lead to those still, quiet waters. Most of us give up just before getting there. In our anxiousness, we subvert our peace and settle for a false peace which

Readings

never touches the true self deep within; though it covers the surface, it fails to penetrate the soul. We must continually confront diseased ideas of God, apathy, and the thin disguises of worldly sufficiencies which obstruct His peace. In Thomas A Kempis' time-honored *The Imitation of Christ* written in 1441, a suggested conversation between Jesus and His disciple speaks of the true peace of heart. "Jesus: 'Everyone wants peace, but not all care for what leads to true peace. My peace is with the humble and gentle of heart; your peace will be in exercising great patience...keep in mind that never to feel any disquiet nor to suffer any heartache or physical pain is not the stuff of this present life but of eternity.'"

For those caught up in the rush for worldly solutions for AIDS, this kind of truth is perceived as stressful and pain producing material. In their blindness, the cure-seekers fail to see that it is really the truce with sin that has produced the pain and its damning effects.

I had the privilege last year of being part of a counseling team for Tom and Cris Crabtree. Tom was one of the three for which we interceded. From the start, there was no doubt that Tom was extremely ill; his slow gait and drawn features were visible signs of a physical battle being lost. Their marriage, severely crippled by his infidelities had every reason to crumble and disintegrate with the addition of AIDS. I had to admit there were several times during our intense meetings when I had the option (urge) not to probe, to just stop and let sleeping dogs lie. However, they both chose to keep pushing through their emotional junkyard. A swift settlement of divorce or a peaceful decline unto death might have sufficed for some—but not here. Quite a bit was uncovered. Anxiousness, pain, anger, denial, unforgiveness and shame all paraded themselves before Tom—all the attributes of his false, un-becoming self. Henri Nouwen describes this in *The Way of the Heart* as the "secular or false self which is fabricated by social compulsions." Had Tom or his wife stopped becoming and settled for the status quo, their marriage would have ended tragically, yet predictably, in a worldly way. Although Tom eventually died from complications due to HIV, he was in pursuit of Christ's peace. This was Tom's hope for which he committed himself. In heaven, he has found it. However, amidst the spiritual, emotional and physical tumult of HIV Jesus established His life with Tom—distinguishing His sanctifying peace from the world's despairing solutions. Christ revealed Himself to Tom as immovable in faithfulness, fully alive to his human brokenness and need.

Just like our friend Tom, we are forever challenged to relinquish the old friends of adversity unto the Cross—the only true distiller of our soul. We do this through repentance, forgiveness, renunciation and ongoing accountability to others. Unfortunately, relational accountability is most often forsaken and substituted with a quick solitary vow made in the privacy of one's prayer closet. The power of the confessional is avoided. The tendency of minister or patient, volunteer or client to distance himself from others digresses into a deathly atmosphere and war within.

Oftentimes the cry for help comes too late. The drift away from others happens all the time in AIDS ministry at levels obvious and hidden. There seems to be an ongoing feud with Body life that persistently leads to a descent into self where endless monologues of doubt stifle life. The prayers of others coming alongside a modest member of the Body can uphold and steady him (or her) in holiness and purity. In so doing they reiterate and glorify the truth of Christ's strength and peace to one another and the world. St Paul in II Cor. 1:9-11 writes:

> Indeed in our hearts we felt the sentence of death. But this happened that we might not rely on ourselves but on God who raises the dead. He has delivered us from such a deadly peril and he will deliver us. On him we have set our hope that he will continue to deliver us as you help us by your prayers. Then many will give thanks on our [your] behalf for the graciousness forever granted us in answer to the prayers of many.

In these times of wars and rumors of war, both within oneself and without, the enemy would have us abort our hope. He would have us believe that attempting peace—the Jerusalem of our soul—is foolish and doomed. But unlike the medieval crusaders of old, whose efforts were undermined by false motives and inadequate means, ours is an assured victory. The liberation of Christ is guaranteed

Readings

as we surrender together to the work of His Spirit. Therein lies true peace

> May God himself, the God of Peace sanctify you through and through. May your whole spirit, soul and body be kept blameless at the coming of our Lord Jesus Christ. The one who calls you is faithful and will do it.
> (1 Thess. 5:23)

Desert Stream Ministries Newsletter, Summer 1991

Session 6

Transformation & the role of the cross

NOTES

Jesus said: *"I came that they may have life and have it to the full."* (John 10:10). Experiencing this fullness of life—discovering our true selves in relationship with the Living God—comes only by way of the cross of Jesus Christ. The visual presence of the cross in Christian churches and households is a symbolic reminder that "Jesus Christ crucified" is at the core of the Christian faith.

Sadly, the meaning of the cross is unclear and troublesome to many contemporary minds and has lost much of its true significance and power. For believers brought up in a church where the cross did not play a central part in their spiritual growth and healing, phrases like "carry the cross," "take up your cross daily," or "in the cross" remain abstract and obscure ideas. For others, the cross may have become distorted signifying an object of intense fear and perpetual guilt. Neither perspective is life-giving.

Our concept of the cross affects our experience of God's redemptive work of saving and restoring us to fullness of life as divine image-bearers. (This process of being freed more and more from sin in our lives and becoming more like Christ—the perfect image-bearer—is called *sanctification*.) If the cross is to become a liberating symbol to us, rather than a stumbling block to our healing, our understanding of its meaning must be free of all unbiblical ideas.

Session 6 — Transformation and the role of the cross

NOTES

With a cross physically present discuss the following in the group:

■ What impressions and understandings of the cross, past and present, have you gleaned from the church and elsewhere?

After sharing, take time to pray the following prayer

Heavenly Father, we ask that You would take from us, now, every false, distorted and weakened image and memory of the cross from our hearts and minds.

Remove from us all oppressive and evil perceptions that try to diminish the power of the cross, so that we will be empowered to live holy and righteous lives.

Cleanse us of false imaginations that would oppose the truth of Your work upon the cross for our redemption and healing.

Forgive us, Lord, for cherishing or clinging to any false concepts of Your cross. As we release them to You, we commit ourselves, by Your grace, never to embrace these false concepts again.

We receive, now, the cleansing of Your forgiveness and the goodness of the truth about Your cross for our lives.

We give you praise, Lord Jesus Christ, that all authority and power to complete this prayer rests with You. It is in Your name we pray. Amen.

In this brief chapter we can not possibly explore the full breadth and depth of the cross of Jesus in its varied meanings and roles. We do, however, seek to highlight several aspects of the cross that bear specifically on both our understanding and experiencing of the fullness of life that Jesus offers.

The cross: altar, threshold, way of Christ

Jesus' death on the cross mediates the mercy and love of God in many ways. "Jesus Christ crucified" is God's chosen vehicle by whom He delivers all his gifts of forgiveness, reconciliation, restoration, freedom, healing and fullness of life promised in the gospel. The symbol of the cross itself stands as an emblem of hope, that all God intends for us is truly ours. In a sense, the cross is like a tree of life we learn to embrace, enjoying its life-giving fruit and allowing it to satisfy the deepest needs and longings of the soul.

Practically speaking, for the Christian disciple, the cross functions in three significant ways.

Transformation and the role of the cross — Session 6

Altar of redemption

> For I resolved to know nothing while I was with you except Jesus Christ and him crucified. (1 Corinthians 2:2)
>
> May I never boast except in the cross of our Lord Jesus Christ, through which the world has been crucified to me and I to the world. (Galatians 6:14)

The cross is the *altar* of the New Covenant—the new agreement God has made with us. It replaces the Old Covenant altar with its gold-gilt mercy seat in the Holy of Holies. There, once every year, the high priest of Israel sprinkled the blood of a sacrificial lamb to cleanse the people of their sins.

Our new high priest, however, is Jesus Christ And He is, at the same time, the new sacrificial lamb, pouring out His own pure blood upon the cross. This once-and-for-all sacrifice covers and cancels the guilt of our sin, cleanses us from sin, breaks the power that sin had over us, and reconciles us to God.

The good news of the cross is that we are completely known for who we are and, yet, we are completely loved and forgiven. Jesus beckons all of us to boldly approach His simple wood altar by faith, not shrinking back in fear, but offering our repentance and receiving hope.

Threshold of life

> ...you have taken off your old self with its practices and have put on the new self, which is being renewed in knowledge in the image of its Creator. (Colossians 3:9-10)
>
> ...put on the new self, created to be like God in true righteousness and holiness. (Ephesians 4:24)

The cross also serves as the *threshold* through which we enter into full and abundant life and experience our true humanity.

Jesus' death on our behalf has the effect of taking our sin away from us in exchange for the perfect righteousness of Jesus which God assigns to us as if it were our own. By way of the cross of Jesus, we pass over a threshold, whereupon the filthy rags of the old self are removed and replaced with the Designer's robe of righteousness. This beautiful new robe covers us. The effect is that whenever God looks upon us, He sees the righteousness of Jesus instead of our sin. At the same time, we experience a freedom, a

NOTES

Session 6 — Transformation and the role of the cross

NOTES

reinvigoration and power that only His new set of clothes can bring.

This spiritual exchange is analogous to an event that takes place every evening in downtown Los Angeles and other metropolitan cities that house the homeless. A friend of mine, who worked at the Los Angeles Mission described for me the process that every person goes through before they bed down for the night at the facility:

Everyone is required to give up their dirty, infested, street clothes and then shower thoroughly. Having done so, they are given a fresh change of clothing to wear which they get to keep. Should they choose to, they can stay on to go through the rehabilitation program which involves Christian discipleship.

This image resembles our entry into life with Christ. At the cross, we forsake the old in repentance and confession, are cleansed in the waters of our baptism, and then given a new identity.

The way of life

> ...If anyone would come after me, he must deny himself and take up his cross daily and follow me. For whoever wants to save his life will lose it, but whoever loses his life for me will save it. (Luke 9:23,24)

Once we pass over the threshold of the cross we are called to follow Christ. As imitators of Jesus Christ who is himself our path, our concerns are intended to be in harmony with the One who has predestined us to do good works in Him. Following Jesus involves *carrying the cross* as a way of life.

But what does it mean to deny oneself and take up the cross?

The cross was Imperial Rome's answer to anyone who defied the will of Caesar. That answer, in so many words, was, "Either submit yourself to Caesar and conform your will to the will of the state, or we will do it for you by nailing you and your rebellious will to a cross!"

Jesus takes this powerful image and uses it to teach us something about discipleship. With his call to deny ourself and take up the cross, Jesus is saying, "In the same way, submit yourself to my Father in heaven and conform your will to the will of His Kingdom. Deny your rebellious, self-serving will and its demands to run your life. Put your will to death by nailing it to the cross. Do it every day. Then you will be free to follow me and get on with Life! In other words, obey me and my Father's will." That is what it means to "take up" or "carry" the cross.

Transformation and the role of the cross — Session 6

At the cross, we confess sin before one another and God; we receive forgiveness; we forgive others; we continue to renounce sinful ways when tempted. We walk the way of the cross in the daily refinement of sanctification and service to Jesus.

Our commitment to these things, empowered by the Holy Spirit at work within us, brings forth the true self (our subject for next week's lesson).

> ...God made you alive with Christ. He forgave us all our sins, having canceled the written code, with its regulations, that was against us and that stood opposed to us; he took it away, nailing it to the cross. And having disarmed the powers and authorities, he made a public spectacle of them, triumphing over them by the cross. (Colossians 2:13-15)

> May God Himself, the God of peace, sanctify you through and through. May your whole spirit, soul and body be kept blameless at the coming of our Lord Jesus Christ. The one who calls you is faithful, and he will do it.
> (1 Thessalonians 5:23-24)

Our daily posture is one of kneeling before the cross and offering Jesus our brokenness and sin, asking Him to replace our unrighteousness with His resurrection life.

In your quiet time with the Lord, meditate upon the cross. Study the assigned Scriptures that refer to the cross. Ask God to reveal their import and bring clarity and richness to your experience of the cross. God's unfolding gift of eternal grace impels us to declare together with the Apostle Paul:

> May I never boast except in the cross of our Lord Jesus Christ, through which the world has been crucified to me and I to the world...[W]hat counts is a new creation. Peace and mercy to all who follow this rule...
> (Galatians 6:14-16)

NOTES

Session 6
Transformation and the role of the cross

NOTES

SCRIPTURE READINGS
Isaiah 53; Matthew 20:28; Colossians 2:13-15;
1 Corinthians 1:17-18; Romans 5:6-11; 6:1-19; Matthew 10:38

RECOMMENDED READING
The Cross of Christ by John Stott

THOUGHTS FOR JOURNALING
John Stott, in his book *The Cross of Christ* writes:

"Paul's whole world was in orbit around the cross. It filled his vision, illumined his life, warmed his spirit. He 'gloried' in it. It meant more to him than anything else. Our perspective should be the same." (p. 351)

How has your perspective on the cross been altered since you have been diagnosed?

Readings

From:

"The Cross of Christ"

by John Stott

Paul's great affirmations about the cross in the letter to the Galatians

First, the cross is the ground of our justification. Christ has rescued us from the present evil age (1:4) and redeemed us from the curse of the law (3:13). And the reason why he has delivered us from this double bondage is that we may stand boldly before God as His sons and daughters, declared righteous and indwelt by His Spirit.

Secondly, the cross is the means of our sanctification. This is where the three other crucifixions come in. We have been crucified with Christ (2:20). We have crucified our fallen nature (5:24). And the world has been crucified to us, as we have been to the world (6:14). So the cross means more than the crucifixion of Jesus; it includes our crucifixion, the crucifixion of our flesh and of the world.

Thirdly, the cross is the subject of our witness. We are to placard Christ crucified publicly before people's eyes so that they may see and believe (3:1). In doing so, we must not bowdlerize the gospel, extracting from it its offense to human pride. No, whatever the price may be, we preach the cross (the merit of Christ), not circumcision (the merit of man); it is the only way of salvation (5:11; 6:12).

Fourthly, the cross is the object of our boasting. God forbid that we should boast in anything else (6:14). Paul's whole world was in orbit around the cross. It filled his vision, illumined his life, warmed his spirit. He "gloried in it. It meant more to him than anything else. Our perspective should be the same.

If the cross is not central in these four spheres for us, then we deserve to have applied to us the most terrible of all descriptions, "enemies of the cross of Christ" (Phil. 3:18). To be an enemy of the cross is to set ourselves against its purposes. Self-righteousness (instead of looking to the cross for justification), self-indulgence (instead of taking up the cross to follow Christ), self-advertisement (instead of preaching Christ crucified) and self-glorification (instead of glorying in the cross)—these are the distortions which make us "enemies" of Christ's cross.

Paul, on the other hand, was a devoted friend of the cross. So closely had he identified himself with it, that he suffered physical persecution for it. "I bear on my body the marks of Jesus" (Gal. 6:17), he wrote, the wounds and scars he received in proclaiming Christ crucified, the stigmata which branded him as Christ's authentic slave.

The stigmata of Jesus, in the spirit if not in the body, remain a mark of authentication for every Christian disciple, and especially every Christian witness. Campbell Morgan expressed it very well:

> It is the crucified man that can preach the cross. Said Thomas 'except I shall see in his hands the print of the nails...I will not believe'. Dr. Parker of London said that what Thomas said of Christ, the world is saying about the church. And the world is also saying to every preacher: Unless I see in your hand the print of the nails, I will not believe. It is true. It is the man...who has died with Christ, ...that can preach the cross of Christ.

G. Campbell Morgan, Evangelism, pp. 59-60.

Copyright 1986 by John R.W. Stott, pp350-351. Used by permission of InterVarsity Press, P.O. Box 1400, Downers Grove, IL 60515.

Our new identity

Session 7

NOTES

"The true self is dead" Walter Truitt Anderson declared in his book, *Reality Isn't What it Used to Be*. His contemporary psychology arrives at a sorry conclusion, although without God's Spirit, we might find ourselves agreeing with Anderson's belief. His perspective is that we are fragmented beings whose identities shift, depending on the role played at any given moment. Tragically, many people, including some Christians, think Anderson is right!

Our true identity in Christ

> The fear of the Lord is the beginning of wisdom, and KNOWLEDGE OF THE HOLY ONE IS UNDERSTANDING.
> (Proverbs 9:10). [emphasis JH]

The revelation of the true self cannot occur apart from the gospel of Jesus Christ and His cross. Christ's bodily resurrection demonstrated the credibility and authority of the gospel concerning the redemption and restoration of our souls. Becoming born again by His Spirit enables us to understand who we truly are as *He* defines us by *His* true word. Only in union with Him can we discover who we are destined to become.

Apart from the Redeemer of souls, we are unrealized beings, subject to every lie, whim and scheme that the world, the devil and our fallen nature can conjure up. Fr. Thomas Keating in *Intimacy with God* writes:

> Jesus has taken upon himself ALL the consequences of our sins and sinfulness. In other words, the false self with the accumulation of wounds that we bring with us from early childhood and our childish ways of trying to survive. (Keating, p. 34)

Session 7

Our new identity

NOTES

This week's lesson is intended to help secure and increase our understanding of Jesus' transforming life within us.

The false self vs. the true self

It may be helpful to begin with an explanation of what the false self is. Henri Nouwen in *The Way of the Heart*, says, "The secular or false self is the self fabricated...by social compulsions." Thomas Keating defines it in more detail:

> [The false self is]...the self developed in our own likeness rather than the likeness of God; the self-image developed to cope with the emotional trauma of early childhood. It seeks happiness in satisfying instinctual needs of survival/security, affection/esteem and power/control, and bases its self-worth on cultural or group identification.
> (*Intimacy with God*, Fr. Thomas Keating, p.163)

The true self is only apprehended when one is indwelt with the Holy Spirit, who applies to our lives Jesus' work on the cross and conforms us to his image. It follows that the true self bears the likeness of the one who is true—Jesus Christ. St. Paul emphatically states: *"...what counts is a new creation"* (Galatians 6:15b).

The new creation or emerging true self within us may or may not be discernable at first. Jesus was not instantly recognized as the Son of God by the disciples. Only in inspired moments were they fully aware of the One they beheld! We, too, can fail to recognize the restoration of His image within us. Worse, we can ignore even refuse to respond to the promptings of His Spirit.

The true self (that which is in union with Christ) can be obscured and hidden under the false self and its layers of emotional decay and spiritual alienation from God. Our sanctification becomes the process of removing those layers so that the true self may be seen and heard with ever-increasing clarity by ourselves and others. It is a process of uncovering the real.

Our "uncovering" is not instantaneous but a lifelong work. Patience and perseverance are required in the believer. Near the end of his life and in prison, the Apostle Paul himself wrote

> ...I press on to take hold of that for which Christ Jesus took hold of me... I do not consider myself yet to have taken hold of it. But one thing I do: Forgetting what is behind and straining toward what is ahead, I press on toward the goal to win the prize for which God has called me heavenward in Christ Jesus. (Philippians 3:12-14)

Our new identity

Session 7

NOTES

Our restoration often comes in healing prayer through our brothers and sisters, as God uses them to call out the true self. Such prayer is vital for our health and well being. It affords members of the body of Christ the opportunity to participate with God in the creative process of bringing forth life in another—truly the most creative act that any of us can enter into!

> Now you are the body of Christ and each one of you is a part of it...
> (1 Corinthians 12:27)
> From him the whole body, joined and held together by every supporting ligament, grows and builds itself up in love, as each part does its work.
> (Ephesians 4:15-16)

While we are "in process," we are also called into service. We are, as Henri Nouwen said, "wounded healers." Whether giving or receiving prayer, all are totally dependent on God's power and touch for healing to occur. On that common ground of faith the Lord's pleasure (and glory) is derived. His perfect love is intimately expressed, from one to another, through the healing touch of imperfect hands. In this manner God has ordained the restoration process to be one of receiving *and* giving (Isaiah 58:6-12). Together, in the Body of Christ, we work to uncover not only our individual selves, but the true Church.

The emergence of the true self is only possible through the crucifixion of those things within us that do not produce life and relationship with God. The soul's weaning from destructive ways of thinking and acting must begin and end in faith: *"And without faith it is impossible to please God, because anyone who comes to him must believe that he exists and that he rewards those who earnestly seek him"* (Hebrews 11:6). Prayer and obedience are transforming acts of faith.

Our identification with Jesus Christ and his grace produces true change. *Only* in Christ is there the authority and power to bring about transformation. His advocacy for us is amply described in the Scriptures. As he states in John 10:10: *"I have come that they may have life, and have it to the full."* Christ's words for us are substantive words of living hope, an eternal feast, far more nutritious and satisfying than anything the world can offer.

Session 7 — Our new identity

NOTES

Restoration of a divine work of art

> We are, not metaphorically but in very truth, a Divine work of art, something that God is making and therefore something with which He will not be satisfied until it has a certain character.
> (The Problem of Pain, C.S. Lewis, p.31)
>
> We look to Christ, not inwardly, in order to receive the truth of our self-worth. As Christ peered through Peter's impulsive, brash exterior and called forth the rock (Matt. 16:18) so does He see through our brokenness in order to behold the jewel of the true self, fashioned according to God's design and wisdom.
>
> He wills for us to embrace and walk in the truth of that self and His favor upon it.
> (*Living Waters Program*, Andrew Comiskey, p.119)

Pictures can often convey a clear understanding of what is happening in the unseen spiritual realm. The following example may prove helpful to your understanding of God's restoration of your true self.

The figure in the four panels on the back cover of this guidebook is a minute portion of one of the greatest works of art ever created—Michelangelo's fresco found on the ceiling of the Sistine Chapel in the Vatican. After centuries of pollution, poor attempts at preservation, and damp weather, the beauty of the masterpiece had become damaged and obscured (notice panel one). To undertake its restoration, many craftspersons were solicited for advice. After viewing the first exposed sections, the experts were at odds as to whether they should or could undertake the entire project. Some critics resisted the uncovering, convinced Michelangelo would never ever have painted with such a bright palette. Their arguments for leaving the fresco alone were based more on their imagined notion of the artist's style than any written records left by Michelangelo himself. They reasoned that the public would take their side of the debate and disdain the bright colors, too. Thankfully, the naysayers lost out. The fresco today is totally restored to its original glorious state.

Like that great work of art, the Lord wants those created in His image to be restored to true brilliance (His original intent). He is continually in the process of cleansing away dirt, removing debris and repairing the damage done to us by sin and worldly abuse. Encrusted layers of spiritual and emotional grime have accumulated from years of neglect and lack of resources. Our Creator can see to our core, the true self laboring beneath the muck and mire of godlessness, aching to be released. And, as C.S. Lewis said, God won't be satisfied until we resemble his Son, aglow with His restoration.

Our new identity

Session 7

NOTES

Panel one represents the start of our souls' restoration. The layers of grime are removed with tender care rather than with harsh abrasives. Progress is made layer by layer.

Colors and forms subtly emerge in the second panel, although cleansing is by no means finished. While the fresco restoration could have ceased at this point (the same could be said in our own healing), the possibilities for even greater discoveries compelled the restorers to go further. Can we not imagine ourselves in that same place as we allow our brothers and sisters to go deeper with us in healing prayer?

Panel three represents the self fully engaged in restoration, yet perhaps feeling at odds with the process—red and raw from the exposure of old wounds.

Finally, we emerge (see the last panel). Our scars are visible, but we are a beautiful sight to behold! The final outcome produces a defined figure that could be likened to the boundaries of our newly discovered, true self, clear and distinct. (This is a relief from the blurredness and confusion of the wounded, false self.)

Just as those figures on the ceiling of the Sistine Chapel, we image-bearers shine forth in ever-increasing brilliance our Creator's original intent. Thus we become *"... a light shining in a dark place"* (2 Peter 1:19), the unobscured love of God now gloriously visible to the world.

As the Lord reveals the beauty of our true selves in union with Him, He gives us the choice: *Will you stop here and go no further in your restoration, or will you press on for the prize of completion?* Michelangelo's painting could not call out to the restorers, "Keep going! Don't stop now!" But we can. Turning to our Creator, our Father, and asking Him to continue the work He has begun in us is the privilege He reserves for those He calls by His name.

† Lord, only You who created my inmost being can call forth my true self.

In my restoration, I ask for the courage and strength to press on to the goal of Christ-likeness.

Fortify my will to choose the way of the cross—to follow You wherever and however You lead me in the process of my sanctification.

Where possible, Lord Jesus, use me to minister hope and restoration to others who, like myself, are on the journey toward wholeness. Amen

Session 7

Our new identity

NOTES

Answer together the following questions:

- Which stage of restoration (as represented by the panels of the fresco) best illustrates where you find yourself today?

- What hindrances to your restoration and growth are you encountering?

Take time to pray for one another concerning those areas where the person feels stuck in disappointment, anger or fear in their restoration process. Prayerfully encourage one another on to the next step.

SCRIPTURE READINGS

Galatians 2:20; Isaiah 53; Ephesians 4:15-16; Colossians 3:9-10; Romans 6:6

THOUGHTS FOR JOURNALING

Can you discern the difference between those thoughts and actions that emanate from the false and true self?

What do you do (if anything) about those things coming from the false self?

Has your physical condition helped or hindered you in the restoration of your true self?

Did you draw any additional analogies from the example of the fresco restoration?

Embracing Life Series: International Copyright © 1998 by Embracing Life Ministries. All Rights Reserved

Forgiveness, the beginning of healing

Session 8

NOTES

"Forgive as the Lord forgave you." (Colossians. 3:13)

While on the cross, consumed by excruciating pain, Jesus looked down on His taunting executioners and said, "Father, forgive them for they know not what they are doing" (Luke 23:34). His words resound with a mercy so profound that eternity is not long enough for humanity to fathom its depths. His forgiveness is the means to our healing, words we must always reckon with to be restored persons.

The cross: source of forgiveness

> Compared with the miracle of the forgiveness of sin, the experience of sanctification is slight. Sanctification is simply the marvellous expression of the forgiveness of sins in a human life, but the thing that awakens the deepest well of gratitude in a human being is that God has forgiven sin.... When once you realize all that it cost God to forgive you, you will be held in a vice, constrained by the love of God.
> (*My Utmost for His Highest,* Oswald Chambers, Nov. 20)

Session 8 — Forgiveness, the beginning of healing

NOTES

Because of Jesus' perfect submission and the Father's answer to his prayer, we have received God's forgiveness and experienced His restorative power. There is no greater gift. As King David exclaimed: "Blessed is he whose transgressions are forgiven, whose sins are covered" (Psalm 32:1).

The story of Jesus healing the paralytic in Mark 2:1-5 confirms the priority of forgiveness. After being lowered through the roof by his friends, the paralytic is laid before Jesus. The Lord's first response to their bold act was to forgive the paralytic's sin. The man's physical healing came afterwards when Jesus commanded him to take up his mat and walk. Everyone in that room left having witnessed the power of Jesus' forgiveness.

In turn, the promise of forgiveness must be declared by us as restored persons in Christ. If the cross is the focal point of our healing, then the words spoken from that cross must become ours as well. His words of forgiveness become our invitation to the world to be reconciled to God (2 Corinthians 5:18-21).

Forgiving others

Not only do we announce God's forgiveness, we extend it to those who have hurt us. However simple and basic in principle forgiveness may be, we typically hold back and refuse to give it. Our tendency is to cling to our grievances against another, especially if it means avoiding our own sinful contribution to the hurtful situation. Withholding forgiveness may even be an element that sustains some of our infirmities. Certainly the Scriptures attest to the possibility of some kind of connection between repentance, forgiveness and physical healing.

> For I take no pleasure in the death of anyone, declares the Sovereign Lord. Repent and live! (Ezekiel 18:32)

> ...If he has sinned, he will be forgiven. Therefore confess your sins to each other and pray for each other so that you may be healed. (James 5:15b-16a)

With the possibility of such hope for healing held out to us, we who are continually reminded of the destructive force of disease must learn to regard forgiveness as our lifeline to renewal.

> For if you forgive men when they sin against you, your heavenly Father will also forgive you. But if you do not forgive men their sins, your Father will not forgive your sins. (Matthew 6:14-15)

Forgiveness, the beginning of healing

Session 8

NOTES

In Sessions Six and Seven we talked about the emergence of the true self that comes from the daily application of the cross to our lives. Jesus and his cross mediate the forgiveness of God. Through the cross, God's image is restored in our humanity.

Walking humbly in Jesus' steps, in the way of the cross, is part of that restoration process. Denying ourselves means releasing our claim to justice or vengeance against another who has hurt us. Taking up our cross means submitting our claim to the One who forgave us. Taking our cross and following Jesus means we must forgive the other. Forgiving others is not an option for those who follow Jesus.

When we forgive the other, we forgive as Jesus forgave, releasing new life in the process. By the grace and power of God we change our world. By the act of forgiveness we reflect God's image as a creative being. Lewis Smedes writes:

> [W]hen we forgive, we come as close as any human being can to the essentially divine act of creation...We create healing for the future by changing a past that had no possibility in it for anything but sickness and death. (*Forgive and Forget*, Lewis Smedes, p.152)

If we stubbornly refuse to release others from real or imagined wrongdoing, our lives become loaded down with all kinds of sin: envy, covetousness, malice, vengeance, pride, self-righteousness, judgements and condemnation. Instead, we should be running to the cross to unload all our unrighteous thoughts. At the altar of the cross, we exchange our burdensome, controlling thoughts of retribution for the Lord's way of forgiveness, liberation and healing. "Therefore confess your sins to each other and pray for each other so that you may be healed" (James 5:16).

The way to forgiveness is fraught with opposition and obstacles—Satan, man and our false selves. The evidence is all around us; our culture claims the right to hold a grudge. Releasing another from our judgements by forgiveness is an alien concept to be ridiculed and associated with weakness. Instead, vengeance is glorified. Nowhere is the self-appointed vigilante more exalted than in our media icons—consider some of the characters portrayed by Charles Bronson and Clint Eastwood. With such a dark pantheon of "heroes," is it any wonder that our imaginations are inflamed with payback fantasies of blowing people away?

Henri Nouwen in *The Road to Daybreak* captures the feelings many of us have when we have "been wronged."

Session 8   Forgiveness, the beginning of healing   **Embracing Life Series**   95

Session 8

Forgiveness, the beginning of healing

> It is hard for me to forgive someone who has really offended me, especially when it happens more than once...Maybe the reason it seems hard for me to forgive others is that I do not fully believe that I am a forgiven person. If I could fully believe that I am forgiven and do not have to live in guilt and shame, I would really be free. My freedom would allow me to love others seventy times seven times. By not forgiving, I chain myself to a desire to get even, thereby losing my freedom. A forgiving person forgives... This lifelong struggle lies at the heart of the Christian life. *(Nouwen, p.68)*

Forgiveness and healing

It could be said that all aspects of spiritual and emotional healing revolve around and include prayers of forgiveness. We seek forgiveness from God (1 John 1:9), we forgive others in prayers to God and we ask God to forgive others (Colossians 3:13). Others seek God's forgiveness for hurting us and others forgive us in their prayers (Ephesians 4:32). We ask God to help us forgive ourselves. During and after those prayers we (and others) experience healing (Psalm 103:1-5).

To describe in detail the various kinds of healing prayer and their interplay with spiritual, emotional and physical illnesses is beyond the scope of this course. Nevertheless, the essential ingredient needed for effective healing prayer for any situation is found in the cross—the forgiveness made available to all in the death and resurrection of Jesus Christ. The cross of our Lord is the power source of all forgiving prayers that truly heal.

> When you were dead in your sins and in the uncircumcision of your sinful nature, God made you alive with Christ. He forgave us all our sins, having canceled the written code with its regulations, that was against us and that stood opposed to us; he took it away, nailing it to the cross. And having disarmed the powers and authorities, he made a spectacle of them, triumphing over them by the cross. (Colossians 2:13-15)

96   **Embracing Life Series**   Forgiveness, the beginning of healing   Session 8

Forgiveness, the beginning of healing   Session 8

Practicality and prayer

Practically speaking, what goes on in prayers of forgiveness? Consider the following:

- Getting in touch with what needs to be forgiven, being specific about the offenses (naming the wrong)
- Expressing your hurt and anger before God or an objective person (how it damaged)
- Releasing the offending person from personal judgement (the debt you feel they owe)
- Releasing the person from your expectations
- Releasing harsh destructive feelings toward the person including thoughts of retribution
- Pursuing forgiveness as an act of the will, regardless of whether it coincides with feelings of well being for the other at the time
- Releasing the offense to the Lord, believing that in time the negative emotions associated with it will be healed
- Acknowledging that forgiveness does not require that the other person conform to what we want
- Realizing reconciliation may never occur
- Loving, praying for, and, if possible, doing good for that person
- Accepting the person so that we can speak the truth in love
- Seeking (when appropriate) the other person's forgiveness for your sinful reactions toward him or her.

(from earlier edition of *Living Waters Guidebook*, Andrew Comiskey, p.77-79)

In the time remaining, break up in pairs and go over the following exercise. First, read over the prayer guide and get familiar with it. Then, pray through it with your partner.

NOTES

Session 8 — Forgiveness, the beginning of healing

NOTES

†

Father God, I choose, as an act of my will to forgive _____. I forgive _____ for _____ (list offenses specifically).

Father, I ask that You forgive _____ for these things and that You not hold these charges against him/her on my account. As I release _____, I ask You to release him/her as well.

Father, I ask that You forgive me for holding unforgiveness, bitterness, and resentment in my heart toward _____. I receive Your forgiveness now and Your cleansing in my heart from all unrighteousness.

I choose to forgive myself at this time for not being perfect, for the hatred, bitterness, and other negative responses I've had, and for any judgment I am placing on myself for the pain of this situation.

Father, I also choose not to hold any bitterness toward You for allowing these hurts to happen to me. I affirm that You are loving, powerful, and good. I release any notion that You owe me an explanation or an apology.

Father God, if there are any more stored up negative feelings in me toward _____, I ask that You cleanse me of them. I will be open to replace these negative emotions with the fruit of Your Spirit (love, joy, peace, patience, kindness, goodness, faithfulness, gentleness, self-control).

Heavenly Father, I ask that You heal now the wounded places of my soul. Heal my memory of those offenses so that I can look back on them realistically, knowing that they were hurtful, but also knowing that You, Lord, have healed the hurt. And use those experiences for the healing of others with whom I come into contact.

Now, Father, I ask that You bless _____ with Your abundant mercy. Prosper _____ in every way: body, soul, and spirit.

(From earlier edition of *Living Waters Guidebook, Comiskey, p.80-81*)

Forgiveness, the beginning of healing

Session 8

SCRIPTURE READINGS

Psalm 32:1-5; Proverbs 24:17, 29; 25:21-22; Matthew 5:7, 39-41; 18:21-35; Mark 11:25; Luke 6:35-37; Romans 12:14, 17, 19; Ephesians 4:32; Colossians 3:13; 1 Peter 3:9

RECOMMENDED READINGS

Restoring the Christian Soul Through Healing Prayer by Leanne Payne

Authority to Heal by Ken Blue

THOUGHTS FOR JOURNALING

Have you experienced the power of prayers of forgiveness in your life (apart from conversion)? Write about them.

Use the prayer guide with another brother or sister present to release any people or organization you may need to forgive.

NOTES

Readings

From:

"The Healing Light"

Agnes Sanford

Ch. 11: Healing of Emotions

The last chapter brought out a danger in spiritual healing—the danger of becoming either emotionally sterile or emotionally unstable. It suggested a defense against this danger—the rooting and grounding of the emotions in the supernatural love of Jesus Christ, expressed through the natural channels of everyday life.

There may be many roundabout ways of securing an emotional release, but for the sake of those who need it I will set down here the most effective way that I have found so far. I found it after much searching and after great need... I realized that I needed forgiveness, and that forgiveness would restore my emotional balance. I had thought a great deal about forgiving others, but I had never thought of being forgiven because I was not in the least conscious of sin.

Through the advice of a friend, I tried the confessional. "The confessional is the church's way of passing on power," she told me. And I retranslated these words to mean "The confessional is the church's way of giving a healing treatment."

I was astonished beyond measure. "If that is so, why have I lived all these years without being told?" I demanded. "Why have I been allowed to think that the confessional was only an escape for neurotics or desperate measure for criminals?"

To this question the friend had no answer.

"Just the same, it is so," she said. "The confessional sets free in you the power of God through the forgiveness of Jesus Christ. It releases power in the way that is the most simple and wholesome and human. If you try and get that power all by yourself, you are apt to overstrain your spiritual energies. The only way you can go on and on getting it alone is to close your eyes to humanity and try and live on a spiritual plane. That method isn't new. It has been tried in the middle ages and given up. It is good as far as it goes, but it doesn't go far enough. And unless one combines it with the sacramental method, it tends to spiritual dryness and exhaustion. Some people can overcome that and go on, living more and more on a spiritual plane. But that separates them from other people. They deny their humanity instead of redeeming it, and so they get farther and farther away from ordinary human beings. They get cold and remote. They build a wall around themselves so that people cannot get near them."

All of this I recognized. It had all happened to me. But I still did not understand the need of the confessional.

"I know that if you believe in Jesus Christ He forgives your sins," I puzzled. "I've known that all my life. Then why do I need to go to any other person and confess my sins so as to be forgiven?"

"Try it and you will find out," said my advisor.

"Well, all right," I replied. "I'll try anything once. After all, that's the way I've found out everything else-by trying it. What do I do?"

Upon this my new friend gave me careful and particular instructions which I shall set down precisely as I received them. I do so, not because everyone who reads this book will rush to the confessional. Having been brought up strictly in the Presbyterian fold I know full well how impossible this would be for many people. But the principles worked out in the following method are universal. They are the best ways that I know for obtaining an emotional balance. And if one is unable to use them in the form of the confessional because one cannot find a minister who believes in it, they can be adapted and used in other forms.

The suggested method for that form of soul-searching that the Bible calls repentance is as follows. Choose the same time and the same place every day for an act of preparation for confession. Relax and lift the mind into the presence of God, and do so with a pencil and paper in the hand. Then divide one's life into seven periods.

Readings

Throw the mind back, on the first day, into the nearest period. Ask the Holy Spirit of God to bring into the remembrance any unforgiven sins (or any uncomfortable memories, as we would probably call them) from these years that still linger in the subconsciousness. Write down these sins as they come to mind. Write them down simply, briefly, without using names or mentioning circumstances or any kind of alibis. Having done this, set aside the paper and forget the whole matter until the next day.

On the next day at the same time and the same place take the second period of one's life and do the same thing. And so on through the seven days.

The little things that come to mind may seem childish, and so they are. But the method is nevertheless right. For why would childish things linger just below the level of consciousness all these years unless there were in them some unhealed hurt—some unforgiven sin? They are like splinters in the hand. The thing may be invisible, but as long as it is there it festers a bit. So the splinters of uncomfortable memories (unforgiven sins) fester in the subconsciousness and throw out into the conscious mind various symptoms of fears, nervous tensions, etc., of whose cause we are completely unaware.

Upon the last of these days, my adviser told me, it might be well to make a retreat of twenty-four hours so as to put my mind entirely upon this thing. She also advised me to go to a priest whom I did not know.

So I made a first confession, very uncomfortably, with the shades of my Scotch Presbyterian ancestors peering around the corners. I followed the strict cut-and-dried form of the church. I read the opening prayer in which I stated that I was guilty of certain sins, by my fault, my own fault, my own grievous fault. I thus had no chance to call these things errors rather than sins as I would undoubtedly have called them otherwise. It was not possible to use the words "negative thought-habits" or "unfortunate decisions" or "nervous tendencies." Neither was it possible to make an excuse or alibi of any kind. There was no dotted line in the form of confession set before me on the prayer desk for any "But he did so-and-so, or she said so-and-so, or life treated me after this or that fashion." I was forced to look squarely upon all my failings, to call them sins and to accept full responsibility for the same. Others may have sinned ten times more than I concerning a certain thing. That made no difference. I was responsible in the sight of God for my own sin, not for that of anyone else. If someone had gossiped about me, lied about me, slandered my name and ruined my life it was nevertheless my duty to confess only to the sin of resentment toward him.

Thus I was forced by an ancient, simple, cut-and-dried method to a self-searching and a straight-thinking that was as uncomfortable and as cleansing as a strong cathartic.

Having read through my list, without comment, I then ended with the printed prayer on the desk before me in which I said I was truly sorry for these and all my other sins that I could not at the time remember and that I intended to do better.

Whereupon the priest made one statement and only one. He said, "Although so few people know it, the church through Jesus Christ really does have the power and authority to forgive sins. Therefore I am sure that these your sins will be forgiven." He then pronounced the absolution, as I had heard the priest pronounce it many a time in the communion service, and I rose and went out, still without comment.

This was done by an act of will and of will only. There was no emotion connected with it except a feeling of distinct discomfort. To kneel in the presence of another person, even though I knelt to the cross and not to him, was not a pleasant experience. There was not even in my mind a feeling of faith or of expectancy. Indeed, my adviser had made it very plain that I must not expect any feeling of joy or of release because the power of God worked in varying ways and the emotions were not a correct indicator of the power of its working. So I arose and went out feeling stiff and cold both in my knees and in my mind.

But I had hardly gone out of the place before I was flooded from head to foot with the most overwhelming vibrations. I felt a high ecstasy of spirit such as I had felt before when very spiritual people had prayed for me...I knew by the inner warmth and tingling that my nerves and glands were being healed of their overstrain and weakness. And indeed a healing process did begin in me at the time. But in addition to these manifestations of the grace of God through the forgiveness of Jesus Christ I felt

Readings

something else that I cannot put into words. I can only say that I felt for the first time that Jesus loved me. Something touched my heart. A stream of tenderness was released within me. And I knew that this was the forgiveness of Jesus Christ—His life, given for me.

Jesus saw that we need not only His teachings but also His life. He tried saving people by His teachings alone and it did not work. His principles were right, but they were continually short-circuited by the forces of evil in this world. The sins of man had created a thunder-cloud, as it were, that shut out the free shining of God's love. So our Lord in the garden of Gethsemane undertook the great work that we call the atonement—the *at-one-ment* which reunited man with God.

For this also He died. Having received our sins into Himself by an effort so great that it literally broke His heart, as the account of the crucifixion shows, He then sent out to us the love of God in a rush of power that broke down the dam of man's hate. He did this upon the cross, so that His death might be a matter of state record, testified to beyond any doubt. But His death, taking place in three hours, was not caused by the cross. It was caused by the weight of man's sins upon a heart that had known no sin. We are fond of blaming His death upon those people whom He chose as His brothers and His friends, His apostles and His martyrs—the Jews. We would do better to consider those sins of our own that formed part of the burden that He bore...He removed the thunder-cloud of man's hate and released the clear shining of God's love...Thus He set flowing a stream of life within life, like the Gulf Stream within the ocean or like the main current within a river. This does not contradict anything about the universal love of a God who sends His rain on the just and on the unjust. It only adds something to it. It adds a specific and personal current of love to that love which is universal. It adds love to love—power to power—life to life.

This costly gift has staggered the imagination of the wise for two thousand years and has been received with simplicity by the childlike.

If we are too wise to receive it, that is no reason why we should abandon any help we may have gained from universal love of the God of all men. A magnifying glass can provide for us a concentrated sunlight that can set on fire a piece of paper placed beneath it. But if we have no magnifying glass or if we do not care to experiment with so great an energy, that is no reason why we should stay out of the sunlight. Some who read this book may not be able to accept this chapter. If so, they would be wise to lay it on the table, as it were, and proceed with their methods of self-help until such time as they need a deeper power. Or if that time never comes, they would still be wise to absorb as much of the universal life of God as He graciously sets free for them.

If I were to place a piece of paper beneath a strong magnifying glass in the sunlight and see it catch on fire, I might not understand the reason for the phenomenon, but nevertheless seeing it I would believe that it was so.

Through the confessional my heart caught on fire. Its dullness and boredom was burned away, its coldness was turned to warmth, its pride was melted into humility. From that time forth I owed all things to all men, for the sake of Him who loved me and gave Himself for me. But at first I did not understand the reasons for this marvelous grace of God. Why, I thought, was it necessary for me to have a mediator of the forgiveness of God in order to receive this grace? Why had I not been able by myself to repent of my sins and to receive full forgiveness? I had always believed in the forgiveness of sins through Jesus Christ. Then why had it not worked for me by my own efforts?

In the same way I had wondered years ago why healing had not come to my baby through my own prayers.

I could give many reasons for this. I could point out the difficulty of seeing our own sins, much greater than the difficulty of seeing our own illnesses. I could explain the value of two minds working together, the one to accomplish an act of repentance, the other to send forth the word of power, the assurance of forgiveness. But the words of the Bible are so absolutely clear and plain on this subject that my own seem trivial beside them. In John 20:22,23, we read, "Receive ye the Holy Ghost; whosesoever sins ye remit, they are remitted unto them; and whosesoever sins ye retain, they are retained." In James 5:16 this direction is given, "Confess you faults one to another, and pray one for another, that ye may be healed."

Readings

And in St. John's first epistle we have this fact presented again and again with brilliant clarity by the disciple who best understood the mind of the Master. "The blood of Jesus Christ His Son cleanseth us from all sin. If we say that we have no sin, we deceive ourselves, and the truth is not in us. If we confess our sins, He is faithful and just to forgive us our sins and to cleanse us from all unrighteousness. If we say that we have not sinned, we make Him a liar, and His word is not in us."

No words of mine could be so straight and so definite as that...However, I had always known this. I had been brought up in the knowledge that the blood of Jesus Christ cleansed from all sin, and had never doubted it for a moment. Yet I was not released from that bondage until I tried the confessional and since then my release has come step by step as I have seen more and more clearly my need of forgiveness.

Merely believing that God has the power to cure diseases does not cure the disease. I had found out by experience that one needed to be more specific and definite than this. In order to be a channel for God's healing to another I had to believe that God had the power and the will to heal that specific disease of that person through me, at that time. In the same way I found out by experience that just belief in Jesus Christ and His power to forgive sins does not make one into a perfect person. One needs to be more specific and more definite than that. One needs first to see one's own faults clearly, and secondly, to believe that God is able to remove those faults then and there, and to create in one precisely the opposite virtues. If one can and does do this without the aid of priest or spiritual friend, psychiatrist or medical adviser, well and good. I know a few people who can, and do. But they are saints and this is a book for ordinary little people. Very few of us ordinary people do this by our own efforts. It is comforting to know that if we have not and cannot do it for ourselves there is still a way open to us, even though it is a way that seems difficult at first.

It seems as a matter of fact, more difficult than it is. It is like jumping into cold water. After the plunge, it is all right! And the hardness of that first plunge is due quite simply to one specific sin—pride. We who have sought Him with our minds do not like to fall upon our knees and to receive Him in our hearts. It flatters our intellects to think that we can learn and practice what He taught. It does not flatter us to think that we can receive His life through a humble acceptance of His forgiveness. Yet that forgiveness is His very life given for us—His perfect love given for our feeble and imperfect love, His strength for our weakness, His health for our illness, His life for our death. For the current of His forgiveness sweeps through the shallows of this world toward the deep waters of everlasting life.

Copyright 1947 Macalaster Park Publishing Company. Used by permission. (pp116-133 Ballatine edition).

Readings

From:

"Jesus Lamb of God"

David Atkinson

Excerpts from Ch. 3: The Sacrificial Lamb Forgiveness

Surprisingly, forgiveness is a term which hardly ever features in psychological or psychiatric textbooks. And yet as guilt is a near universal phenomenon, forgiveness is a universal need.

The Christian understanding of human life reminds us that all of us constantly need the forgiveness of God. This is the reason why the daily office in our prayer books begins with the confession of sin. It is not there to make us feel bad as we try to dredge up every little wrong thought we have had during the past day or past week. It is to remind us that we stand before God in worship only on the basis of his forgiveness and merciful grace. It is also there to remind us that, this side of heaven, we will to some extent, always get things wrong.

I once came across a version of the Ten Commandments, which were expressed in reverse—in negative terms—as "the Ten Commandments of self-defeat". They were depicted as the devil's instructions for ensuring fear, worry, anxiety and depression on the earth. One of the devil's commandments of self-defeat reads, "Thou shalt never make mistakes." Of course we shall make mistakes. I will hurt you, you will hurt me. There will be disappointment and frustration. There will be failure. Faith in God is no protection against failure, suffering and a sense that everything is wrong.

But forgiveness is a way of saying that life can still go on. Forgiveness does not pretend that things are not wrong. It does not say: "There, there, it does not matter." Forgiveness does not live the lie of saying everything is fine when in fact a person is hurting because wrong things have been done and said. But forgiveness is a way of rebuilding life and relationships in spite of wrong, and in the light of wrong, in the most creative way possible. Forgiveness is not about brushing things under the carpet. It acknowledges where wrong has occurred and looks it full in the face, but also says that in grace the one who is wronged will not allow the wrong for ever to get in the way of the relationship being restored. Forgiveness is costly, but it can be healing.

This is the rich gift which the burnt offerings in Leviticus point towards.

The Law of Retaliation

Much of contemporary society is built upon the law of retaliation: "You owe so you must pay." This quickly becomes the law of bearing grudges, holding resentments, standing on rights, exposing other's failures to ridicule. It is a law from which the Christian family is not immune. Too quickly we can react with authoritarian demand, or by putting one another into categories, or by refusing to let the other person be themselves, because they have offended in some way. Wherever it is found, and even if wrong has truly been done, the law of retaliation can only be destructive. In many human situations, for example for people who may have been sexually abused, the deep feelings of the need for revenge, justice, retribution are sometimes all too powerfully present—and they can be destructive. This is crippling and stifling to the freedom of love.

By contrast, the gospel tells of something more positive, more creative, more joyous, though much more costly: the healing power of forgiveness. That is not to say that to deal with painful feelings for someone who has been abused is ever easy or painless. On the contrary, it can be a hard journey of recovery, sometimes later on in life, and usually needing specialist counseling help. But there are many examples of people who have found or are finding help on the way towards moving away from the law of retaliation and retribution.

Forgiveness also breaks down idealizations; it reminds me that both I and you are neither devil nor angel, but sinful and fallible human beings trying to live for Christ, with a lot of the life of Adam still there, but in grace seeking to grow and to change. That is why the writer of the letter to the Ephesians calls on the church to "put up with one another in love." (Ephesians 4:2 "bearing with one another").

Forgiveness is constantly creative of new beginnings. How often because someone has fallen into what we think is error, we are ready to write them off. They may have made an error, but God's grace does not write them off.

Forgiveness can be healing, but as we have said, forgiveness is costly. It costs the whole of the precious lamb for the worshipper. It cost Hosea the sacrifice of going out

Readings

searching for his adulterous wife, finding her up for sale in the market place, and nonetheless bringing her home. It was to cost Jesus Christ no less than the giving of his life.

The Sacrifice of Christ

It is to illustrate the costliness of Christ's self-giving that the New Testament applies to him much of the Old Testament imagery of the sacrificial lamb. This is particularly true of the letter to the Hebrews. There it is made clear that the Old Testament sacrificial system is a shadow. The reality of which this is a shadow is seen in the life and death of Jesus. The Old Testament sacrifices foreshadow the one sacrifice for sins for ever, which is how the writer to the Hebrews understands the death of Christ. By his own will he laid down his life: "By that will, we have been made holy through the sacrifice of the body of Jesus Christ once for all" (Hebrews 10:10).

The letter goes on immediately to indicate how the sacrificial death of Jesus opens to us a new way of life for Christian believers. Guilt is removed and consciences can be cleansed. And it is a way of life which is meant to be shared. In one paragraph, filled with Old Testament imagery, we read:

> Therefore, since we have confidence to enter the Most Holy Place by the blood of Jesus, by a new and living way opened for us through the curtain, that is, his body, and since we have a great priest over the house of God, let us draw near to God with a sincere heart in full assurance of faith, having our hearts sprinkled to cleanse us from a guilty conscience and having our bodies washed with pure water. Let us hold unswervingly to the hope we profess, for he who promised is faithful. And let us consider how we may spur one another on towards love and good deeds. Let us not give up meeting together, as some are in the habit of doing, but let us encourage one another—and all the more as you see the Day approaching. Hebrews 10:19-25

So, the thinking is clear: God's forgiveness of us, through the costly self-giving of his sacrificial lamb, is meant to lead to mutual fellowship and acceptance within the community.

Forgiveness in Practice

How can forgiveness be applied in modern life?

Forgiveness in Personal Relationships

Let us focus on the interpersonal dimension to forgiveness; that is forgiving other people, and forgiving myself. One of the New Testament parables is told by Jesus in response to Peter's question "Lord, how many times shall I forgive my brother when he sins against me?" (Matthew 18:21)

Jesus compares the kingdom of heaven to a king who wished to settle accounts with his officials, one of whom owed him a massive debt and could not pay. The official implored the king for patience, and the king out of compassion released him and forgave him the debt. The same official, however, refused similar compassion to a fellow worker who in his turn owed him a trifling few pence. The official returned to the law of retaliation: you owe, so you must pay! The king was understandably enraged at this, and delivered the official to the jailers. Clearly the refusal to display forgiveness to one of his fellows demonstrated that this official had not properly understood and received the forgiveness offered by his lord. Jesus' comment is hard: "This is how my heavenly Father will treat each of you unless you forgive your brother from your heart" (Matthew 18:35).

Forgiveness is thus an act of will to refuse to stand by the law of retaliation, and a determination to reshape the future of the relationship as creatively as possible despite the wrong and hurt.

There is an instructive example of forgiveness in one of the therapeutic journals.[3] It tells the story of a bright, intelligent, hysterical girl, aged twenty-five with a great deal of anger about her upbringing. There had been much trauma in her earlier life, but also her own learned responses had become increasingly aggressive, causing people to turn away from her. Through sustained therapy, she came to the point of understanding something of the kind of upbringing her own parents had received. "With this she was able to see that no less than herself, no less than everyone else in the world, her parents were inevitably caught in the effects of their life experiences and possessed both good and bad qualities." This realization led to a change in attitude in the girl. She abandoned blaming, accepted responsibility for her own behavior, recognized the real, impartial, impersonality of much human suffering and, with tenderness and some ruefulness, forgave her parents. She then fell in love, and shortly afterwards, married.

Some people also use the term "forgiveness" of

Readings

themselves. To come to an appropriate realization of one's own ambiguous state—partly good and partly bad; to refuse to accept an inappropriate burden of guilt; to cease to blame oneself for things for which one is not responsible; to recover a proper sense of self-esteem and self-acceptance: all this is part of the meaning of forgiveness. Many of us need more help in this area of life than we sometimes like to admit.

Copyright 1996 by David Atkinson,
pp 58-64. Used by permission of
The Society for Promoting Christian
Knowledge, London, UK.

[3] *Forgiveness, Retaliation and Paranoid Reactions,* by R.C.A. Hunter, Canadian Psychiatric Association Journal, 23, 1978.

Readings

From:

"Restoring the Christian Soul Through Healing Prayer"

Leanne Payne

Ch. 7: Second Great Barrier to Wholeness in Christ: Failure to Forgive Others

> For if you forgive men when they sin against you, your heavenly Father will also forgive you. But if you do not forgive men their sins, your Father will not forgive your sins. (Matthew 6:14-15)

The failure to forgive another is a most formidable barrier to wholeness. One can only begin to comprehend its danger to the soul by meditating on Christ's words above. Most moderns, including Christians, have lost even the language with which to speak of the soul. Therefore, the soul's motions are largely lost to them. For that reason, I will write briefly of what seems to me to be the most common "categories" of this failure in order to help us identify our own needs to forgive, as well as to help us be of greater help to those for whom we pray.

Always, at the bottom of everything that is amiss, we will find pride. We need to confess it. And so it is in our failure to forgive the merely petty things in life. Let's look at that category first.

Forgiving Petty Offenses

We tend to overlook this category when we are praying for folks, but often the need to forgive will be just here. It's the *everydayness* of such irritations and transgressions that gets to us, and we can easily come to despise those who offend us in these ways.

Besides that, we should like to pick and choose those who are eligible to offend us. The implication here, of course, is that the offender is something of a snippet and grossly inferior to us in some way. The remedy is to confess the sin of *pride*, calling it precisely that, and then forgive the offender.

Christ does not see others as we see them. To stop for a moment, practice His Presence, and ask to see this person through His eyes can give us an entirely different perspective. In doing this, we often see strengths we've overlooked in the other person, while at the same time we may be painfully reminded of our own weaknesses and Christ's patience with the petty within ourselves.

I witnessed a remarkable physical healing in a woman who realized her need to forgive a petty offense. This woman was part of a prayer group that met regularly to pray for the healing of the sick. She had become increasingly crippled by arthritis, and no matter how often she received healing prayer, she slowly worsened. Several years into her illness, we were praying once again for her healing when the matter of her upstairs neighbor came forcibly before her. This neighbor was an invalid, and she took lunch to her every day at noon. Invariably, however, a few minutes before she could carry the steaming plate of food up the stairs, the phone would ring, and a whiny voice would moan, "Are you coming?"

Her thoughts toward this neighbor grew darker as this behavior continued, but rather than facing the poor soul with the fact that the daily phone call sorely tried her patience, she simply held her tongue with its growing list of unspoken retorts. But she "thought them" loudly enough. After several years of this, her insides were fairly shouting, "Don't I always come! Do I ever miss!" and so on. She got to the point that she would tense up just before the call came. So things went on, day in and day out.

On the day of her healing, she painfully bent her arthritic knees before the altar, and as we prayed with

Readings

her, she realized her need to forgive the upstairs invalid and to ask God's forgiveness for her reactions. This she did, and she was instantly healed of her very painful arthritic condition. People who have never seen something like this have difficulty believing it. Such a healing dramatically illustrates the power of forgiveness and the way it can open us more fully to God's Healing Presence.

Humility and longsuffering, those great Christian virtues, are not often expounded or understood these days. Not all who seem to have them (by never thinking about themselves, for example), in fact, do have them. Christians bent toward one another in idolatrous and codependent ways sometimes mistake this condition for one of humility and service to others. In actuality, these conditions merely enable sick and sinful behavior in others.[1] "Humble yourselves—feeling very insignificant—in the Presence of the Lord, and He will exalt you. He will lift you up and make your lives significant" (James 4:10, *The Amplified Bible*).

To confess the sin of pride and to go on to forgive is marvelously simple, but many stumble right here. We find we must enroll in a primary level of the Holy Spirit's school of prayer. "Father, I am nothing apart from You, have mercy on me; I have been seeing *apart from You*; if you leave me for an instant, I shall be even more prideful, more self-serving." When we learn to pray this prayer, without the least taint of the wrong kind of self-hatred on the one hand or a feeling of superiority on the other, we will be well on our way to maturity in Christ.

Where there are ongoing petty offenses, it is important that we forsake the subjective (reactionary) position and then—listening to God for instruction—step into the free air of an objective position. In this manner, my friend could have dealt honestly with her neighbor's daily whining question and phone call and then ministered Christ's love to the real problem—the invalid's intense loneliness and fear of abandonment.

Failure to Forgive Due to Being Out of Touch with One's Heart

In this day when people's heads are so out of touch with their hearts, many have unforgiveness and do not realize it until, in prayer for healing, the Holy Spirit reveals it.

Often when praying with such persons, I find that a memory of abusive or abnormal behavior by another will come up. The person will not know he needs to forgive the offender. I will have to say, "You must confess this as a sin against you, and you must name it specifically for the sin that it is, and then, before God, extend forgiveness to (offender's name)." The specific naming of the sin and of the offender is important. This is no abstract transaction, but a very real dealing before and with our God.

These persons will invariably be surprised, as if they have never thought about the matter in this light. This is especially true when the need to forgive another involves a parent. But once the deed or circumstance has been acknowledged as an offense, and forgiveness has been extended to that person, healing comes quickly.

Often these people do not know what normal is. They are from dysfunctional homes in which the members do not relate to one another in a healthy fashion. In addition, as children these persons usually were taught to deny their feelings. Even when normal thoughts and feelings were expressed, these were not validated. So there will be a deep inner knowledge of injustice and/or frustration and, at some level of their being, a knowledge of the need to forgive. I know this is so because when they restate (at my request) the offense and extend forgiveness, great anger begins to surface. I then have them raise their hands to Christ on the cross, and they "see" the anger and unforgiveness come up and out of them and flow into the One who, in our stead, takes and carries all our sin and darkness. After this is accomplished, we ask Christ to fill all those spaces where this pain, anger, and unforgiveness have been with His healing love and light.

Judy's story, recounted in chapter 6 of *Crisis in Masculinity*, is a good example of how emotionally sick and confused persons can be when they need to forgive another but do not realize it. The story also shows that we remain tied to parents in unhealthy ways until we extend forgiveness to those parents. In fact, we fail to fully separate our own identity from our parent's and end up hating ourselves.

Readings

Forgiving the Unforgivable

In all their distress he too was distressed, and the angel of his presence saved them. (Isaiah 63:9)

> Agony means severe suffering in which something dies—either the base thing, or the good. No man is the same after an agony; he is either better or worse, and the agony of a man's experience is nearly always the first thing that opens his mind to understand the need of Redemption worked out by Jesus Christ. [2]

Sometimes we must forgive actions that go far beyond the petty offenses to our pride and prejudice. For the young person, twisted in mind and spirit, robbed of even the simplest pleasures of childhood and youth due to the overbearing hatred and mistreatment of a crazed or perverted parent, forgiving can at first seem impossible. Many and varied too are the more subtle sins against the human spirit and soul that are equally hard to forgive. The minister errs who simply throws out the Scripture "forgive your enemy" to such persons without helping them into the Presence of God in such a way that they can both forgive and receive consolation and healing.

I have often heard people say to me, "I cannot forgive." And when they tell me the circumstances, I fully understand their difficulty. In *The Healing Presence*, pages 88-90, I tell about my own experience of forgiving the "unforgivable," how through an entire afternoon I cried out to God for the power to forgive and knew only too well how helpless I was without His grace. As I wrote:

> There were terrible moments in that interminable afternoon when I wondered what I would do if God failed to help me, if I would simply have to cry out like this the rest of my life. Then came a moment when instantly my pleading was interrupted by an amazing awareness of Christ in me, and from that center where He and I were mysteriously one, forgiveness was extended to my enemy. It was as if Christ in and through me forgave the person (who can explain such a thing?)—yet I too forgave. [3]

Note here that it was not until I reached full identification with Christ that I was able to forgive. On the cross He identified Himself with my sin, my suffering—the very pain I was at that moment experiencing. In reaching that place of identification with Him, I could, as it were, stand in the cross and hurt—with Him.[4] One with Him in His dying, I was able to release my unforgiveness, with all its feelings of rage and woundedness, to Him in utter trust. In unison with Him, I could pray: "Father, forgive them, they know not what they do." All my hurt, fear, inability to forgive flowed into Him, and in exchange He gave me freedom. Having taken my place in His dying, now one with Him still, I took my place in His rising. And I knew joy. There is no better theology than this. It's the message of the cross. And it applies to all of us. This is the way of Christian forgiveness.

On the basis of Scriptures and from my own personal experience and that of helping many, many others with the worst imaginable situations, I can always assure these dear ones, "Oh yes, you can forgive. And I will gladly show you how. We will go to prayer, and 'you shall receive power' (Acts 1:8)—the power to forgive even your worst enemy." This enemy often will be your "beloved enemy." It is those nearest to us who have the greatest power to wound and maim us.

The story of "The Doctor Who Hated His Face in the Mirror," first recounted in *Crisis in Masculinity*, pages 70-76, illustrates the way of helping others forgive the more subtle but equally devastating kinds of sins parents commit against them. In this story, we deal with the childhood oath, and the fear that forgiving may open oneself again to another's power to hurt.

The Doctor's Story

A Christian physician, loved by everyone who knows him, had a most difficult time in accepting himself fully. Every morning, as he shaved, he was reminded of this need because he did not like to see his own face in the mirror. He is a man wonderfully used of God, and therefore one who has prayed continuously for the grace to overcome the problem of self-hatred, if for no other reason than in order to accept the vocation God has given him. Anointed by God to pray for the sick, he has *had* to live from the

Readings

Center, at least part of the time. But he knows the danger of running from God's perfect will for himself when, judging himself unacceptable, he steps alongside and looks at himself with excessive distrust and unlove.

As he grew in the favor and admiration of others, and in success both as a physician and as a Christian serving in the public eye, his self-hatred pained him all the more. All kinds of new fears about himself set in: "Why do I seek out friendships with good-looking, handsome, athletic men?" Before his involvement in Christian ministry, he had kept his feelings, fears, yearnings, needs and loneliness to himself. In fact, before his experience of renewal in the Spirit, he had kept a stern authoritarian control over both himself and his family, a control that kept true conversation with them at a safe distance. Rarely, therefore, could he share meaningfully even with his wife. To do so might mean to look, even for a moment, at his fears, and then he would have to believe the worst of himself. But gradually, as he came present to the Lord, he came present to his own heart and gained the courage to look at his feelings and fears. After hearing me speak and reading *The Broken Image*, he realized and faced the fact that although he did not have a sexual neurosis, he was severely cut off from his masculine side. He simply could not accept himself as a man.

He came to talk to me about his fears, the main one being, "Why am I so desperate for male companionship? Is there really something wrong with me? I have never looked at myself as being masculine; by that I mean 'handsome, rugged, athletic.' I see myself as being different, odd, seeking male approval and companionship. I like to be creative, do gardening, read, travel, dress well, and I am 'people-oriented.' I'm a 'hugger.' And I feel I must apologize for being this way, that I must try to hide my creativity and my gifts."

As we talked, his agitation concerning his father quickly became apparent: "I have never felt loved or affirmed as a son or as a man by my father. I don't ever remember him holding me, telling me he loves me, that I am good, or that he is proud of me."

If ever a man needed to be lifted from the subjective to the objective position where his father was concerned, this good man did. He still yearned for his dad's love and affirmation; he still grew angry with him for not giving it. He looked for his father to change, and he went through all the gamut of emotions over and over again as he reached out to his father and as his father remained precisely the man he had always been: unloving, unreasonable, and always accusing others of neglecting him. At my suggestion that he, the physician, must gain the objectivity to see and accept his father as he in fact was, and that we would pray to this end, the pitch of his voice must have risen an octave: "But you don't know what you are asking! We can't accept him *that* way."

And out came the picture of what it had meant to try to grow up straight in the midst of an evil perversity. His father, a rich man, was also a miser. Although he owned thousands of acres of rich orchards in Oregon, he never gave anything to his wife or children that cost him anything—whether in the way of loving actions or even the lowliest gift. One of the doctor's most agonizing charges against his father was, "He never once gave me a gift. He is a rich man, and for my birthday he gives me coupons that cost him nothing." Throughout his school and college years, the son had spent vacations laboring in the father's orchards. Although he was well-paid, he had no sense of partnership with his father in this enterprise. His father remained as aloof toward him as toward the other workers. Through his work he came to know the magnitude of his father's holdings and remarked to me in bitterness, "My mother died without having even the most common labor-saving devices or a penny to jangle in her pockets. He even did the grocery shopping."

As he shared about his father's words and actions toward himself, I saw him as a miracle sitting before me. A "miracle," true enough, who was not yet affirmed in his masculine identity or as a person, and one who had yet to gain the objectivity needed to creatively handle the problem with his father. But few sons survive such a negation of themselves as this father was able to dish out. A man who negated life and love, this father had failed to snuff out the essential spirit, the *life* in his son. It was almost as if he had tried, albeit unconsciously. He had wounded him dreadfully, and if God had not helped this son, that son could have (by hating or failing to forgive his father) become a little more like him every year.

This is the problem with the childhood oath, with

112   **Embracing Life Series**   Session 8

Readings

the childhood determination to "never be like my father." Apart from accepting and forgiving our parents *as they are*, we cannot get our identities separated from them and go on to accept ourselves. We are therefore in danger of becoming more and more like them. To fully forgive is divine, and divine intervention is required to do it. "Yes," said the doctor to this insight, "before I found Christ in a deeply meaningful way and began the work of forgiving, I was becoming more like him every year."

Nevertheless, the work of forgiveness to be done was not finished in Dr. L.'s life. He was now face to face with his need to receive the gift of divine objectivity, to be raised from the subjective little-boy position in relationship to his father to one of adult maturity with its capacity to stand above a problem, see it for what it is, name it before God, utterly forgive it, and no longer be grievously entangled in it. It's one thing to suffer a problem while looking down upon it from a free perch, and quite another to suffer it while still having one's feet, like a captive bird caught in the net. For Dr. L. to achieve the objective position, he must now accept his father as the man he in fact is and always has been. After explaining to him his need, I helped him to pray in the following fashion:

"I forgive you, Dad, for being unable to love me, unable to give to me or to my mother, my brother, and my sister. I face the illness and wickedness of your particular brand of miserliness, and I name it as the evil it is, as an evil with the power to wound my mother and my sister (even fatally perhaps, for they both died early of physical diseases), and myself. That you could never see or treat us as *persons*, that you could not affirm the life that was given us, but could only see everything in terms of your own small and even perverted desires, I forgive you. I forgive you for not becoming all God created you to be; I accept you as you have chosen to be, and I will no longer strive uselessly, demanding that you change, demanding that you love me, that you recognize me as a person with needs, feelings, aspirations, and desires. But because I can now truly forgive you, I will no longer give you the power to wound me or my own wife and children. We name the evil, and in the name of Him who is our light and life, we surmount it, we transcend it in the power of the Spirit. We can now bless you as you let us, expecting nothing in return.

We do not accept your attempts to scapegoat us, but with the word of truth, that wisdom that comes from God, we turn your accusations and projections back upon your own head, and we leave you to deal with them. We know now that this is love, the love that 'is more stern and splendid than mere kindness.' It is the love, this word of truth, that will help you overcome the evil that binds you to yourself. We do not judge you, Dad, but we do judge the evil that has wounded us all.

"And now, Heavenly Father, I thank You for hearing this prayer, for enabling me to accept and fully forgive my father, and for enabling me to no longer subjectively flail under the evil that has afflicted us all, but to rise into that true objectivity that will perhaps someday enable me to be a channel of Your healing love to my father."

In this way, Dr. L. came into that green and spacious place where he began to know God the Father's affirmation of himself as a son and as a man. He began to hear the voice of the ultimate Affirmer. "On my first eight-day retreat, I heard the Father tell me He loved me, that I was precious in His eyes, and that He needed me to do His work. This permeated my entire being...'I love you and now call your sexuality [masculinity] into order so that you can grow in My love and then minister to men I call you to.'

In this way, listening to the affirming words of God the Father, he began to "bond" with Him; he made contact with ultimate masculinity, which in turn struck fire to his own. And he began to gain, slowly at first, the gift of divine objectivity.

Dr. L. could now see that his deep desire for male relationships, never a bad thing in itself but rather needful and healthy for all men, was frightening to him because he had a fear of rejection by other men and such an overwhelming need for their affirmation of himself as a man. He had never bonded with his father and unconsciously sought this masculine bonding through other men. His need for masculine approval and love had been so great, therefore, that he had had to repress it, and rankling as it did, deep in his unconscious, it began to erupt as fear, guilt, odd thoughts, genital responses, impotency with his wife, and finally, as time went on, to an unhealthy fantasy life in order to perform sexually.

As Dr. L. came present to and understood his

Readings

own heart, all repression of his need for father-love and masculine approval stopped. Then once it moved into the conscious where it could be laid before the Lord, it could no longer erupt in odd ways. He repented of and put to death the fantasy life he had adopted in response to his fears and guilt; his problems with impotency, inappropriate genital responses, and odd thoughts subsided and disappeared.

From then on he could begin to relate to men. He was no longer afraid to put his arms around the man who needed his touch, hold him tight, and pray with him—whether this was in his capacity as a physician treating the ill and diseased, or as a layman called to pray with and for others. Dr. L. had a medical practice in a large West Coast port. His large medical practice brought him all conditions of men and women. As a specialist in his medical field, he is often called upon to treat medical problems that are specific to practicing homosexual males. Before his healing, these patients could bring to life the worst fears he had about himself. Now, however, in his own words, "I can talk with, pray with, cry with" the homosexual person. "I have become more lovingly authoritative or firm in speaking about sexual behavior to the men who come to me." Dr. L. now has, in fact, a most significant ministry to men suffering with sexual neuroses and, because of the cosmopolitan nature of his city, has helped people from many lands.

As infants snuggling in our mother's arms, sons and daughters alike are affirmed in their feminine side. We get in close touch with the feminine within our mothers and therefore within ourselves. Dr. L., having had a loving, understanding mother, was highly developed in his feminine side. And this was a very good thing indeed. But, being insecure in his masculine side, he had been fearful and ashamed of his giftedness. He had even tried to hide the creativity that came directly out of being in close touch with his intuitive, feeling, compassionate self. "As Leanne and I prayed about masculinity/femininity and their balance, I began to see myself differently. I began to see myself in the light of Jesus. I also saw the balance within Jesus; His masculinity/femininity became more obvious, and His relationships with both men and women."

As this physician understood this, he recognized and accepted his own unique gifts.

An important prayer we pray over the one who has been so deeply wounded by the sins and sicknesses of others is one of "binding and loosing" (see Matthew 18:18). In the Scriptures these terms refer to loosing people from their sins and from the effects of being sinned against.

In the effective doing of this, we take an important principle from the prophets of old who, one with their people who had sinned, acknowledged their part in the corporate sin of the nation. Daniel's prayer (9:4-19) is one of the most beautiful illustrations of this principle, as is Nehemiah's prayer (1:5-11).

> I confess the sins we Israelites, including myself and my father's house, have committed against you. (Nehemiah 1:6)

> They stood in their places and confessed their sins and the wickedness of their fathers. (Nehemiah 9:2b)

When praying for someone who is grievously sinned against, we confess those sins before God that have so deeply pierced the soul of the one for whom we pray. This does not mean that the evildoer's sin is hereby remitted. It does mean that with this confession and our extension of forgiveness to the sinning one, the power of that sin to continue to wound and to shape the sufferer is broken....

1) We do not forgive evil (per se).
2) We do not forgive Satan.
3) We do not forgive demons and evil principalities.

But we do forgive *persons* in the clutches of that evil. Only in the Healing Presence of God are we enabled to pray this way. But this sin too He has already endured for us and experienced the awful turning of His Father's face from Him as he took upon Himself and into Himself the sin of a fallen world.

A Cleansing Grief

Truly, as the doctor, and all of us find out, it is in being humbled to the ground with sorrow and loss that we as Christians can find both the grace and the option of mourning before Almighty God our sins, our sorrows, our grievous losses and injustices.

Readings

From such a stance, we more deeply recognize the human condition, that we too are sinners, that we too are capable of wounding others. We know that if we do not find the grace to forgive, within our hearts a coldness and a hardness will increase, and we will as sinners grow more monstrous. But if in this state of woundedness and mourning, we cry out to Him for the power to forgive, we receive healing and mercy. Our hearts softened and pliable now in a way for which our greatest successes could never have prepared us, we go on to true victory over the world, the flesh, and the devil. This is why it is not in our successes and victories, but in the fires of sorrow that we find our truest selves. When we truly forgive (that vital principle at the very heart of Christ's cross and the Christian gospel), we find that He is with us (and has been all along) in the fiery affliction. If I fail to forgive, I turn from Him, and lose the real "I." An icy hardness begins to form in my heart, and I am the loser.

Though suffering is the way we can best learn, not all are helped by it. As Oswald Chambers has said, "it makes some people devils."

> We all know people who have been made much meaner and more irritable and more intolerable to live with by suffering. Suffering perfects only one type of person—the one who accepts the call of God in Christ.[5]

...Thanks be to God, I have seen very few who refuse to forgive once they understand that the grace to forgive and be forgiven is available to them. Once in a while, however, I do see it. It is not something one easily forgets, for of all that is tragic, this is the most. As Oswald Chambers reports:

> There is no suffering to equal the suffering of self-love arising from independent individuality which refuses to submit to God or to its nobler self.[6]

---

[1] For more on this, send for tapes on codependency to Pastoral Care Ministries, P.O. Box 17702, Milwaukee, Wisconsin 53217.

[2] Oswald Chambers, *Oswald Chambers, The Best from All His Books* (Nashville: Thomas Nelson, 1987), p. 345.

[3] Leanne Payne, *The Healing Presence* (Wheaton, IL: Crossway Books, 1989), p. 89.

[5] Chambers, *Best of All His Books*, p. 345.

[6] *Ibid.*, p. 344.

Copyright 1991, pp 67-102.
Used by permission of Baker Book House Company, Grand Rapids, MI.

Dealing with shame & self-hatred

Session 9

NOTES

Our focus on the cross, the true self and forgiveness gives us a firmer sense of our identity as emerging persons in Christ. With this essential knowledge we can more clearly discern the destabilizing elements of our past. In our past are voices that run contrary to God's Word, that try to threaten our security in Christ. Our ability to get free from those negative influences (often rooted in our childhood) is grounded and realized in Jesus Christ, the Lord over all creation (Colossians 1:16) and over time itself (Hebrews 13:8). This week's study focuses on our liberation from the tyranny of those voices that hinder our soul's growth.

The stigmas and prejudices associated with life-altering illnesses feed into deep-seated, diseased ideas and perceptions about ourselves. Shame and self-hatred comprise a polluted seedbed of destructive thoughts. Shame and self-hatred often result from a child's wounded soul left to its own devices, continually accusing and blaming itself. As adults, our damaged souls may regard the Lord's healing with suspicion, our hearts hardened from too many broken promises in childhood. At best, we mentally embrace what the Scriptures say, yet our hearts are constantly on alert for disappointment.

Self-hatred

In an earlier session, we looked at the "Who I am in Christ" list and chose Scriptures that spoke to each of us particularly. We discussed how the restoration of the image of God must proceed from the cross and the Lord's

Session 9 — Dealing with shame & self–hatred

NOTES

forgiveness of our sin. From there, the layer-by-layer removal of lies and misperceptions begins in earnest. Just as important, the Holy Spirit is intent on freeing up the passageway between what the head knows and what the heart experiences—if we let Him. If not, the cut-off heart will remain isolated by its own imprisonment of self-judgement.

We may sincerely believe our reasons for hating ourselves are valid, even biblical. However, that is clearly a misinterpretation of the Scriptures which call us to "deny" ourselves. (See this week's reading from Seamands.) The folly of our self-hatred becomes clearer as we look at the Scriptures more closely.

> "Love your neighbor as yourself." (Jesus—Matt. 22:38b)
>
> Yet to all who received Him, to those who believed in His name, he gave the right to become children of God—children born not of natural descent, nor of human decision or a husband's will, but born of God. (John 1:12-13)
>
> He chose to give us birth through the word of truth. (James 1:18)
>
> I have been crucified with Christ and I no longer live, but Christ lives in me. (Galatians 2:20)

The Lord calls us, as his children, to participate in our liberation from the lies of self-hatred. A decision to not embrace or entertain self-hatred has to be made *by* us, not *for* us. Leanne Payne writes in her book, *Restoring the Christian Soul Through Healing Prayer*:

> The renunciation of self-hatred is a deliberate (volitional) step we take, and we keep our eyes on the Source of our salvation, not on our subjective feelings, which are unreliable and even 'diseased' due to the habitual attitudes we've formed.
>
> As we do this, God honors our transaction and showers His grace upon us. We then do battle with all the diseased and negative thoughts and imaginings, lifting them up to Him as they arise in our hearts and minds. (Payne, p. 21)

Recognize that we are not talking about the negation of self, rather our selfish intentions. Selfishness stems from our insecure need for self-assertion and self-rule. When we renounce self-hatred, we learn to *receive* and *accept* the precious gift of life and affirmation that the Lord has given us in Himself. We believe it when God says that He loves us. Furthermore, we grow and mature by *acting* upon his words! *"Man does not live on bread alone but by every word that comes from the mouth of the Lord"* (Deuteronomy 8:4).

118 Embracing Life Series

Dealing with shame & self-hatred

Session 9

Leanne Payne wrote a beautiful prayer for renouncing self-hatred, edited and adapted here.

> ***Every person in the group is to participate in praying this prayer out loud.***

For God caused Christ, who himself knew nothing of sin, to be sin for my sake, so that in Christ I might be made good with the goodness of God. (2 Corinthians 5:21 J.B. Phillips)

✝

HOLY FATHER, thank You for Your Son Jesus Christ...that His death and resurrection has enabled me to have life and intimate relationship with You. Faith in Christ cleanses my heart from my sins and my wounding reactions to the sins of others against me. Because of your Son, Father, I can now share in Your perspective of myself and others. Thank You, Heavenly Father for this gift of life and hope.

JESUS CHRIST, Son of God, in You I live and breathe and discover who I am created to be. Thank you, Lord of my life, Holy One, crucified for me—Your blood justifies me. And now, in union with You, Your goodness is mine.

HOLY SPIRIT, thank You for sharing the love of the Father and the Son with me. You give me the grace to receive my full inheritance as a child of God. Strengthen me now to renounce the sin of self-hatred and empower me to press on toward the goal of fully accepting my identity as a child of God the Father, the Son and Holy Spirit.

Pray quietly, giving thanks. If diseased feelings start to surface, simply allow them to flow, one at a time, up and out of your heart and mind and into the Crucified One. Note them later in your prayer journal, not only so you can converse with God about them, but recognize and refuse them if and when they return asking readmittance to your heart. Now see Him dying on the cross and taking those things into Himself. Then see Him risen again, ascending to the Father, there to intercede to the Father for you, to pour out upon you His Holy Spirit, to send you words of Life that engender in you new and wholesome feelings and attitudes. And give thanks.

Now, Lord in Your name and with the grace You shower upon me, I renounce the sin of self-hatred.

(*Restoring the Christian Soul Through Healing Prayer*, Leanne Payne, p.23-24.)

NOTES

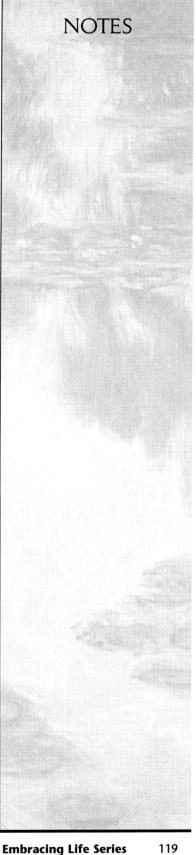

Session 9 — Dealing with shame & self–hatred

NOTES

Shame

"Today, if you hear his voice, do not harden your hearts." Psalm 95:7-8a

Once the lid of self-hatred has been removed, the underlying complex of toxic shame may be exposed. John Bradshaw in *Healing the Shame that Binds You* describes this shame as:

> ...an excruciating experience of unexpected exposure. It is a deep cut felt primarily from the inside. It divides us from ourselves and others. In toxic shame we disown ourselves. And this disowning demands a cover-up. Toxic shame parades around in many garbs and get-ups. It loves darkness and secretiveness. (Bradshaw, p.3)

Pastor and counselor Craig Lockwood writes of the origins of shame:

> ...shame enters the heart early in the developmental stages of the child's life, getting its vitality from the internalized negative messages sent during abandonment, abuse, and shaming actions of parents with no internal well-being of their own.
>
> Because of his lack of individuation a child has developed no internal boundaries. This makes him vulnerable to being shamed by experiencing and being forced to carry, the negative feeling reality of his parents.
> (SALT Program unpublished notes)

The previous prayer of renunciation prepares our spiritual senses to receive healing words from our Heavenly Father. May there be no doubt that by putting to death the old, self-loathing, religious self, we are more free and able to deal with the underlying shame and its many manifestations. In response to its discovery, we are called to deposit our burden of shame *on Him who knew no shame*, assured that it will be thoroughly disposed of.

> Let us fix our eyes on Jesus, the author and perfector of our faith, who for the joy set before him endured the cross, scorning its shame, and sat down at the right hand of the throne of God. Consider him who endured such opposition from sinful men, so that you will not grow weary and lose heart.
> (Hebrews 12:2-3)
>
> Thus you will know that I am in Israel, and that I am the Lord your God and there is no other; and my people will never be shamed. (Joel 2:27)

Listening for God

"Speak for your servant is listening." (1 Samuel 3:10)

The intensity and volume of destructive voices in our heads (couched in painful memories) will decrease as we seek the Lord for a new

120 **Embracing Life Series**   Dealing with shame & self–hatred   Session 9

Dealing with shame & self-hatred   Session 9

sensitivity to His voice, for His words of affirmation and life. Our inner ear can become trained to discern the edifying and encouraging words of our true Father. Our spiritual hunger for His life-producing words can, in time, produce a distaste within us for things false and uncharacteristic of God.

> ...and the sheep listen to his voice. He calls his own sheep by name and leads them out...his sheep follow him because *they know his voice.* (John 10:3-4) [italics JH]

In this discovery of our Father's voice, journaling becomes more and more important. Leanne Payne writes of the results of listening prayer after we have been liberated from the solitary confinement of self-hatred:

> With this renunciation, a multitude of accusing [shame-based] thoughts—the root causes behind the self-hatred—may begin to surface. Simply write them down in your prayer journal, acknowledging them, and then listen for the thought or illumination God is sending you. For this will be the word from Him that not only replaces the diseased thought pattern but will flood you with understanding. (Restoring the Christian Soul, p. 24)

King Solomon wrote in the voice of divine wisdom:

> My son [and daughter], pay attention to *my* words; incline your ear to *my* sayings. Do not let them depart from your sight; keep them in the midst of your heart. For they are life to those who find them, and health to their whole body. (Proverbs 4:20-22) [italics JH]

Destructive, shameful words have crippled our souls. The identification and removal of those false labels requires a ruthless honesty and courage in allowing the pain from our past to freely surface. Robert McGee in *The Search for Significance* notes:

> Day after day, year after year, we tend to build our personalities upon the rubble of yesterday's personal disappointments.
>
> But nothing forces us to remain in the mold of the past. By the grace and power of God we can change! We can persevere and overcome! No one forces us to keep shifting our feet in the muck of old failures. We can dare to accept the challenge of building a new life...
>
> Our past relationships may involve the intense pain of neglect, abuse and manipulation. If we do not begin the process of healing from those broken relationships, however, we will be unable to experience the joy, and yes, the challenge of potential failure in the present. (McGee, p. 84)

Session 9 — Dealing with shame & self-hatred

NOTES

Releasing the labels of shame

> Here I am! I stand at the door and knock. If anyone hears my voice and opens the door, I will come in and eat with him and he with me. (Revelation 3:20)

When we engage in listening prayer we are asking the Lord to reveal the destructive words we hear in our internal dialogues. All kinds of derogatory, berating words may surface. As they do, we offer them to the Lord for his disposal. We then ask Him to give us His word or words to replace them. He will be faithful to do so. Learn to distinguish His response from others. The Lord's word will be encouraging, edifying, or exhortive and always scriptural—in character with His nature as revealed in the Word. Those words which are not His are destructive, slanderous and berating. They emanate from the fallen or false self, the demonic, or worldly influences we have taken into ourselves.

In their book *Listening Prayer,* Dave and Linda Olson clearly communicate the essence of what we are seeking as human beings *in relationship* with God:

> Most people feel that prayer is asking God for what we need and telling Him what we want to tell Him. In listening prayer, however, we wait on God to answer. In listening prayer, we believe that He might have something to say to us at the moment rather than some later date. Listening prayer means dialogue, rather than monologue. We are absolutely convinced that the Lord loves us and would like to share His heart with us as we share our hearts with Him.
>
> Think about it: God's whole purpose and plan when He created the world was to have someone outside the Trinity with whom He could have relationship. He created mankind a little lower than the angels. He did not want another entity simply to serve Him, as the angels do. He wanted someone to love, to talk to. He longed for close relationship. (Olson, p. 8)

Though there are other ways our Father communicates to us—for instance through the Scriptures, mental pictures, counsel and prophetic words from others or simply a strong intuition "in our gut"—hearing His still small voice may prove to be the most underdeveloped. In your attempts to develop acuity for hearing his voice, you may experience some momentary failures but don't give up; this is normal. Contemplative writer Henri Nouwen wrote:

> The root choice is to trust at all times that God is with you and will give you what you most need. Your self-rejecting emotions might say, "It isn't going to work. I'm still suffering the same anguish I did six months ago. I will probably fall back into

Dealing with shame & self-hatred — Session 9

NOTES

the same old depressive patterns of acting and reacting. I haven't really changed." And on and on. It is hard not to listen to these voices. Still you know that these are not God's voice. God says to you, "I love you, I am with you, I want to see you come closer to me and experience the joy and peace of my presence. I want to give you a new heart and new spirit. I want you to speak with my mouth, see with my eyes, hear with my ears, touch with my hands. All that is mine is yours. Just trust me and let me be your God. (*The Inner Voice of Love*, p. 113)

In just a moment we are going to do a prayer exercise that entails listening…listening with your "spiritual ears." We will be listening for that still, small voice of God…of the One who is desiring to speak to us. As we listen intently, trust Him to reveal Himself to you. He truly does want *all* of His children to discern Him. You have not been born again only to be born deaf to your heavenly Father's voice! Believe it.

The following is a listening exercise that can be done alone or in a group where the leader initiates the prayers and participants repeat afterward.

[Note: have pen and paper or use this guidebook to write in.]

Follow the indications for the prayers to be said out loud. Listening prayer done in this manner will help you distinguish between the audible sound of your voice and that of the still, small responsive voice of the Holy Spirit inside.

We will first ask the Lord to reveal the negative descriptive words we have taken in about ourselves. We'll then note them on paper and offer them to the Lord. Following that, we'll pray to Him again, asking Him to replace the destructive words with His life-giving words of truth. As we hear them, we will note them on paper. …Let's take a moment to pray over this exercise.

† Father, we long to hear from you; Your counsel, Your words of encouragement, Your words of life. As Your children, we want to learn to recognize and respond to Your voice and no other. We ask You, Lord, to help us recognize those deeply embedded, obstructive, critical words and voices—all that has interfered with hearing the voice of Your Holy Spirit. We humbly ask that You would replace that which is false with your loving words of truth, according to Your Word and who we are in Your Son Jesus Christ.

Session 9 — Dealing with shame & self-hatred

NOTES

[Out loud, together] Lord, please reveal to me those negative and destructive words about myself that I've accepted and embraced-words I've allowed to name and define me. Help me to hear them clearly. I am listening.

- *Write the words down as they come up.*

- *When finished, draw a bold cross over the words. Look at the words, let the reality that these words are covered by the cross settle in.*

- *With eyes closed, offer the list to the Lord. If you see Him disposing of the list in any way, note it.*

- *Prepare to pray out loud again. We will be asking the Lord to replace those words with healing, life-giving words, listening to what He says about us through His Holy Spirit.*

✝

[Out loud, together] Lord, I ask that You might speak to me now. Replace the old false words, with Your words of truth. Your words are life to me. So I ask, Father: Let me hear Your voice, tell me what You think of me as Your child. I am listening.

- *As before, write down what you hear His voice saying inside.*

- *His response will come quickly and simply. [Note: You may want to repeat the prayer, out loud, more than once]*

- *Remember these are words coming from the Lord who loves you. His voice (the Holy Spirit within you) will be familiar and kind. The manner in which He speaks is neither lecturing nor like a sermon. He always lovingly encourages, builds-up or corrects His children. His heart's desire is to reveal His love and the truth of who we are that we might eagerly seek Him.*

- *Close the exercise with a short prayer of thanksgiving.*

Important note to the leader: In the group setting, time should be given for participants to talk about what they have heard. Sharing the responses before others unmasks the enemy, reveals God's love and lifts the shame as they realize the commonality of their experiences. After each person shares, affirm their ability to hear God's voice, bless the healing words they received from God and pray for the ongoing dialogue they will have with Him.

Dealing with shame & self-hatred — Session 9

SCRIPTURE READINGS

2 Corinthians 5:21; Colossians 1:22-23
Psalm 69:6; Romans 8:12-16

RECOMMENDED READINGS

Restoring the Christian Soul Through Healing Prayer by Leanne Payne
(Part I, "The Virtue of Self-Acceptance")

The Three Battlegrounds by Francis Frangipane
(Part 1, "The Battleground of the Mind")

Listening Prayer by Dave and Linda Olson

Putting Away Childish Things by David Seamands

THOUGHTS FOR JOURNALING

What kind of verbal affirmation did you receive growing up? Did shame play an important part in the ways you interacted with others? Continue to journal the shame-based thoughts and feelings that come to the surface. In keeping with the prayer exercise we completed, note the words the Lord gives you to replace the negative self-talk.

NOTES

Readings

From:

"Putting Away Childish Things"

by David A. Seamands

Ch. 10: Childish Concepts of Self & Self-Surrender Regarding Self-Disparagement

There are Christians who equate self-denial with self-disparagement. They do this because they do not understand the proper place of self-love in the Christian life. They reject self-love because they see it as the very essence of sin. It is dangerous to think of self as something detached and essentially evil.

Jesus said that we should love God with our whole hearts and love our neighbor as we love ourselves. Love for self is as necessary for maturity and wholeness and holiness as is love for God and for other people. Indeed, loving God and loving my neighbor require a measure of self-acceptance and self-love in which I hold my own selfhood in esteem, integrity, identity, and respect.

In the great marriage passage of Ephesians, we read that the measure of a man's love for his wife is his love for himself (5:28-29). Commenting on this chapter, John Wesley wrote: "Self-love is not a sin; it is an indisputable duty." Selfishness is a sin, as is self-centeredness, for these are distortions and perversions of love. Never fall into the trap of thinking that crucifixion of the self, self-denial, or self-surrender mean self-contempt or self-despising. Even the word selflessness is very misleading. The opposite of pride and self-centeredness is not selflessness or self-contempt, but God-centeredness. "I live, yet not I." Yes, my ego is still alive, but it is not a self-centered, self-filled ego. It is a Christ-filled, Christ-centered ego. Don't make self-belittling or selflessness the goal of your Christian life.

St. Augustine said many wonderful things, but he also made some horrendous blunders. It has taken us centuries to get over some of his extremities regarding the body and sex and self. One of those blunders is in *The City of God*: "The difference between the city of the world and the city of God is that the one is characterized by love of self to the contempt of God, and the other (the city of God) is characterized by love of God to the contempt of self." This is very wrong, very unbiblical, and the way many of us live. We think we are pleasing God. We think we are producing the sanctified and holy life through this kind of counterfeit holiness. In reality, we produce a guilt-ridden piety, a joyless self-negation, an unattractive goodness. Instead of delivering us from self-centeredness and pride, self-contempt leads us into religious self-centeredness and pride.

In his famous letters to Wormwood, that abominable genius Screwtape gives some subtle advice on the matter. Wormwood is on his first assignment. He always refers to the young Christian he is tempting as the patient. Screwtape writes to Wormwood, "You must therefore conceal from the patient the true end of humility. Let him think of it not as self-forgetfulness but as a certain kind of opinion (namely, a low opinion) of his own talents and character" (*The Screwtape Letters,* C.S. Lewis, Macmillan, p. 72).

Another time when Wormwood has tried all forms of temptation and the young Christian is not falling for any of them, Screwtape writes him, "Your patient has become humble; have you drawn his attention to the fact?' (p. 71)

Self-despising is not pleasing to God, and it is not the answer to the problem of pride. It actually increases the problem. Psychologist Karen Horney has said, "Self-hate is pride's inseparable companion, and you can't have one without the other." How often self-incrimination becomes an inverted form of good works, of inner penance which we must do, thinking we are pleasing to God. It is a badge of membership in an elite holy club which prides itself for self-belittling and guilt. So an amazing thing happens: condemnation of self becomes the basis of "a good conscience."

Readings

Some of us wouldn't know how to live if we didn't feel guilty; we'd go to pieces from spiritual anxiety. That guilty self becomes the basis of a "good conscience," while a good conscience somehow creates a feeling of guilt. It reminds me of a cartoon I saw. Two convicts in a prison courtyard are whispering about a third. The first convict says to the second, "You know, the thing I can't stand about that guy is his guiltier-than-thou attitude."

"Love your neighbor as you love yourself," said Jesus. Self-love, not selflessness, is the basis of interpersonal relationships. Selflessness between people can turn out to be mere compliance and appeasement. It is often used to rationalize copping-out on the tough, real-life questions of right and wrong. And, of course, selflessness in the hands of a Christian bully can become an exquisite instrument of torture, of spiritual and emotional blackmail. If he can make you feel guilty by saying to you, "You're thinking about yourself," then he can control and manipulate you into doing whatever he wants.

The heart of the Christian life is love, loving God with the whole self and loving others as you love yourself. Don't translate that—"Love your neighbor instead of yourself." "Love your neighbor as yourself," Jesus said. This requires not less of a self, but more of a self filled with power and love.

Copyright 1982.
Used by author's permission.

128 **Embracing Life Series** Session 9

Breaking free from the spirit of death

Session 10

NOTES

A foreboding sense of death is one of the most troubling and persistent experiences common to humankind. Thankfully, through the liberating truth of the gospel, prayerful vigilance and consistent relational support, one can become free of death's pervasive influence. With confidence we look to Jesus Christ who has triumphed over death. Jesus frees us from death's intimidation and claim to power. *"Christ was raised from the dead...death no longer has mastery over him"* (Romans 6:9).

The importance of this week's lesson cannot be overstated! What we will call "the spirit of death" is very real in this world. It is opposed to the fullness of life that Jesus Christ and his cross represent. We understand the "spirit of death" to be a spiritual influence, a shadow over our days that colors our vision and shapes a fatalistic mindset. We are not speaking of the universal experience of physical death but of a lying voice (from the false self or the enemy) that tries to refute Christ's promises of ever-increasing life. This voice introduces thoughts of death and destruction and seeks to thwart our ability to receive healing, as well as casting doubt on God's desire to heal us.

Non-Christians and Christians alike are under the influence of the spirit of death. Its debilitating effect over lives will continue to spread unless its presence is exposed and deposed.

Session 10 — Breaking free from the spirit of death

NOTES

"The valley of the shadow"

The imagery used by King David in the Twenty-third Psalm poignantly describes what many of us experience. For a good reason it is one of the most frequently used Scriptures at funeral and memorial services. We all can relate to that bewildering "valley of the shadow of death."

> The Lord is my shepherd, I shall not be in want.
> He makes me to lie down in green pastures,
> he leads me beside quiet waters, he restores my soul.
> He guides me in the paths of righteousness for his name's sake.
> Even though I walk through the valley of the shadow of death,
> I will fear no evil, for you are with me;
> your rod and your staff they comfort me.
> You prepare a table before me in the presence of my enemies.
> You anoint my head with oil; my cup overflows.
> Surely goodness and love will follow me all the days of my life,
> and I will dwell in the house of the Lord forever.   (Psalm 23)

"Though I walk through the valley of the shadow of death" is an evocative word-picture. It describes that place on the road of a sojourner's life where many of us feel stranded—four flat tires, no cell phone, no Auto Club card, no help in sight. Some of us feel like we've been raised in the "valley of the shadow" since birth, a legacy we've inherited from our parents. It's dreary, but it's real estate! Years of living in that threatening emotional and spiritual state have driven some to the erroneous conclusion that it is the Lord's will that they remain there, a penance without end.

The Lord never intended for us to be stuck in such a lifeless place. King David writes of the Good Shepherd's means for guiding us through that valley to green pastures and still waters. Comfort for the journey comes from the Shepherd's rod and staff. These can be viewed as symbols representing the cross: the vertical piece of the cross being the rod—signifying Christ's authority, protection, guidance and rescue; the horizontal piece of the cross represented by the staff—signifying the load-bearing support the Lord gives us on our journey through life.

Reassuring as those verses are, they can quickly get swallowed up by the more familiar, fearful symbols of dread. Unfortunately, it is the image of the threatening "shadow" and not the trustworthy Shepherd that quickly resonates in many souls. If that is so for you, what follows will be familiar ground you've already tread.

130   **Embracing Life Series**

Breaking free from the spirit of death — Session 10

Manifestations of death

Those experiences and influences that facilitate the manifestations of the spirit of death in a person's life are many and varied. Examples include: birth traumas (being the child of an unwanted pregnancy or a failed abortion); suicide attempts; crippling or isolating, childhood diseases; living in a violent, emotionally-abusive home; sexual molestation; caring for an ill relative for an extended period of time; sudden death of a cherished loved one.

The way death works

The subtle shadow of darkness can affect us in profound and personal ways by keying into our diseased thought patterns and habits. The enemy is familiar with human fallenness (he was there at its inception) and he uses that loaded information to continually lie to and slander us. We are only too ready to agree with him. Unless our fallacious ways of thinking and acting are confronted (named, repented of and consistently renounced), our relationship with the Lord will continue to suffer. Our unhealed, twisted and erroneous thoughts about God, our identification with depression, anxiety, loneliness, hopelessness, passivity, suicidal thoughts and death fantasies, all can take up a consuming amount of our time and imagination. They are collectively a "house made of thoughts," as author Francis Frangipane describes, taking up space intended for thoughts of the Lord. And they will continue to occupy our minds until *we participate in dismantling them.*

> **We demolish arguments and every pretension that sets itself up against the knowledge of God, and we take captive every thought and make it obedient to God.** (2 Corinthians 10:5)

The origins of our perceptions and imaginings go back to our childhood—memories which we have repressed or forgotten, including how, when and from whom we learned them. Proverbs 18:21 says: *"The tongue has the power of life and death."* Our sponge-like souls, absorbing what we heard from those in authority, received many damaging messages about our personhood, words like: *stupid, klutz, ugly, good for nothing, ungrateful, selfish, whore*—the list goes on and on. Those poisoned words accumulated in our minds, occupying more and more space—a fortress of sorts. The price paid for its maintenance has severely taxed our well being.

Is it a wonder that words that the Lord intended to convey life—*birth, family, marriage, home, intimacy*—take on a negative connotation when they pass through our experiential grid? They are quickly awash with bitterness and disappointment. Those significant word-symbols, spoiled by the overload of deadly experiences stored inside of us, can (in some cases) even become

NOTES

Session 10 — Breaking free from the spirit of death

NOTES

repellent to us. We grow up to view God's creation through the matrix of unbelief, cataracts that prevent us from perceiving and experiencing life more fully. *Frangipane* writes in *The Three Battlegrounds*:

> Their thoughtless words went so deep that, in recoiling from the pain, you have involuntarily remained in the recoiled or withdrawn position. Since then, you have refused to place yourself in situations where you can become vulnerable to criticism. You may not even remember the incidents, but you may not have stopped recoiling, even until today. *(Frangipane, p. 28)*

Over-identification with dark thoughts and faulty religious assumptions about God effectively help to reinforce a jaundiced worldview. The result: impoverished personal relationships and enfeebled ministries. By harboring those destructive thoughts we aid and abet the enemy in his strategy to keep Christians from effectively mediating Christ's "Good News."

Christians under the influence

Is the inference here that *Christians* may be ministering while under the influence of death? In a word—YES! It is a sad irony that those who serve in the helping professions (most notably in hospitals, convalescent centers, hospices and compassion ministries) are the very ones who least suspect they are under death's influence...because they're under it! One can, find oneself in helping ministries before realizing what the underlying impetus was for pursuing it in the first place.

Proverbs 16:2 says: *"All a man's motives seem innocent to him, but motives are weighed by the Lord."* We must be willing to pray through our motives for serving to see what the Lord unearths. Perhaps the Lord would like to do a little housecleaning with us before we continue doing the "same old, same old."

Note from the author

My personal history holds many examples and obvious signs of having accommodated the spirit of death in its various forms. It wasn't until several years after becoming director of Embracing Life, however, that I began to examine my motives for involvement in a ministry with so much illness and death.

Self-questioning arose when a friend—after observing my reaction to the deaths of three of our patients—remarked how altogether used to death I appeared to be. My prideful self took immediate offense at his comment

Breaking free from the spirit of death

Session 10

NOTES

(though in truth, he wasn't being critical). I had thought my tolerance of death was a gift, not something negative or unhealthy. This started me thinking about the state I was in: Had I become emotionally numb to the death around me? Was I overly-familiar with death? What might my underlying motives *really* be for doing this work?

In the ensuing months, the Lord revealed to me that while growing up I had actually made a false peace with death. My parents were not born again believers. The subjects of death and evil were never discussed in our family; in fact, such subjects were carefully avoided. In response to the tragedies and misfortunes that befell our family, my parents typical reply was: "That's just the way things happen in life." The thought never entered my mind that there might actually be spiritual strategies opposed to life.

"Death is naked before God; Destruction lies uncovered" (Job 26:6). Indeed, with ongoing, vigilant prayer my compliance with death was exposed and laid bare. Looking back over my family history, it was clear there was a generational pattern of passive accommodation of sorrow and death. It was a spiritual tie that I had to *personally* sever in prayer.

The indispensable, insightful prayers of Christian brothers and sisters helped reveal the extent to which the spirit of death and its influences had infected my life and shaped my fatalistic my worldview. My prayer partners were crucial in helping me get free from the dominance and familiarity of those dark thoughts and spirits.

To this day, we stand together in prayer in *staying* free from death's influence over our lives as we continually oppose it through the victorious cross of Jesus Christ.

The need for corporate prayer

Isolation from the truth of God's Word and the body of Christ is the enemy's foremost tactic for wearing us down and killing us off. That is why we pray *together* (before God and with our brothers and sisters) in renouncing the spirit of death. We make our oath before "a cloud of witnesses;" we recall that to the enemy later on when he tries to deceive us with lies: "You didn't really mean that prayer you prayed back then." And accuse us again he will! Death's presence does not depart once, forever. That time is reserved for the day when death and Hades are thrown into the lake of fire (Revelation 20:14). For us to live free from the influence of darkness takes repeated consistent routing until the spirit of death no longer finds us an attractive place to hang around. This will take courage and vigilance on our part as we engage the will again and again. Proverbs 15:24 says: *"The path*

Session 10 — Breaking free from the spirit of death

NOTES

of life leads upward for the wise to keep him from going down to the grave." God will supply the strength to accomplish the work he has begun in us (Philippians 1:6).

Paul writes in Romans 7:24, *"Who will deliver me from this body of death? Thanks be to God–through Jesus Christ our Lord!"* There is freedom from the persistent presence of the spirit of death, testifying to the Lord's faithfulness to his word. We can confidently proclaim, along with Paul, *"Where, O death, is your sting? Where, O death, is your victory?"* (1 Corinthians 15:55)

C. S. Lewis writes:

> He is the first fruits, the 'pioneer of life'. He has forced open a door that has been locked since the death of the first man. He has met, fought, and beaten the King of Death. Everything is different because he has done so. (*Miracles*, p. 145)

Our Father in heaven desires that His children enjoy the fullness of His life, unencumbered by darkness, unhindered by death's schemes. He beckons us today and every day to approach him in faith in order to access the life richly distributed by His Son Jesus Christ through the Holy Spirit. Together we will do that in renouncing the spirit of death.

As we pray the following prayer out loud, eagerly anticipate the forthcoming promise of Jesus Christ: *"I came that they might have life and have it to the full..."* (John 10:10).

Prayer Action Points:

1. Confessing pride, which is giving access to the spirit of death.
2. Proclaiming the Lord and His healing word for us as the final Word.
3. Renouncing treaties, friendships, substitutionary vows and appeasements with death and its influences.

    Note on *substitutionary vows:* a vow where one asks that a loved one be freed from their illness and that the illness be transferred to them (the person praying).

4. Inviting the Lord to go to the depths of our being to release us from hiddenness and shame, induced by the enemy.

Breaking free from the spirit of death — Session 10

Prayer for the Renunciation of the Spirit of Death

> **Set your books aside and simply focus on hearing and repeating the prayer.**
>
> **As the leader prays the following phrases one at a time, repeat them out loud after him or her.**

"I am not born of natural descent or a human decision or a husband's will but born of God." (John 1:13)

"I am born of the imperishable seed." (I Peter 1:23)

"I can do all things through Christ who strengthens me." (Philippians 4:13)

- Heavenly Father, Lord Jesus Christ and Holy Spirit, I come before you with my fellow brothers and sisters as witnesses, to declare my freedom from the spirit of death and its influences.

- By the power and authority granted me by my Lord Jesus Christ and in whose name I pray, I renounce the spirit of death and all unclean spirits associated with it. I declare any and all attachments, agreements, appeasements and treaties with those spirits nullified and cancelled. Henceforth I will make no false peace with my enemy.

- I renounce all identification, activity and preoccupation with suicidal thoughts, death fantasies, illness, despair, hopelessness, depression, isolationism, perfectionism, passivity, bitterness, rage, anxiety, fear, abandonment, rejection, violence, racism, witchcraft, heresies and medical pronouncements of impending death. Separate them from me, now, Lord, as far as east is from the west.

- I sever with the sword of the Spirit of Truth, any attachments to generational spirits going back ten generations, placing the cross of Jesus Christ between me and each one of them.

- I repent of any substitutionary agreements, reasserting that it is by Jesus Christ's sacrifice and sufferings that I am saved and healed.

- I will make a conscious effort to forgive all those who knowingly or unknowingly wounded me and thereby enabled death to gain influence over me. I ask You Lord to give me ongoing revelation as to whom I need to forgive.

NOTES

Session 10 — Breaking free from the spirit of death

NOTES

- Forgive me Lord for holding unforgiveness, anger, hatred, pride, bitterness, revenge and any other sinful reaction against them. I will continue to release those people and the feelings as You make them known to me.

- I receive from You, Lord, the cleansing of Your forgiveness in return.

- Please continue to reveal any other hidden destructive influences in and over my life, that I may send them to Your cross to be nailed there.

- I will continue by Your strength, love and power *and* in Your authority to confess, to repent, to renounce and to resist the spirit of death and its influences. As I align my will with yours, I am proclaiming Your will for me is to know abundant life.

- Now I choose to embrace the fullness of life You have for me, Lord.

- I praise You and thank You for always upholding me and always covering me in Your everlasting love.

  AMEN.

[In the moments that follow, allow the Lord, to bring to the surface any lingering, dark influences that need to be released to His cross. Ask Him to replace them with the fullness of His presence and truth.]

I have put my words in your mouth and covered you with the shadow of my hand—I who set the heavens in place, who laid the foundations of the earth, and who say to Zion, "you are my people." (Isaiah 51:16)

Fight the good fight of the faith. Take hold of the eternal life to which you were called when you made your good confession in the presence of many witnesses.   (1 Timothy 6:12)

Embracing Life Series: International Copyright © 1998 by Embracing Life Ministries. All Rights Reserved

Breaking free from the spirit of death — Session 10

SCRIPTURE READINGS
Isaiah 25:7-9; Isaiah 28:14-18; Deuteronomy 30:19-20; John 14:6

RECOMMENDED READINGS
The Three Battlegrounds by Francis Frangipane
The Screwtape Letters by C.S. Lewis
Breaking Free...from the spirit of death by Jonathan Hunter

THOUGHTS FOR JOURNALING
Since renouncing the spirit of death,
what has the Lord shown you about its influence on your life?

NOTES

Cultivating intimacy with Jesus

Session 11

"......let us draw near to God with a sincere heart, in full assurance of faith" (Hebrews 10:22)

I heard a pastor on the radio ask his audience, "When was the last time you heard a Muslim say he had a personal relationship with Mohammed, or a buddhist say he had a personal relationship with Buddha?" Of course, the answer is "never." *The uniqueness of being a Christian is the personal relationship we have with God.*

In this short chapter on intimacy with God, there will be no new insights into God's character, just time to briefly reflect on our relationship with Him. For instance, do we experience God as *immanent* (with us) as well as transcendent? Do we relate to God as if we have a genuine, personal relationship with Him? Our answers may prove significant if we hope to successfully walk out the healing we receive and form healthy, loving relationships with others in the future.

NOTES

Session 11 — Cultivating intimacy with Jesus

NOTES

Jesus our bridge

> But when the kindness and the love of God our Savior appeared, not because of righteousness which we have done, but because of His mercy. He saved us through the washing of rebirth and renewal by the Holy Spirit, whom He poured out on us generously through Jesus Christ our Savior" (Titus 3:4-6)

Jesus Christ came to restore relationship between God and humankind so that we might intimately commune with Him. All other religions have chasms between people and God, separations that *humans* have the responsibility to bridge. Our saving grace is the initiative *God* extended to us through the bridge of His Son Jesus Christ, resulting in a personal friendship with God. Incomparable!

This "friendship" concept introduced by Jesus is a crucial element in our restoration. The existential loneliness inherent in humanity's sin and brokenness cries out for a Savior to rescue us. Jesus is a trustworthy friend who knows our soul, a wise, loving companion to accompany us through life. That person is also God and His Spirit lives in us. Relationships don't get any closer than that!

In a world of ever-diminishing returns, His commitment to us is more profound than we could possibly imagine. Jesus is the truest companion anyone could ask for: *"...Surely I am with you always, to the very end of the age"* (Matt. 28:20).

In the next session we will study the disciplines of the Spirit that support relational growth with God. Here, we remain focused on the idea of friendships and our faithfulness in them.

■ What do you feel intimate friendship entails? What is the most important criteria? List your criteria in order of importance below.

-
-
-
-
-
-

140   **Embracing Life Series**

Cultivating intimacy with Jesus   Session 11

Cultivating intimacy with Jesus   Session 11

Whose heart is breaking?

> [Friendship]...implies a commitment to the relationship. Commitment is what characterizes friendship. We can walk away from casual acquaintances, but we cannot walk away from friendship once it has been established without breaking somebody's heart, including our own.
> (*Intimacy with God*, Fr. Thomas Keating, p. 33)

Our hearts, as Keating points out, get damaged when we forsake True Love for someone or something else. By refusing the "fullness of joy," we settle for lesser gods, mediocre enjoyment and bad counsel. What a tragic mistake we make: *"A man who strays from understanding comes to rest in the company of the dead"* (Proverbs 21:16). We all have stories galore that speak of the price we've paid.

Some time ago, the Lord exhorted me about the "secret" sexual fantasies I had been entertaining in my mind. His words came like a two-edged sword piercing right through my delusions of mental privacy: "Son, why do you seek pleasure in the things that are dead?" I had come to a reckoning in my relationship with Him. Either I could continue offending His Presence with my illicit fantasies or repent and allow Him to re-seed my mind with His creative life. Thankfully I chose the latter. The sexual fantasies disappeared straight away. His work of mental sanctification purified my imagination, a powerful, holy response to a small act of obedience on my part.

It begins with desire

Like you, I am a novice at all this. I write more from a desire for intimate relationship than from a long history of it. My desire however, is rooted in faith—faith in His Word, and taking Him up on it. That is the basis for all the healing we've sought in this series. In previous lessons, the Lord ministered to us in the areas of shame, self-hatred, unforgiveness and the effects of the spirit of death. In order to sustain that healing we need to also rely on the promises of care, counsel and yes, friendship with the One who fully understands our human condition. As we discussed in an earlier session, having spiritual ears to hear Him when He speaks is crucial for our friendship to be one of mutual dialogue. If we turn a deaf ear to Him we are easy prey for a fall.

Session 11 — Cultivating intimacy with Jesus

NOTES

A longing fulfilled

We can't ever afford to forget the extent God went to in order to allow us to have true, intimate communion with Him. Proverbs 13:12 says: *"Hope deferred makes the heart sick, but a longing fulfilled is a tree of life."* The tree of life is the cross, the symbol that reminds our heart of Jesus' ultimate sacrifice on our behalf. Our friendship with God exists because of His atonement. His divine invitation offers us access to God in a way previously unknown except by Adam and Eve before the Fall.

> Greater love has no one than this, that he lay down his life for his friends. You are my friends if you do what I command, I no longer call you servants, because a servant does not know his master's business. Instead *I call you friends,* for everything I learned from my Father I have made known to you. (John 15:12-15) [italics JH]

Our current relational state with the Lord, may seem weak if compared to other friendships we claim to have. It is easy to get stuck in a place of immaturity, wanting all the benefits associated with His name without pursuing an intimate relationship with Him. We choose to remain milk-fed babes while missing out on more substantial fare at the dinner table with Jesus. In short, it can become a very one-sided friendship if we aren't more intentional about it and follow through. (See "Baca" article.) Who's heart are we breaking this time?

Obstacles to intimacy

Granted, intimacy with Jesus Christ may seem more religious fantasy than relational reality because we are fearful of intimacy in our human relationships. Memories of painful relationships throughout our lives have instilled fear and mistrust in our hearts. Jesus is the answer once again if we will invite Him in. We have to learn to trust Him as faithful in all matters of the heart for He is love.

Mercifully, the redemptive power of the cross can heal our wounded souls and reactions. "In me you may have peace. In this world you will have trouble. But take heart! I have overcome the world (John 16:33).

Jesus' love is undaunted by our painful memories. By reaching deep into the soul He created, His skillful Creator's hands are able to fashion peace in our innermost being so that we might accept His friendship and entrust Him with all our time and affections. *"He who loves me will be loved by my Father, and I too will love him and show myself to him"* (John 14:21).

Cultivating intimacy with Jesus — Session 11

May we, by God's grace, become like the apostle Paul who wrote:

> I am convinced that neither death nor life, neither angels nor demons, neither the present nor the future, nor any powers, neither height nor depth, nor anything else in all creation can separate us from the love of God that is in Christ Jesus our Lord. (Romans 8:38-39)

Obedience in love

Intimate friendship with Christ calls for obedience. It requires taking up the cross (the burdens he allows us to share with Him).

His friendship doesn't demand, but instead asks for a demonstration of our affection, our love for Him. You can express this anywhere you find yourself. Pastor, author and friend to Jesus, Mike Bickle writes:

> There are no rules that say we all have to open our bank accounts, close the doors of our businesses and take the next plane to Africa. Never make the mistake of thinking Jesus demands extravagance. He requires only the simple giving of our hearts in love and obedience, the taking up of our crosses and following Him. (*Passion for Jesus*, p. 193)

He wants an exclusive relationship with your whole being ...right where you are. You can include Him right now: *"Seek the Lord while He may be found; call on Him while He is near"* (Isaiah 55:6).

Yielding our schedules

Do you feel like an under-achiever in your pursuit of intimacy with God? This is normal. It keeps us in pursuit of more. Praise God that there is always more, infinitely more to be had in our friendship with God: *"Blessed are those who are poor in spirit for theirs is the kingdom of God"* (Matt. 5:3). His love is poised for response if we will yield to him.

> How do you waste your life on Jesus? Easy. It's no secret. Make the decision in your mind, and your heart will catch up. Get in His presence. Reject sin. Cry out to Him in prayer. Lift your soul to Him in worship. Read and meditate on the Word until your heart is filled with the things that fill God's heart. Utterly abandon yourself to Him, for intimacy with God takes time, and there is no substitute for waiting in His presence. Like Mary, choose to forego, some of the less important things going on around you in order to make more time to cultivate a relationship with Him. Lavishly, extravagantly pour out your life as a drink offering upon the holy altar of God.

Session 11 — Cultivating intimacy with Jesus

NOTES

Allow yourself to be broken and spilled out for the priceless One whose body was broken and whose precious life's blood was spilled out for you. Lord Jesus, in sweet abandon, let me be spilled out and used up for You! (*Passion for Jesus*, Mike Bickle, p. 197)

Is Mike's cry to the Lord your cry too? Good! Rearrange your schedule and your heart's priorities for communing with Him. As Mike says God doesn't demand extravagance, but if we choose it there are rich rewards. Deepening intimacy with Jesus will naturally produce a genuine love for our fellow human beings, the overflow of Christ's love in our hearts pouring out to others: *"...my cup overflows. Surely goodness and mercy will follow me all the days of my life, and I will dwell in the house of the Lord forever"* (Psalm 23:6).

"Practicing His presence"

"Practicing His presence," a phrase introduced by the sixteenth century monk, Brother Lawrence, aptly describes the act of becoming familiar with Emmanuel (literally "God with us"). It takes practice, an ongoing exercise of the will, determination and a desire to have friendship with Him. In short, we must believe he will respond to us, even in the minutest details of our life.

A more contemporary brother in Christ, Frank Laubach, also discovered the joys of friendship with God through practice. In your readings for this week, you are given an excerpt from his journal written in the 1930s while a missionary on the island of Mindanao. You will find Laubach's observations both winsome and stirring! His guidelines are also very practical. Important is his exhortation not to despise small beginnings nor to compare our relationship with Jesus with another. Both tendencies are self-defeating.

Celebrate, instead, all that has already taken place in you through Christ. Continue to move forward. Press on for that prized friendship. Praise God for all Christ is able to do in you and through you. Daily choose to be free from sin. All your efforts toward that end are pleasing to Him and He will lovingly supply.

Cultivating intimacy with Jesus   Session 11

Things to expect

Some things to expect in our pursuit of intimacy:

1. The gentle but constant pressure of our resistant wills.
2. The need to persevere in spite of poor results at the onset.
3. A call to complete surrender; when we willfully rebel, we lose a sense of His presence.
4. The need for ongoing fellowship with like-minded people seeking Jesus, as we are. (Laubach, Ch. 8).

Laubach writes:

> You may not win all your minutes to Christ, or even half, but you do win a richer life. There are no losers excepting those that quit...Our unseen Friend becomes dearer, closer and more wonderful everyday until at last we know him as "Jesus, lover of my soul," not only in song but in blissful experience. Doubts vanish; we are more sure of Him being with us than of anybody else. This warm ardent friendship ripens rapidly, and it keeps on growing richer and more radiant every month. (Laubach, p. 35-36)

An old familiar hymn for our prayer in closing:

> What a friend we have in Jesus, all our sins and griefs to bear!
> What a privilege to carry, everything to God in prayer!
> O what peace we often forfeit, o what needless pain we bear,
> All because we do not carry, everything to God in prayer.
> Have we trials and temptations? Is there trouble anywhere?
> We should never be discouraged, take it to the Lord in prayer!
> Can we find a friend so faithful, who will all our sorrows share?
> Jesus knows our every weakness—Take it to the Lord in prayer!
> Are we weak and heavy laden, cumbered with a load of care?
> Precious Savior, still our refuge—Take it to the Lord in prayer!
> Do thy friends despise forsake thee? Take it to the Lord in prayer!
> In His arms He'll take and shield thee—Thou wilt find a solace there.
> ("What a Friend We Have in Jesus" by Joseph Scriven & Charles Converse)

"Let us fix our eyes on Jesus, the author and finisher of our faith."
(Hebrews 12:2)

Session 11 — Cultivating intimacy with Jesus

NOTES

SCRIPTURE READINGS
John 14-17; Ephesians 1; Song of Solomon

RECOMMENDED READINGS
Practicing the Presence by Brother Lawrence and Frank Laubach
Passion for Jesus by Mike Bickle
The Healing Presence by Leanne Payne
Listening to God by Joyce Huggett

THOUGHTS FOR JOURNALING
After reading the excerpt from Frank Laubach's "Practicing the Presence," write a letter to the Lord expressing your desires for a closer relationship with Him.

Readings

From:

"Practicing the Presence of God"

Brother Lawrence & Frank Laubach

Practical Help

We shall not become like Christ until we give Him more time.

A teacher's college requires students to attend classes for twenty-five hours a week for three years. Could it prepare competent teachers or a law school prepare competent lawyers if they studied only ten minutes a week? Neither can Christ, and He never pretended He could. To His disciples He said: "Come with me, walk with me, eat and sleep with me, twenty-four hours a day for three years." That was their college course. "He chose them," the Bible says, "that they might be with Him," 168 hours a week!

All who have tried that kind of abiding for a month know the power of it—it is like being born again from center to circumference. It absolutely changes every person who does it. How can a man or woman do this? Indeed, unless we "turn and become like children" we cannot succeed.

Try to call Christ to mind at least one second of every minute. You do not need to forget other things nor stop your work, but invite Him to share everything you do, say or think. There are those who have experimented until they have found ways to let Him share every minute until they are awake. In fact, it is no harder to learn this new habit than to learn the touch system in typing, and in time a larger part of the day's minutes are given over to the Lord with as little effort as an expert needs to type a letter. This practicing the presence of Christ takes all our time, yet it does not take from our work. It takes Christ into our enterprises and makes them more successful.

Practicing the presence of God is not on trial. It has already been proven by countless saints. Indeed, the spiritual giants of all ages have known it. The results of this effort begin to show clearly in a month. They grow rich after six months, and glorious after ten years. This is the secret of the saints of all ages. "Pray without ceasing," said Paul, "in everything make your wants known unto God." "As many as are led by the spirit of God, these are the sons of God."

Nobody is wholly satisfied with himself. Our lives are made up of lights and shadows, of some good days and many unsatisfactory days. We have learned that the good days and hours come when we are very close to Christ. Clearly, then, the way to more such days and hours is to take Him into everything we do or say or think.

Experience has told us that good resolutions are not enough. We need to discipline our lives to an ordered regime. So many of us have found the idea of turning to Christ once every minute to be enormously helpful. It is a practice as old as Enoch, who "walked with God." It is a way of living which nearly everybody knows and nearly everybody has ignored. Some will at once recognize it as a fresh approach to Brother Lawrence's "Practicing the Presence God." It is a delightful experience and an exhilarating spiritual exercise; but we soon discover that it is far more than even that. Some people have compared it to getting out of a dark prison and beginning to live. We still see the same world, yet it is not the same, for it has a new glorious color and a far deeper meaning.

You will find this just as easy and just as hard as forming any other habit. You have hitherto thought of the Lord for only a few seconds or minutes a week, and He was out of your mind the rest of the time. Now you are attempting, like Brother Lawrence, to have the Lord in mind each minute you are awake. Such drastic change in habit requires a real effort at the beginning.

How to Begin

Select a favorable hour, an easy, uncomplicated hour. See how many minutes of the hour you can

Readings

remember, or touch, Christ at least once each minute; that is to say, bring him to mind at least one second out of every sixty. You will not do so well at first but keep trying, for it constantly becomes easier, and after a while is almost automatic. When you begin to try this you discover that spiritually you are still a very weak infant. A babe in the crib seizes upon everything at hand to pull himself to his feet, wobbles for a few seconds and falls exhausted. Then he tries again, each time standing a little longer than before.

Suppose you have enjoyed a good time in the presence of the Lord, and then you find yourself with a group of friends engaged in ordinary conversation. Can you recall the Lord at least once every minute? This is hard, but there are some helps. Keep humming to yourself (inaudibly) a favorite hymn—for example, "Have Thine Own Way, Lord, Have Thine Own Way." Keep whispering inside, "Lord you are my life," or "You are my thought."

Here are a few aids that have proven helpful:

When at the table remember Jesus words, "Eat this in remembrance of me." This can be applied to ordinary meals so that every mouthful is His "body broken for you."

When reading, keep a running conversation with Him about the pages you are reading.

If you lean back to consider some problem, how can you remember the Lord? By forming a new habit! All thought employs silent words and is really conversation with your inner self. Instead of talking to yourself, form the habit of talking to Jesus Christ. Some of us who have done this find it so much better that we never want it any other way again. no practice that we have found has ever held the mind as much as this: making all thoughts conversation with the Lord. When evil thoughts of any kind come, say, "Lord, these thoughts are not fit to discuss with you, Lord, you do the thinking. Renew my mind by your presence."

When you are strolling out of doors alone, you can recall the Lord at least once every minute with no effort. If you wander to a place where you can talk aloud without being overheard, you may speak to the invisible Companion inside of you. Ask Him what is most on His heart and then answer back aloud with your voice what you believe God replies to you. Of course, we are not always sure whether we have guessed His answer correctly, but it is surprising how much of the time we are very certain. It really is not necessary to be sure that our answer is right, for the answer is not the great thing—He is! God is infinitely more important than His advice or His gifts; indeed, He Himself is the great gift. The most precious privilege in talking with Christ is this intimacy which we can have with Him. We may have a glorious succession of heavenly minutes. How foolish we are to lose life's most poignant joy, seeing it may be had while taking a walk alone! But the most wonderful discovery of all is, to use the words of Paul, "Christ liveth in me." He dwells in us, walks in our minds, reaches out through our hands, speaks with our voices, if we respond to His every whisper.

Make sure your last thoughts are of Christ as you are falling asleep at night. Continue to whisper any words of endearment your heart suggests. If all day long you have been walking with Him, you will find Him the dear companion of your dreams. Sometimes, after such a day, we have fallen asleep with our pillows wet from tears of joy, feeling His tender touch on our foreheads. Usually, you will feel no deep emotion, but will always have a "peace that passeth all understanding." This is the end of a perfect day.

On waking in the morning, you may ask, "Now, Lord shall we get up?" Some of us whisper to Him our every thought about washing and dressing in the morning.

Men have found they can keep the Lord in mind while engaged in all types of work, mental or manual, and find that they are happier and get better results. Those who endure the most intolerable ordeals gain new strength when they realize that their Unseen Comrade is by their side. (To be sure no man whose business is harmful or whose methods are dishonest, can expect God's partnership.) The carpenter can do better work if he talks quietly to God about each task, as surely Jesus did when He was a carpenter.

There are women who cultivate Christ's companionship while cooking, washing the dishes, sweeping, sewing, and caring for children. Aids which they find helpful are: whisper to the Lord about each small matter, knowing He loves to help. Hum or sing a favorite hymn.

Students can enjoy the presence of the Lord even when taking an examination. Say, "Father, keep my mind clear, and help me remember all I have learned. How shall we answer this next question?" He will not

Readings

tell you what you have never studied, but He does sharpen your memory and take away your stage fright when you ask Him.

Troubles and pain come to those who practice God's presence, as they come to Jesus, but these seem not so important as compared with their new joyous experience. If we have spent our days with Him, we find that when earthquakes, fires, famines or other catastrophes threaten us, we are not terrified any more than Paul was in time of shipwreck. "Perfect love casteth out fear."

Some Prices We Must Pay

The first price is the pressure of our wills, gentle but constant. But, what prize is ever won without effort?

The second price is perseverance. Poor results at the outset are not the slightest reason for discouragement; everyone has this experience for a long while. Each week grows better and requires less strain.

The third price is perfect surrender. We lose Christ's presence the moment our will rebels. If we try to keep even a remote corner of life for self or evil, and refuse to let the Lord rule us wholly, that small worm will spoil the entire fruit. We must be utterly sincere.

The fourth price is to be often in a group. We need the stimulus of believers who pursue what we pursue, the presence of Christ.

What We Gain

You may not win all your minutes to Christ, or even half, but you do win a richer life. There are no losers excepting those who quit.

We develop what Thomas a Kempis calls a "familiar friendship with Jesus." Our unseen Friend becomes dearer, closer and more wonderful every day until we at last know Him as "Jesus, lover of my soul," not only in song but *in blissful experience*. Doubts vanish; we are more sure of Him being with us than of anybody else. This warm, ardent friendship ripens rapidly, and it keeps on growing richer and more radiant every month.

We gain purity of thought, because when we are maintaining the presence of Christ, our minds are pure as mountain streams every moment.

All day long we are contented, whatever our lot may be, for He is with us. "When Jesus goes with me, I'll go anywhere."

It becomes easier to tell others about Christ because our minds are flooded with Him. "Out of the fullness of the heart the mouth speaks."

It is For Anybody

The notion that religion is dull, stupid and sleepy is abhorrent to God, for He has created an infinite variety and He loves to surprise us. If you are weary of some sleepy form of devotion, probably God is as weary of it as you are. Shake out of it, and approach Him in one of the countless fresh directions.

Humble folk often believe that walking with God is above their heads, or that they may "lose a good time" if they share all their joys with Christ. What tragic misunderstanding to regard Him as a killer of happiness! A chorus of joyous voices round the world fairly sing that spending their hours with the Lord is the most thrilling joy ever known, and that beside it a ball game or horse race is stupid. Spending time with the Lord is not a grim duty. And if you should forget Him for minutes or even days, do not groan or repent, but begin anew with a smile. Every moment can be a fresh beginning.

Copyright 1978 pp 29-40.
Used by permission of The SeedSowers
Christian Books Publishing House.

Readings

From:

"Passion for Jesus"

by Mike Bickle

Ch. 11: The Blessings of Intimacy

Some friends of mine remained childless after twenty-three years of marriage, much prayer, two major surgeries to correct infertility, endless rounds of testing and treatment and the expenditure of thousands of dollars. Refusing to be spiritually barren as well, the couple had decided long ago to invest their lives in the kingdom of God by ministering to others. The wife earned a doctorate so she could serve God more effectively in her calling. The husband, a successful businessman, became salt and light through the political offices he held in the metroplex where they lived.

Then God surprised them. A courageous young woman canceled the abortion she had scheduled for the next day, carried her baby full-term and gave it up for adoption at birth, with the stipulation that the infant be placed in the home of a Christian couple who would rear the child for God. You guessed it. Through a series of divine coincidences and interventions, my friends, who hadn't even had their names on an adoption list because they were considered over the age limit to adopt, were blessed with a beautiful little boy just a few days old.

The elated couple understood that completing all the legal paperwork which established the baby's status as a member of their family was only the beginning. The greatest task lay ahead—establishing a deep, secure relationship of love between their adopted baby and themselves. They knew they would love their little son devotedly whether or not he ever returned their love, but they set out to win the child's love by demonstrating their love and affection for him. Bathed in an atmosphere of love, stability and lots of hugs and kisses, their son was a picture of contentment and security.

Time passed, and one afternoon as the couple drove up in front of their lovely home, their little boy exclaimed, "*My* house!" It was indeed. Everything that hard-working father and mother owned had been willed to him from the moment he'd become a member of their family. All they had was his.

Then the day came when the couple's little son began to return their affection. His father kissed him on the cheek and whispered, "I love you," just as he'd done a thousand times before. The little boy looked up, smiled and said, "I you!" As the "I you" eventually expanded to "I love you," juicy kisses and countless hugs, that father felt something of what God must feel when His children begin passing beyond the stage of self-centered receiving and start returning love to Him.

Can we ever hope to comprehend the depth of love God has demonstrated for us by making us sons and daughters in His own house? As J. I. Packer writes in his book *Knowing God*, "The New Testament gives us two yardsticks for measuring God's love. The first is the cross (1 John 4:8-10); the second is the gift of sonship (1 John 3:1). Of all the gifts of grace, adoption is the highest."

God the Father adopted you and me as His children, gave Himself to us as our loving Father and made us fellow heirs with Jesus because He chose to, not because He had to.

The Motive for Spiritual Growth

What best motivates a child to want to be like his parents? Is it intimacy, love and respect, or isolation, fear and guilt? The same principle is true in the spiritual realm. Using wrong motivations to encourage believers to pursue intimacy with Christ—fear, force, guilt trips or manipulation—may seem to obtain quick results, but those results won't last. Even spiritual disciplines such as prayer, fasting, Bible study and witnessing often result in legalism, pride, insecurity or morbid introspection if pursued with the wrong motivation.

Christians will sometimes move into action faster if they are told God is angry and losing interest in them; or that they're going to fail miserably, losing everything that's dear to them on earth if they don't get busy performing and producing. However, in the long run, some very sincere believers will wind up damaged, discouraged and burned out because

Readings

they've built their spiritual lives on faulty foundations.

The heart knowledge of God's deep affection and full acceptance for you and me as His own beloved children is the best motivation for consistent spiritual growth. As Paul explained to the Roman believers, "you have not received a spirit of slavery leading to fear again, but you have received a spirit of adoption as sons by which we cry out, 'Abba! Father!'" (Rom. 8:15). Our spirits cry and long for more of Him when we see His loving adoption of us as His children, rather than condemnation.

Being rooted and grounded in the strong, secure love of God motivates us to greater consistency, spiritual passion and maturity. As we begin to understand the Father's affection and the price Jesus paid to redeem us, our hearts melt with devotion and gratitude. We long for a fuller, more intimate knowledge of God and for heart-to-heart fellowship with Him. We desire to become wise children who bring joy to our Father. Instead of becoming prodigal sons or the "black sheep" of His family, we want to "hang out" with Jesus, our elder brother, and grow up to be just like Him.

As you and I pursue intimacy with Jesus, it will become apparent that we are God's royal children. *We will manifest our family's likeness* by conforming to Christ. *We will seek to further our family's welfare* by loving our brethren. *We will maintain our family's honor* by avoiding what our Father hates, pursuing what He loves and seeking His glory. As we cultivate intimacy with Jesus, out of the riches of His glory we will be "strengthened with power through His Spirit in the inner man" (Eph. 3:16).

Seven Blessings of Holy Passion

The first step toward experiencing intimacy with Jesus is our decision to pursue *Him* more than we pursue other good things such as anointing, happiness and success. When you set your heart to seek the Lord, your life will begin to change in many ways. Here are a few:

1. A Focus on Intimacy Washes Our Spirits.

Jesus loved the church and gave Himself up for her "that He might sanctify her, having cleansed her by the washing of water with the word, that He might present to Himself the church" in glorious splendor (Eph. 5:26-27).

Just as you or I need a daily physical bath, we also need a daily spiritual bath to remove some of the "grime" and defilement. If it is allowed to accumulate, it will lead to spiritual dullness and insensitivity in our spirits. Inner corruption such as anger, slander, impatience and sensuality grieves the Holy Spirit and makes our spirits insensitive and unable to respond fully to Him.

When we fix our hearts on the *person* of Jesus and dialogue with Him, the Word of God washes our spirits. Defilement from our daily contact with a fallen world is cleansed away. The accumulation of information about the Scriptures and the mental discipline of hours of Bible study will never thoroughly cleanse the inner man in the way that devotional, worshipful meditation upon God's Word will. In Bible study alone, we store up important scriptural facts and concepts. But when our Bible study leads into personal dialogue with Jesus as we meditate upon His cleansing Word, we also experience growth in spiritual hunger, sensitivity and nearness to Him.

2. A Focus on Intimacy Protects Our Souls.

We will never possess true purity without inward affection for Jesus. External disciplines and standards of holiness without devotion for Jesus have very little real power or life in them. A person named Jesus—not rules and regulations—guards our souls. Affection for Him creates a hindrance to the added temptations plaguing our souls. Let me share one practical example.

When passion for Jesus is built into our spiritual foundations, this resolution in our spirits automatically repels the sensual communications others send us. It returns the message "No, I'm not available." That strong, clear message rises from within our spirits, nipping temptation in the bud.

We are filled with such longings and affections for Jesus that we refuse to become involved in sensuality and wrong relationships. It's not a matter of being afraid we might get caught. It's not an issue of fear that we might be shamed and lose honor, position, privileges or even the anointing. We have higher motives for resisting temptation than a fear of AIDS or of coming under divine discipline. Our hearts are shielded by our love and reverence for Christ.

Readings

One of the greatest glories of Christ's church is her cleanliness, her purity. The believer deeply in love with Jesus—the soul aggressively engaged in pursuing intimacy with Him—is positioned to overcome temptation. This is true even in natural relationships. Not very many people are tempted to become romantically involved with someone other than their new spouse while on their honeymoon. Most newlyweds are so aware of the love they share with one another, the temptation to have an affair with someone else seems absurd. On the other hand, the passive soul wandering from fantasy to fantasy and lacking affection for God is vulnerable to almost any temptation that happens along.

In our pursuit of intimacy with Jesus, you and I must realize that feelings will come and go, swinging from holy passion to spiritual barrenness. We will have seasons of deep, fervent, longing love for Jesus, when we pray with great feelings of inspiration. But we will also experience seasons when we pray without any feeling of God's presence. Yet, as we persist, we will begin to realize that even in the dry, barren seasons our hearts are growing more fervent in mature love toward Jesus. Our focus is on Jesus, not upon feelings which seem to have fled forever.

As Paul declares, "The greatest of these is love" (1 Cor. 13:13). Love is our greatest motive. It is our greatest strength, joy, protection and perseverance. The breastplate of Christ's love for us and our love for Him is the greatest piece of our spiritual armor. Only foolish presumption dares enter into spiritual warfare without it.

3. A Focus on Intimacy Motivates and Inflames Our Hearts.

When we are "sowing to the Spirit" (Gal. 6:8), we are exposing ourselves to the presence of God whether we feel it or not. As focusing upon Him becomes the habit of our souls, we receive the wonderful anointing spoken of in Hebrews, "Who makes His...ministers a flame of fire" (1:7). The flaming heart of Christ ignites our hearts. Fire begets fire.

I love the verse from the Song of Solomon where the beloved speaks to his bride and says,

> Put me like a seal over your heart,
> Like a seal on you arm.

> For love is as strong as death,
> Jealousy is as severe as Sheol;
> It's flashes are flashes of fire,
> The very flame of the Lord
> (Song of Songs 8:6).

The holy flame is relentless and consuming. It will ignite a focused soul, even though it may be barren, and release deep emotions of hunger for Jesus. However, if we are too busy, easily offended, bitter or self-absorbed, the flame will be diminished.

It's important that we understand this principle: While it is true that a Christian's careless living will cause the flame to die down, this does not mean God's *love* has decreased toward the believer. You and I must refuse to believe the subtle lie of the enemy that says God's love for us goes up and down with our own vacillating spiritual feelings and attainments. The flame we're talking about here doesn't represent God's love and affections for us: It represents our passion and zeal for Him. We can lose our passion for Jesus without losing God's love for us.

4. A Focus on Intimacy Satisfies Our Human Spirits.

Intimacy satisfies the deep longing in our spirits. People who are born again are not always filled with a sense of the nearness of God. Effective ministry produces a satisfaction that comes through helping others and being useful in God's kingdom, but it is not a permanent, deep satisfaction. Nothing but an intimate relationship with Jesus will satisfy this inner cry birthed by the Holy Spirit.

The Holy Spirit may give spiritual gifts to believers and release the benefits of redemption upon us, but none of those things will ultimately satisfy the desire in our spirits for Jesus Himself. When our spiritual hunger is not being satisfied, you and I will experience frustrating boredom and holy restlessness. The Spirit of God is trying to stir up our spirits to seek more of God.

5. A Focus on Intimacy Frees Us From Insecurity and Fear of Man.

Intimacy with Jesus brings a deepened security and rest in the inner man. As we interact in a deeply personal way with Him, we grow in our knowledge that we are accepted and cherished by God. This

Readings

knowledge progressively frees us from feelings of insecurity and the intimidating, paralyzing fear of others' opinions or actions against us.

A focus on Jesus ultimately leads us to the knowledge of His heart of affirmation. This is absolutely vital. As important as human affirmation is, it is woefully inadequate without God's affirmation of us. It is the knowledge that we are loved, accepted and valued by God that gives us a sense of value and true self-worth. When we are secure and confident in God's love, we grow out of our fears. When we know we are pleasing Him, criticism and offenses from others won't affect us as easily. "Proving" our value to others ceases to be the dominant drive in our emotional makeup. God's pleasure and His approving smile are all we need.

6. A Focus on Intimacy Heals Inner Wounds of the Heart.

I believe that counseling is a part of the process of emotional healing. Like almost everything God restores to the church, counseling and inner healing have been abused and taken to extremes in some cases. But that doesn't mean these ministry tools should be shunned. The cure for abuse is *proper* use, not *dis*use. However, if a person's wounded heart is to experience true, lasting wholeness and healing, that individual needs to be introduced to the Healer Himself and encouraged to build a relationship of intimacy with Him.

Human hearts can be wounded in many ways. Almost daily we hear another tragic story of sexual, physical, verbal or emotional abuse. Victims range in age from tiny infants to the elderly. Man's inhumanity to man seems to defy all limits. Yet, when I think about this subject of healing inner wounds of the heart, I can't help but think of my brother, Pat. Few human hearts have been dealt harder blows than Pat's heart suffered after becoming a quadriplegic at the age of seventeen. Then he lost the most precious person in the world to him only eight months later when Dad died.

I watched Pat fight an enemy that could be worse than paralysis or death, and I saw him win. My brother refused to allow bitterness to conquer him. I can tell you this: My brother is a champion of courage.

He is still paralyzed from the neck down. But my brother's spirit is now unhindered by weights of self-pity, hatred or bitterness. For many years now, Pat has loved Jesus with a passion. Over the years he has been a man of prayer, bearing the burdens of others and lifting their needs up to God. Watching my brother's example has affirmed to me many, many times that an intimate relationship with Jesus can heal *any* wound of the human heart.

How are the inner wounds of the heart healed? We have to give everything to God, including our bitterness, self-pity and desire for revenge. Our grief, anger, shame and pride—even our hopes, dreams and ambitions—must be laid on God's altar, along with our personal rights and the desire to run our own lives. Jesus Christ must become the focus of our hearts—not our tragedies, our past or all that might have been. Only Jesus can transform self-pity into praise or tears into triumph. A focus on intimacy with Jesus heals the inner wounds of the heart. My brother's life daily affirms that fact.

7. A Focus on Intimacy Is an Effective Means of Spiritual Warfare.

The strength of spiritual warfare is passion for Jesus. The enemy's strategy is to shift us from an offensive mode into a defensive mode where we're attempting to ward off temptation and sin through the power of our own wills and resolution. He fears offensive Christianity that pursues the person of Christ and fills our lives with purpose. If Satan can separate us from our passion and from our purpose, then we became passive and aimless—an easy prey for sin.

Let's look at two scriptural principles illustrating the wisdom of maintaining an offensive posture when dealing with the enemy: The principle of increasing and decreasing and the principle of light and darkness.

The Principle of Increasing & Decreasing

"He must increase, but I must decrease" (John 3:30). This principle can be applied outside of its original context where John was allowing Jesus' ministry to replace his own. It also applies to how we grow as individuals.

Increase in our knowledge of God comes before decrease in our bondage to darkness. That's God's divine order. Trying to decrease in sin when Jesus has

154 **Embracing Life Series** Session 11

Readings

not first increased in us is difficult and ineffective. Once the knowledge of God's personality penetrates our human spirits, it has a sanctifying impact on our emotions. As Jesus becomes more real to us, the inevitable result is a desire to give ourselves to Him and to decrease those things in our lives that are working in opposition to Him.

The Principle of Light and Darkness

Believers combat spiritual darkness in their lives with spiritual light! John speaks of Jesus in terms of light: "In Him was life, and the life was the light of men" (John 1:4). John continues, "And the light shines in the darkness, and the darkness did not comprehend it." Darkness is driven out of the human spirit by the light of the revelation of Jesus Christ through the Word of God. No darkness in the life of a sincere believer has the force to overpower His light.

Attempting to drive the darkness out of our hearts by ourselves is frustrating and futile, but when the person of Christ is unveiled to us, and His light enters our hearts, the darkness flees. The same is true of natural light in a room, for the darkness in a room disappears when we turn on the light. Rather, we allow the light to enter, and darkness is automatically overpowered. We wear ourselves out by trying to prepare and make way for more light by focusing on trying to drive out the darkness. Instead, we should indirectly attack the darkness in our lives by focusing on the release of more light.

Satan is not intimidated by the shouts and boasts of believers who do not have an intimate relationship with Jesus. He knows that as long as darkness reigns unchallenged and unconquered in many areas of their own lives, those believers pose no real threat to his kingdom. Jesus is the One whom Satan fears. If believers are not filled with the reality and knowledge of Christ, Satan knows it is only a matter of time until they will become victims, not victors.

Satan is troubled by believers who are undistracted from the purity and simplicity of devotion to Jesus. He flees before the sword of the Spirit when it is wielded by men and women who have a history of faithfulness and obedience through their intimacy with God. He is hindered through the prayers of godly intercessors that pierce the darkness, exposing and destroying his strongholds (2 Cor. 10:5).

Isaiah declares, "Neither has the eye seen a God besides Thee, who acts in behalf of the one who waits for Him" (64:4). No matter how weak, imperfect and immature we are, if we will set ourselves to seek God's face and wait upon Him, continuing to persevere in prayer, God's mighty hand will move on our behalf. Divine acts are loosed even in response to weak humans who wait upon the Lord.

A focus on intimacy is an effective means of spiritual warfare, for Satan is hindered by passion for Jesus, purity and persevering prayer. The weakest, most immature believer who has a heart focus of holy passion will become a threat to Satan's kingdom.

Invited to Intimacy

As we continue to focus on intimacy with Jesus, we will be rewarded and enriched by the release of these seven supernatural benefits in our lives. Let's review them once more.

1. Our spirits will be washed from defilement by the Word of God.

2. Our souls will be strengthened against temptation by the breastplate of faith and love affecting our emotions.

3. Our inner man will be motivated and inflamed by a release of divine hunger and zeal as our spirits are exposed to Jesus' flaming heart.

4. The deep cry in our spirits for intimacy with Jesus will be satisfied.

5. We will be freed from insecurity and the fear of man.

6. Inner wounds of the heart will be healed.

7. We will be equipped for spiritual warfare.

The choices are clear-cut: Passion or passivity? Victor or victim? Blessings or barrenness?

You and I are invited to pursue a person actively, for intimacy does not come accidentally. Intimacy comes through the hunger and yearning of our hearts and through sowing to the Spirit. As we hunger and thirst for Jesus, seeking Him and spending time in His presence, we will fall in love with Him.

Copyright 1993, pp 144-156.

Used by permission of Creation House.

Readings

From:

"Intimacy with God"

Father Thomas Keating

The movement inward to the Divine Indwelling suggests that our relationship with Christ is an interior one, especially through his Holy Spirit who dwells in us and pours the love of God into our hearts. We are really identifying with the Paschal mystery. Without going through a theological reflection each time, it becomes a kind of context for our prayer, so that when we sit down in our chair or on the floor, we are relating to the mystery of Christ's passion, death, and resurrection, not as something outside of us but as something inside of us. That is why we experience fairly soon an identification with Christ in his temptations in the desert. Later we experience our identification with Christ in the garden of Gethsemane, and finally our identification with Christ on the cross. In our Christian perspective, Jesus has taken upon himself all the consequences of our sins and sinfulness, in other words, the false self with the accumulation of wounds that we bring with us from early childhood and our childish ways of trying to survive.

As we sit, we may receive the consolation of the Spirit. But after several years of this prayer, we always find ourselves in the desert, because that is the way to divine union. There is no way of getting well from the wounds of our early childhood except through the cross. The cross that God asks us to accept is primarily our own pain that we bring with us from early childhood. Our own wounds, our own limitations, our own personality defects, all the damage that people have done to us from the beginning of life until now, and our personal experience of the pain of the human condition as we individually have experienced it—that is our true cross! That is what Christ asks us to accept and to allow him to share. Actually in his passion he has already experienced our pain and made it his own. In other words, we simply enter into something that has already happened, namely, our union with Christ and all that it implies, his taking into himself all of our pain, anxiety, fears, self-hatred, and discouragement.

It is all included implicitly in his cry on the cross, "My God, why have you abandoned me?" That is the big question. Here is God's son, the beloved to whom we are to listen—Christ who has based his whole mission and ministry on his relationship with the Father—and it has all disappeared. His disciples have fled. His message is torn to shreds. He stands condemned by the religious and Roman authorities. There is nothing left of his message, humanly speaking. Yet this is the moment of our redemption. Why? Because his cry on the cross is our cry of a desperate alienation from God, taken up into his, and transformed into resurrection. As we sit there and sweat it out and allow the pain to come up, we realize that it is Christ suffering in us and redeeming us.

Copyright 1994, pp. 33-35.
Used by permission of The Crossroad Publishing Company.

Readings

"Through the Valley of Baca: A Sojurn in Healing"

by Jonathan Hunter

The other day I was reading Psalm 84 and the following verses stood out boldly:

> Blessed are those whose strength is in you, who have set their hearts on pilgrimage. As they pass through the Valley of Baca, they make it a place of springs; the autumn rains also cover it with pools. They go from strength to strength, till each appears before God in Zion. (v.v. 5-7)

The psalmist describes the kind of people and life-giving ministry that I hope God is fashioning in me and the men and women of Embracing Life. Our pilgrimage over the years has taken us through many valleys of Baca—translated as both "valley of weeping" in the NIV and "thirsty valley" in the NEB. It is familiar territory for those in AIDS ministry—a desert of weariness for those to whom we minister.

Christ Within Me

My personal sojourn through that wasteland continues to be possible through the grace and affirming love of others who have mediated Christ's will for me to live. But more than that, it has been the awakened realization that Christ lives in me. This experience of real life has forever changed the course and resolve of our ministry-HIS ministry. (Many thankful prayers must go to Leanne Payne for the Pastoral Care Ministry school and her book, The Healing Presence. The PCM conferences both revived and quickened all of us to the true import of Jesus' presence as fundamental to real ministry.)

We are learning that to be those blessed pilgrims of the Lord, we need to be practicing His presence, allowing the Lord to transform our ministries (our lives) into an oasis of life-giving refreshment, a "place of springs" for a weary, parched world. Unfortunately, many pilgrims—I would include myself here—have sojourned without ever truly knowing Christ's indwelling presence. This compels us to try to minister out of our own ephemeral power. Instead of going from "strength to strength" as the Psalm says, we become quickly depleted, a shell of a ministry. What was initially a source of healing and sustenance has become feeble and stagnant. This is a fearful thing to experience and potentially dangerous to others if it continues. Unless redemptive, profound healing comes to these individuals, they end up on the trash heap of burnt out ministries, another casualty of frenetic activism "for the Lord."

His Gifts

Our ministry, like many others, has occassionally fallen into the trap of becoming more enamored with aspects of Christ's ministry than His person. The result has been a vulnerable and undefined ministry. In our earnest desire to see people healed, we were tempted (and acted on it) to worship the gifts rather than the Giver. Repeatedly we stumbled over the truth that without His presence, the gifts become as a "clanging cymbal." The test for us has come not with use of the charismata, but in allowing ourselves to rest in him, to allow His character to be developed in us. In evaluating the quality of our response to people, we've had to ask the Lord if we have reflected His character or have used a religious covering to hide the empty selves inside. Henri Nouwen writes of this in his book, *Lifesigns*:

> "Once we have come to know the truth we want to act truthfully and reveal to the world its true nature...It is not a fearful attempt to restore a broken order. It is a joyful assertion that IN CHRIST [emphasis JH] all order has already been restored. It is not a nervous effort to bring divided people together but a celebration of an already established unity. Thus action is not activism. An activist wants to

heal, restore, redeem, and recreate, but those acting within the house of God point through action to the healing, restoring, redeeming, and recreating presence of God."

Fleshly Activism

These pitfalls of ministry can actually be deadly when perverted by the enemy. But praise be to God He is not remaining passive in the midst of it— may it never be! He is purifying His people and calling us to a holiness that won't support secular activism in His name. He invites us to embrace the Father with the life of the Son. He shows us that the tools of ministry (gifts of the Spirit) are less amazing for their functions and more a natural manifestation of His supernatural presence within us. He wants us to know peaceably and confidently that where Christ is, healing is.

Reaching the Promise

Only the true well springs of Jesus' life will heal and sustain us. In the meantime, [We] have set out hearts on pilgrimage...going *from strength to strength, till each appears before God in Zion."*

> You will seek me and find me when you seek me with all your heart. I will be found by you, declares the Lord... (Jer. 29:13, 14)

DSM Newsletter, Fall 1990

Developing a devotional life

Session 12

NOTES

> Theological realities without practical application mean little. God has given us tools that we can take hold of...These instruments convey Christ to us and enable us to be His agents to others.
> (from earlier edition of *Living Waters Guidebook,* Andrew Comiskey, p. 121)

We've seen both the importance and the great potential of having an intimate relationship with Jesus. In order to cultivate and enjoy the fruit of that intimate relationship, we must commit ourselves to certain practices and habits. These practices and habits constitute what is called a "devotional life." Every Christian who seeks fullness of life in Christ must develop a devotional life.

Each one of us has family members or friends with whom we have regular, perhaps daily contact. Such relationships are known as primary relationships. These people know many of the details of our day-to-day lives, and the details of their lives are known by us.

Developing a devotional life means making Jesus your primary relationship, putting Him above all others. It means He receives the firstfruits of your time and relational energy.

The Apostle Paul knew the importance of the Christian's deepening, personal relationship with Christ. He wrote to the church in Ephesus:

Session 12   Developing a devotional life   Embracing Life Series   161

Session 12

Developing a devotional life

NOTES

> I keep asking that the God of our Lord Jesus Christ, the glorious Father, may give you the Spirit of wisdom and revelation, *so that you may know him better.*
>
> I pray also that the eyes of your heart may be enlightened *in order that you may know the hope to which he has called you,* the riches of his glorious inheritance in the saints... (Ephesians 1:17-18) [italics JH]

Those of us living with life-threatening or life-altering conditions not only need intimacy with Christ, but also the habits of the heart and mind that insure we will "know Him better." Because words of sickness and hopelessness are often spoken over us, it is vital to remian close to the Good Shephard and to know His voice. Jesus said: *"The Spirit gives life; the flesh counts for nothing. The words I have spoken to you are spirit and they are life"* (John 6:63). Although helpful and perhaps necessary, other means of support and encouragement pale in comparison to the power and the peace found in knowing God and knowing Him well.

A definition

A devotional life involves the ordering of your life to become, over time, rooted in the ways and purposes of God, so that you walk in your God-created destiny, mediating His life to others. The goal is to become like Him: to know Him better, to discern His voice apart from others competing for your attention, and to be obedient to what He tells you.

The devotional life of Jesus

Jesus, our ultimate model, accomplished His mission because He listened carefully to what the Father was saying and acted upon what He heard. He was obedient. Jesus revealed the nature of His union with the Father in the Gospel of John:

> ...I say to you, the Son can do nothing of Himself unless it is something He sees the Father doing; for whatever the Father does, these things the Son also does in like manner. For the Father loves the Son and shows Him all things that He Himself is doing... (John 5:19-20 NAS)

Jesus saw what the Father was doing. Even though Jesus was and remains fully God, He was and remains fully human, as well. On earth Jesus' relationship with the Father had to be formed as a human. Jesus pioneered a true life of devotion for the rest of us.

Developing a devotional life

Session 12

Jesus said to his disciples: *"...I say to you, he who believes in me, the works I do he shall do also; and greater works than these shall he do because I go to the Father"* (John 14:12 NAS). Because we have His Holy Spirit indwelling us, we are able to order our lives according to the Father's will—as Jesus did.

What do we know about Jesus' devotional life? We see several things in the account of His temptation in the wilderness and in the events immediately following: Jesus committed His will to godly obedience, He had a commanding grasp of the Scriptures, He withdrew often to pray or rest, and He served people (Luke 4).

The use of our wills

What are the essentials in beginning a devotional life? First, our wills must be activated. In C.S. Lewis' fictional tale, *The Screwtape Letters*, a high-ranking demon shares insights with an apprentice demon on keeping a young man on track to hell:

> The Enemy [God]...has a curious fantasy of making all these disgusting little human vermin into what He calls His "free" lovers and servants—"sons"...Desiring their freedom, He therefore refuses to carry them, by their mere affections and habits, to any of the goals He sets before them: He leaves them to do it on their own. (*The Screwtape Letters*, C.S. Lewis, p. 13)

A devotional lifestyle does not come automatically to us. We are not "wired" so that our eyes pop open every morning at 4:00 AM to spend a couple of hours with Jesus before the day begins. *A lifestyle of worship is not acquired passively.*

We *are*, on the other hand, "wired" to need relationship with our Creator. God could override our resistant wills, but then we would be robots and not His sons and daughters. By the grace of God we take up the cross and *choose* intimacy with Jesus. Because we will be opposed by both our own fleshly desires and the enemy of our souls, we struggle for that intimacy! God is faithful to supply what we need for the fight. He gives his merciful and healing Holy Spirit. Nevertheless, *we* make the choice whether or not to align our hearts and wills with His and pursue intimacy.

The devotional life can be viewed through individual and corporate disciplines (practices). The individual disciplines (reading Scripture and prayer) constitute our inner/private life with Jesus. Corporate disciplines (service and life together in the Church) constitute our outward/public life with Jesus. We will be discussing the outward disciplines in the next session as we look at our place in the Church. Let's look now at the inner/private disciplines.

NOTES

Session 12   Developing a devotional life   **Embracing Life Series**   163

Session 12 — Developing a devotional life

NOTES

The Scriptures: testimony to the Living Word, Jesus Christ

> God speaks to us in what can only be described as supernatural ways when the "imperishable seed," the Word of God, is continually hidden away in our hearts. The Holy Spirit takes the truth of the gospel of both Testaments, anoints it and seals it on our minds and hearts.
> To the extent our minds and hearts are bereft of the Holy Writ, our capacity to listen and discern aright is limited."
> (*Listening Prayer*, Leanne Payne, p. 26)

The Bible is indispensible in our pursuit of intimacy with the Lord. It is our *objective source of Truth*. It is the written Word. Knowing the Word and submitting our lives to its truth yield the greatest of benefits:

1. **The Scriptures are dependable in giving guidance and form to our lives.** (Psalm 119:105; 2 Timothy 3:16)

2. **The Scriptures inform us of the character and intentions of God** as revealed through His dealings with people and all creation in history.

3. **The Scriptures give language for our prayer life.** We learn prayer from others who knew God. Using the prayers, themes, and the language of Scripture ensures that our prayers (which must become our own, not just mimicked) are consistent with the will of God. The Book of Psalms has always been the great hymn book and prayer book of the Church.

4. **God's words administer life.** (John 6:63) As we have seen, this is critical for the person living with a life-threatening condition. The writer of the Book of Hebrews said that the Word of God is living and active, with the sharpest of accuracy, separating the false from the true within our own hearts (Hebrews 4:12).

5. **Reading or hearing, the Word of God always produces something in us** (Isaiah 55:10-11).

6. **The Scriptures have power to silence the devil.** When Jesus successfully countered the temptations the devil offered, our Lord showed that knowledge of the Scriptures enables one to engage in effective spiritual warfare (Luke 4:1-13).

For the Christian, the reading, studying and application of Scripture is a lifelong occupation.

Developing a devotional life

Session 12

Prayer:
response to the Living Word

Prayer is also indispensible to our life of devotion. *Smith's Bible Dictionary* says that prayer is "the approach of the soul unto God." *Our souls engage in relationship with Jesus through prayer.* It is our most personal point of contact with Him. Prayer is our conversation with God.

Studying the Scriptures without prayer is incomplete. For example, one could become an expert on Abraham Lincoln by reading everything written about him, but the ability to *know* him will forever be limited, because it is not possible to have a conversation with him. Yet this is not the case with God! The Creator of the universe has made Himself accessible to us. We can communicate with Him! And know Him, through prayer!

Prayer is expressed in a number of ways. Jesus introduces several of these ways in the "Lord's Prayer" (Matthew 6:9-13). Below we will look at these prayer expressions, each one introduced by a phrase from Jesus' model prayer.

Praise and thanksgiving:
"Our heavenly Father, hallowed be Your Name..."

> ...It is right, and a good and joyful thing, always and everywhere to give thanks to you, Father Almighty, Creator of heaven and earth.
> (*The Book of Common Prayer*, The Great Thanksgiving, p. 361)

Praise and thanksgiving are the beginnings of prayer. "Praise" is simply declaring to God who He is. Praise highlights God's majesty, holiness, and absolute rule. We get a dramatic picture of praise in Revelation 4, where the "twenty-four elders" continually throw their crowns to the ground and fall on their faces to worship the living God (Revelation 4:9-11; 5:11-14). Praise lifts us out of our distorted, earthbound perspective into that heavenly reality.

"Thanksgiving" is adoring and worshipping God for what God does and has done, for others and for us. Psalm 103 begins with praise ("Bless the LORD, O my soul..."), but quickly shifts into thanksgiving ("...and do not forget his benefits") in verse two.

Praise and thanksgiving are weapons against anything in conflict with intimacy with God. The Psalmist says of God's people: *"May the praise of God be in their mouths and a double edged sword in their hands..."* (Psalm 149:6).

NOTES

Session 12 — Developing a devotional life

Intercession:
"Your kingdom come, Your will be done on earth as it is in heaven."

Intercession means to intervene as an advocate for another person. Intercessory prayer is speaking to God about the needs of another person on behalf of that other person. It is identifying with a world in need and talking to God about those needs. When we pray that God's kingdom would come, we are praying that the life of Jesus and the righteous rule of the Father would fill the earth and meet those needs. Intercession calls us out of ourselves. The *Evangelical Dictionary of Theology* states:

> Personal petition would become egocentric if it were not held in balance with intercession, adoration and thanksgiving. We pray not simply for personal happiness or protection (as in primitive prayer) but for the advancement and extension of the Kingdom of God. (Donald Bloesch, *The Evangelical Dictionary of Theology*, Walter Ewell, ed., p. 867)

Petition:
"Give us today our daily bread"

Petition brings to the Lord our personal needs and yearnings. It is important that we do this, so that our needs and desires do not remain unsatisfied longings of the soul. Unspoken, they become an occasion for anxiety or sin, inhibiting intimate communion with God. Leanne Payne writes:

> Until we learn to yield to God all the needs, cries and desires of our hearts in petition, we will know neither Him nor our hearts as we should. *To come present to Him and to our hearts is to cry out our personal petitions.* Then we must have ears to hear His heart for us: His desires, promises, exhortations, and commands.
>
> (*Listening Prayer*, Leanne Payne, p. 75) [italics JH]

Developing a devotional life   Session 12

Repentance and forgiveness:
"Forgive us our debts, as we also have forgiven our debtors. And lead us not into temptation, but deliver us from the evil one."

Leanne Payne writes: "Without forgiveness or freedom from evil we are subject to sickness of spirit, soul and eventually body as well" *(Listening Prayer,* p.97*)* King David prayed: *"...O Lord, have mercy on me; heal me for I have sinned against you,"* (Psalm 41:4). One can infer from David's prayer that unconfessed sin creates vulnerability to infirmity and hinders our ability to receive healing words.

The total sum of our sin—past, present and future—has been forgiven. That forgiveness was purchased by Jesus once and for all on the cross. That once and for all forgiveness was applied to our lives by the Holy Spirit when we first put our trust in Christ and gave our lives to Him. Since that time, and for the rest of our lives, the daily sins we commit—knowingly or unknowingly—need to be confessed to Jesus. The Holy Spirit brings them to our attention. *"If we confess our sins He is faithful and just and will forgive us our sins and purify us from all unrighteousness,"* (1 John 1:9). Confession clears the communication lines. It clears the air. Confession, followed by embracing our status as "forgiven sinners," builds intimacy with Jesus.

Practical helps to order your devotional life

What are some basic principles for developing a devotional life? If we conducted our earthly relationships according to a rigid set of rules, they would not grow and develop. There is no "one way" to be a friend. As time goes on, the rhythm and priorities in a relationship often change. Nevertheless, there are certain constants.

> **1**   ***Set aside time daily and make it non-negotiable.*** *If you wait until you have time, a devotional life will never happen or be given importance. If you have a job during normal hours, the most realistic times are the early morning or the evening. Scripture favors the morning (Mark 1:35, Psalm 5:1-3). As an example, it makes more sense to tune the orchestra before the concert than to do so afterwards. If mornings will not work, then choose another time that is conducive for your communing with God.*

Session 12 — Developing a devotional life

NOTES

2   ***Settings can differ.*** Most of us don't have the idyllic garden or a richly paneled soundproof room with a fireplace and comfortable chair in which to read the Bible and pray. However, there are many ways to improvise depending on your personal options and preferences. Perhaps your workplace provides a proper setting, if you arrive before everyone else. One well-known pastor went to hospital waiting rooms at night. Hardly anyone was in them, and they had free coffee! Other possibilities are parks, your bedroom, or the library. The setting should be a place where you can wait quietly before the Lord without interruption or distraction.

3   ***Have a plan for the reading of Scripture.*** Random reading of Scripture can be blessed by the Holy Spirit. To maximize your time and grasp the context of the whole book, however, it is better to have some structure in your Bible reading. There are Bibles that are laid out to be read in one year. *Through the Bible in One Year* is a good example. *The Book of Common Prayer* provides a reading plan that follows the church calendar: Advent, Christmastide, Epiphany, Lent, Easter, Resurrection, Ascension and Pentecost.

Always ask the Holy Spirit to bless your reading and to reveal the Father and Son to you in it.

4   ***Keep a prayer journal.*** This could be a composition book or a notebook. Journaling can be an enjoyable discipline. It is a way of keeping a record of your dealings with God. Try to journal all the aspects of prayer we have covered: meditation, praise and thanksgiving, intercession, personal petition, repentence, forgiveness and conversations with God (listening prayer).

King David expressed the joys, anguish, anger and confusion in his life through his own personal prayer journal—the Psalms. David refused to sit with his own death-filled and fear-filled feelings and meditations. Over the years, he learned to submit his thoughts and emotions to God as prayers, always expressing his hope that God would meet him no matter how he felt. His journal can provide a model for us.

5   ***Learn to wait before the Lord, listen...be.*** Listening is fifty percent (or more) of prayer. As you pour out your heart to God, wait and listen for Him to respond. Remember, prayer is a conversation, a dialogue. We cannot talk all the time and expect to become acquainted with someone, let alone become intimate

Developing a devotional life

Session 12

NOTES

with that person. Learn to simply *be* in God's presence without audibly speaking. The best of friends can be with each other without words being said. This is a practice that will become more familiar and comfortable over time. (Read the included excerpts by Henri Nouwen.)

6 *Fasting.* As your prayer life develops, you may be led by the Lord to fast. Jesus fasted and recommended fasting for situations that seemed insurmountable (Matthew 4:1-4; 17:21). Fasting involves temporarily abstaining from something in order to focus our attention, our entire being, on God.

We seek to fill up the spiritual emptiness inside of us with many substitutes that can never satisfy. Our self-indulgence fails us. Only God can fill us and give us life. Going without food, or television, or the radio, or alcohol, or something else, reveals what we may be relying on to fill the void.

Fasting is one way of denying yourself and taking up the cross. Fasting is making a deliberate choice to bring your body and will under submission with the goal of greater reliance upon God. The rewards are the refining of your prayer life, preparation for conflict, the reinvigoration of your will, and victory over problems (Mark 9:29; Matthew 4:2; 2 Samuel 12:16-23). Many have reported breakthroughs in their lives following a time of fasting. How should you fast? Pray and the Holy Spirit will show you. Have a purpose.

Discuss the following questions in the group.

- To what extent have you created a place and space for a devotional life?

- What benefits and fruit have you seen? What difficulties have you had?

- Do you feel a need to re-commit yourself to developing a devotional life?

# Session 12 — Developing a devotional life

NOTES

SCRIPTURE READINGS

Below are Psalms that voice a variety of types of prayers in differing circumstances. Read them to determine what kind of praying the psalmist is engaged in (praise, thanksgiving, intercession, petitioning, repentence and forgiveness). Write down phrases that express your heart and begin using them in your prayer times.

Psalms 5, 32, 38, 51, 62, 63, 83, 103, 126, 147

RECOMMENDED READINGS

Listening Prayer by Leanne Payne
The Way of the Heart by Henri Nouwen

THOUGHTS FOR JOURNALING

After reading the assigned Psalms, write your own psalm which expresses your heart to Jesus in the midst of your current circumstances.

Readings

From:

"The Spirit of the Disciplines"

by Dallas Willard

Pertinent sections excerpted from Ch. 9: Some Main Disciplines for Spiritual Life

> But to obtain these gifts, you need more than faith; you must also work hard to be good, and even that is not enough. For then you must learn to know God better and discover what he wants you to do. Next, learn to put aside your own desires so that you will become patient and godly, gladly letting God have his way with you. This will make possible the next step, which is for you to enjoy other people and to like them, and finally you will grow to love them deeply. The more you go on in this way, the more you will grow strong spiritually and become faithful and useful to our Lord Jesus Christ. (2 Peter 1:5-8, LB)

A discipline for the spiritual life is, when the dust of history is blown away, nothing but an activity undertaken to bring us into more effective cooperation with Christ and his Kingdom. When we understand that grace (*charis*) is gift (*charisma*), we then see that to grow in grace is to grow in what is given to us of God and by God. The disciplines are then, in the clearest sense, a means to that grace and also to those gifts. Spiritual disciplines, "exercises unto godliness," are only activities undertaken to make us capable of receiving more of his life and power without harm to ourselves or others.

Though we may not be aware of it, we experience "disciplines" everyday. In these daily or "natural" disciplines we perform acts that result in a direct command of further abilities that we would not otherwise have. If I repeat the telephone number aloud after looking it up, I can remember it until I get it dialed. Otherwise, I probably couldn't. If I train rigorously I can bench press 300 pounds; otherwise not. Such ordinary activities are actually disciplines that aid our physical or "natural" life.

The same thing happens with disciplines for our spiritual life. When through spiritual disciplines I become able heartily to bless those who curse me, pray without ceasing, to be at peace when not given credit for good deeds I've done, or to master the evil that comes my way, it is because my disciplinary activities have inwardly poised me for more and more interaction with the powers of the living God and his Kingdom. Such is the potential we tap into when we use the disciplines.

The Disciplines of Abstinence

> Abstain from fleshly lust which war against the soul. (1 Peter 2:11)

Reminding us that the word "asceticism" is the correlate of a Greek word for *training*, as in athletes training for a race, W. R. Inge notes that disciplines of abstinence should be practiced by everyone, leading to a sober and moderate use of all God's gifts.

> If we feel that any habit or pursuit, harmless in itself, is keeping us from God and sinking us deeper in the things of earth; if we find that things which others can do with impunity are for us the occasion of falling, then abstinence is our only course. Abstinence alone can recover for us the real value of what should have been for our help but which has been an occasion of falling…It is necessary that we should steadily resolve to give up anything that comes between ourselves and God.

He concludes his discussion of abstinence by quoting from Bishop Wilson of the Isle of Man: "Those who deny themselves will be sure to find their strength increased, their affections raised, and their inward peace continually augmented."

Readings

In the disciplines of abstinence, we abstain to some degree and for some time from the satisfaction of what we generally regard as normal and legitimate desires. "Normal" desires include our basic drives or motivations, such as those for food, sleep, bodily activity, companionship, curiosity, and sex. But our desires for convenience, comfort, material security, reputation or fame, and variety are also considered under this heading. Psychologists have no generally accepted classification of these "normal" drives or of their precise interrelationships, though obviously most of the ones just mentioned must be satisfied to some degree for the sake of human life and health.

Keep in mind that the practice of abstention does not imply that there is anything essentially wrong with these desires as such. But in today's distorted condition of humanity, it is these basic desires that have been allowed to run a rebellious and harmful course, ultimately serving as the primary hosts of sin in our personalities.

We can clearly see this by considering the nature of the major types of sin. The seven "deadly" sins recognized throughout church history are pride, envy, anger, sloth, avarice, gluttony, and lasciviousness. Gregory the Great (A.D. 540-604) described these as "a classification of the normal perils of the soul in the ordinary conditions of life." Each is a case of one or more legitimate desires gone wrong. An adequate course of spiritual discipline will single out those tendencies that may harm our walk with God. By the carefully adapted arrangement of our circumstances and behavior, the spiritual disciplines will bring these basic desires into their proper coordination and subordination within the economy of life in his Kingdom.

Solitude

We have already seen what a large role solitude played in the life of our Lord and the great ones in His Way. In solitude, we purposefully abstain from interaction with other human beings, denying ourselves companionship and all that comes from our conscious interaction with others. We close ourselves away; we go to the ocean, to the desert, the wilderness, or to the anonymity of the urban crowd. This is not just rest or refreshment from nature, though that too can contribute to our spiritual well-being. Solitude is choosing to be *alone* and to dwell on our experience of isolation from other human beings.

Solitude frees us, actually. This above all explains its primacy and priority among the disciplines. The normal course of day-to-day human interactions locks us into patterns of feeling, thought, and action that are geared to a world set against God. Nothing but solitude can allow the development of a freedom from the ingrained behaviors that hinder our integration into God's order.

It takes twenty times more the amount of amphetamine to kill individual mice than it takes to kill them in groups. Experimenters also find that a mouse given no amphetamine at all will be dead within ten minutes of being placed in the midst of a group on the drug. In groups they go off like popcorn or firecrackers. Western men and women, especially, *talk* a great deal about being individuals. But our conformity to social pattern is hardly less remarkable than that of the mice—and just as deadly!

In solitude we find the psychic distance, the perspective from which we can see, in the light of eternity, the created things that trap, worry, and oppress us. Thomas Merton writes:

> That is the only reason why I desire solitude—to be lost to all created things, to die to them and to the knowledge of them, for they remind me of my distance from You: that You are far from them, even though You are in them. You have made them and Your presence sustains their being and they hide You from me. And I would live alone, and out of them. O beata solitudo!

But solitude, like all of the disciplines of the spirit, carries its risks. In solitude, we confront our own soul with its obscure forces and conflicts that escape our attention when we are interacting with others. Thus, "Solitude is a terrible trial, for it serves to crack open and burst apart the shell of our superficial securities. It opens out to us the unknown abyss that we all carry within us...[and] discloses the fact that these abysses are haunted." We can only survive solitude if we cling to Christ there. And yet what we find of him in that solitude enables us to return to society as free persons.

Solitude will also pain and threaten our family

Readings

and friends. The author Jessamyn West comments: "It is not easy to be solitary unless you are born ruthless. Every solitary repudiates someone." Others need us to keep *their* lives in place; and when we retreat, they then have to deal with their souls. True, they need God more than they need us, but they may not understand this. We must carefully respect their pain and with much loving prayer make wise arrangements on their behalf; and we must do all possible to help them understand what we are doing and why.

Of all the disciplines of abstinence, solitude is generally the most fundamental in the beginning of the spiritual life, and it must be returned to again and again as that life develops. This factual priority of solitude is, I believe, a sound element in monastic asceticism. Locked into interaction with the human beings that make up our fallen world, it is all but impossible to grow in grace as one should. Just try fasting, prayer, service, giving, or even celebration without the preparation accomplished in withdrawal, and you will soon be thrown into despair by your efforts, very likely abandoning your attempt altogether.

On the other hand, we must reemphasize, the "desert" or "closet" is the primary place of *strength* for the beginner, as it was for Christ and for Paul. They show us by their example what we must do. In stark aloneness it is possible to have silence, to be still, and to *know* that Jehovah indeed is God (Ps. 46:10), to set the Lord before our minds with sufficient intensity and duration that we stay centered upon him our hearts fixed, established in trust (Ps. 112:7-8)—even when back in the office, shop, or home.

Thomas à Kempis distilled more of what was right in the monastic calling than any other, and he had this to say:

> The great holy men, where they might, fled men's fellowship and chose to live to God in secret places. One said: As ofttimes as I was among men I came back a less man, that is to say less holy...If in the beginning of thy conversion thou keep thy cell and dwell well therein it shall be to thee afterwards as a dear and well beloved friend and most pleasant solace. In silence and quiet the devout soul profiteth and learneth the secrets of the Scriptures...Leave vain things to the vain...Shut thy door upon thee and call to thee Jesu thy love: dwell with him in thy cell for thou shalt not find elsewhere so great peace.

Henry David Thoreau saw how even our secular existence withers from lack of a hidden life. Conversation degenerates into mere gossip and those we meet can only talk of what they heard from someone else. The only difference between us and our neighbor is that he has seen the news and we have not. Thoreau put it well. As our inward quiet life fails, "we go more constantly and desperately to the post office," but "the poor fellow who walks away with the greatest number of letters, proud of his extensive correspondence, has not heard from himself this long while. ...'Read not The Times,' he concludes, 'read The Eternities!'"

Silence

In silence we close off our souls from "sounds," whether those sounds be noise, music, or words. Total silence is rare, and what we today call "quiet" usually only amounts to a little less noise. Many people have *never* experienced silence and do not even know that they do *not* know what it is. Our households and offices are filled with the whirring, buzzing, murmuring, chattering, and whining of the multiple contraptions that are supposed to make life easier. Their noise comforts us in some curious way. In fact, we find complete silence shocking because it leaves the impression that nothing is happening. In a go-go world such as ours, what could be worse than that!

Silence goes beyond solitude, and without it solitude has little effect. Henri Nouwen observes that "silence is the way to make solitude a reality." But silence is frightening because it strips us as nothing else does, throwing us upon the stark realities of our life. It reminds us of death, which will cut us off from this world and leave only us and God. And in that quiet, what if there turns out to be very little to "just us and God"? Think what it says about the inward emptiness of our lives if we must *always* turn on the tape player or radio to make sure something is happening around us.

Readings

Hearing is said to be the last of our senses to go at death. Sound always strikes deeply and disturbingly into our souls. So, for the sake of our souls, we must seek times to leave our television, radio, tape players, and telephones turned off. We should close off street noises as much as possible. We should try to find *how* quiet we can make our world by making whatever arrangements are necessary.

Silence and solitude do go hand in hand, usually. Just as silence is vital to make solitude real, so is solitude needed to make the discipline of silence complete. Very few of us can be silent in the presence of others.

Yet most of us *live* with others, so how can we practice such a discipline? There are ways. For instance, many have learned to rise for a time in the middle of the night—to break the night's sleep in half in order to experience such silence. In doing so, they find a rich silence that aids their prayer and study without imposing on others. And though it sounds impossible, meaningful progress into silence can be made without solitude, even within family life. And sharing this discipline with those you love may be exactly what is needed.

As with all disciplines, we should approach the practice of silence in a prayerful, experimental attitude, confident that we shall be led into its right use for us. It is a powerful and essential discipline. Only silence will allow us life-transforming concentration upon God. It allows us to hear the gentle God whose only Son "shall not strive, nor cry; neither shall any man hear his voice above the street noise" (Matt. 12:19). It is this God who tells us that "in quietness and trust is your strength" (Isa. 30:15, NAS).

But we must also practice the silence of *not speaking*. James, in his Epistle, tells us that those who seem religious but are unable to bridle their tongues are self-deceived and have a religion that amounts to little (James 1:26). He states that those who do no harm by what they say are perfect and able to direct their whole bodies to do what is right (James 3:2).

Practice in not speaking can at least give us enough control over what we say that our tongues do not "go off" automatically. This discipline provides us with a certain inner distance that gives us time to consider our words fully and the presence of mind to control what we say and when we say it.

Such practice also helps us to listen and to observe, to pay attention to people. How rarely are we ever truly listened to, and how deep is our need to be heard. I wonder how much wrath in human life is a result of not being heard. James says, "Let every man be swift to hear, slow to speak, slow to wrath" (1:19). Yet when the tongue is moving rapidly, it seems wrath will usually be found following it. God gave us two ears and one mouth, it's been said, so that we might listen twice as much as we talk, but even that proportion is far too high on the side of talking.

In witnessing, the role of talking is frequently overemphasized. Does that sound strange? It's true. Silence and especially true listening are often the strongest testimony of our faith. A major problem for Christian evangelism is not getting people to talk, but to silence those who through their continuous chatter reveal a loveless heart devoid of confidence in God. As Miguel de Unamuno says, "We need to pay less attention to what people are trying to tell us, and more to what they tell us without trying."

Why do we insist on talking as much as we do? We run off at the mouth because we are inwardly uneasy about what others think of us. Eberhard Arnold observes: "People who love one another can be silent together." But when we're with those we feel less than secure with, we use words to "adjust" our appearance and elicit their approval. Otherwise, we fear our virtues might not receive adequate appreciation and our shortcomings might not be properly "understood." In not speaking, we resign how we appear (dare we say, how we *are*?) to God. And that is hard. Why should we worry about others' opinions of us when God is for us and Jesus Christ is at his right hand pleading our interests (Rom. 8:31-34)? But we do.

How few of us live with quiet, inner confidence, and yet how many of us desire it. But such inward quiet is a great grace we *can* receive as we practice not talking. And when we have it, we may be able to help others who need it. After we know that confidence, we may, when others come fishing for reassurance and approval, send them to fish in deeper waters for their own inner quiet.

Here's the testimony of a young person entering into the practice of solitude and silence:

Readings

The more I practice this discipline, the more I appreciate the strength of silence. The less I become skeptical and judgmental, the more I learn to accept the things I didn't like about others, the more I accept them as uniquely created in the image of God. The less I talk, the fuller are words spoken at an appropriate time. The more I value others, the more I serve them in small ways, the more I enjoy and celebrate my life. The more I celebrate, the more I realize that God has been giving me wonderful things in my life, the less I worry about my future. I will accept and enjoy what God is continuously giving to me. I think I am beginning to really enjoy God.

Fasting

In fasting, we abstain in some significant way from food and possibly from drink as well. This discipline teaches us a lot about ourselves very quickly. It will certainly prove humiliating to us, as it reveals to us how much our peace depends upon the pleasures of eating. It may also bring to mind how we are using food pleasure to assuage the discomforts caused in our bodies by faithless and unwise living and attitudes—lack of self-worth, meaningless work, purposeless existence, or lack of rest or exercise. If nothing else, though, it will certainly demonstrate how powerful and clever our body is in getting its own way against our strongest resolves.

There are many ways and degrees of fasting. The desert fathers such as St. Antony often subsisted for long periods of time on bread and water—though we must understand that their "bread" was much more substantial than what we have today. Daniel and his friends would not eat the king's meat or drink his wine; they had vegetables and water only (Dan. 1:12). At another time, Daniel "ate no pleasant bread, neither came flesh nor wine in my mouth, neither did I anoint myself at all, till three whole weeks were fulfilled" (10:3). Jesus in the time of his preparation for temptation and ministry seems to have forgone all food for more than a month (Matt. 4).

Fasting confirms our utter dependence upon God by finding in him a source of sustenance beyond food. Through it, we learn by experience that God's word to us is a life substance, that it is not food ("bread") alone that gives life, but also the words that proceed from the mouth of God (Matt. 4:4). We learn that we too have meat to eat that the world does not know about (John 4:32,34). Fasting unto our Lord is therefore feasting—feasting on him and on doing his will.

The Christian poet Edna St. Vincent Millay expresses the discovery of the "other" food in her poem entitled "Feast":

> I drank at every vine.
>
> The last was like the first
>
> I came upon no wine
>
> So wonderful as thirst.
>
> I gnawed at every root.
>
> I ate of every plant.
>
> I came upon no fruit
>
> So wonderful as want.
>
> Feed the grape and the bean
>
> To the vintner and the monger;
>
> I will lie down lean
>
> With my thirst and my hunger.

Hence, when Jesus directs us not to appear distressed and sad when we fast (Matt. 6:16-18), he is not telling us to mislead those around us. He is instead explaining how we will feel—we really will not be sad. We are discovering that life is so much more than meat (Luke 12:33). Our belly is not our god, as it is for others (Phil. 3:19; Rom. 16:18); rather, it is his joyful servant and ours (1 Cor. 6:13).

Actually fasting is one of the more important ways of practicing that self-denial required of *everyone* who would follow Christ (Matt. 16:24). In fasting, we learn how to suffer happily as we feast on God. And it is a good lesson, because in our lives we *will* suffer, no matter what else happens to us. Thomas à Kempis remarks: "Whosoever knows best how to suffer will keep the greatest peace. That man is conqueror of himself, and lord of the world, the friend of Christ, and heir of Heaven."

Persons well used to fasting as a systematic practice will have a clear and constant sense of their

Readings

resources in God. And that will help them endure deprivations of *all* kinds, even to the point of coping with them easily and cheerfully. Kempis again says: "Refrain from gluttony and thou shalt the more easily restrain all the inclinations of the flesh." Fasting teaches temperance or self-control and therefore teaches moderation and restraint with regard to *all* our fundamental drives. Since food has the pervasive place it does in our lives, the effects of fasting will be diffused throughout our personality. In the midst of all our needs and wants, we experience the contentment of the child that has been weaned from its mother's breast (Ps. 131:2). And "Godliness with contentment is great gain" (1 Tim. 6:6).

Fasting, though, is a hard discipline to practice without its consuming all our attention. Yet when we use it as a part of prayer or service, we cannot allow it to do so. When a person chooses fasting as a spiritual discipline, he or she must, then, practice it well enough and often enough to become experienced in it, because only the person who is well habituated to systematic fasting as a discipline can use it effectively as a part of direct service to God, as in special times of prayer or other service.

Copyright 1989
by Dallas Willard, p. 156-175. Used by
permission HarperCollins Publishers, Inc.

*All persons, and especially those with
life—altering conditions, should consult their
physician before beginning a fast.

Readings

From:

"Seeds of Hope"

excerpts from writings of Henri Nouwen
edited by Robert Durback

Words & Silence

1

One of our main problems is that in this chatty society, silence has become a very fearful thing. For most people, silence creates itchiness and nervousness. Many experience silence not as full and rich, but as empty and hollow. For them silence is like a gaping abyss which can swallow them up. As soon as a minister says during a worship service "Let us be silent for a few moments," people tend to become restless and preoccupied with only one thought: "When will this be over?" Imposed silence often creates hostility and resentment. Many ministers who have experimented with silence in their services have soon found out that silence can be more demonic than divine and have quickly picked up the signals that were saying "Please keep talking." It is quite understandable that most forms of ministry avoid silence precisely so as to ward off the anxiety it provokes.
The Way of the Heart

2

Recently I was driving through Los Angeles, and suddenly I had the strange sensation of driving through a huge dictionary. Wherever I looked there were words trying to take my eyes from the road. They said, "Use me, take me, drink me, smell me, touch me, kiss me, sleep with me." In such a world, who can maintain respect for words?

All this is to suggest that words, my own included, have not lost their creative power. Their limitless multiplication has made us lose confidence in words and caused us to think, more often than not, "They are just words."

Teachers speak to students for six, twelve, eighteen, and sometimes twenty-four years. But the students often emerge from the experience with the feeling: "They were just words." Preachers preach their sermons week after week and year after year. But their parishioners remain the same and often think: "They are just words." Politicians, businessmen, ayatollahs, and popes give speeches and make statements "in season out of season," but those who listen say: "They are just words. . . just another distraction."

The result of this is that the main function of the word, which is communication, is no longer realized. The word no longer communicates no longer fosters communion, no longer creates community, and therefore no longer gives life. The word no longer offers trustworthy ground on which people can meet each other and build society.
The Way of the Heart

3

Silence is the home of the word. Silence gives strength and fruitfulness to the word. We can even say that words are meant to disclose the mystery of the silence from which they come.

The Taoist philosopher Chuang Tzu expresess this well in the following way:

> The purpose of a fish trap is to catch fish and when the fish are caught, the trap is forgotten. The purpose of a rabbit snare is to catch rabbits. When the rabbits are caught, the snare is forgotten. the purpose of the word is to convey ideas. When the ideas are grasped, the words are forgotten. Where can I find a man who has forgotten words? He is the one I would like to talk to.

"I would like to talk to the man who has forgotten words." That could have been said by one of the Desert Fathers. For them, the word is the instrument of the present world and silence is the mystery of the future world. If a word is to bear fruit, it must be spoken from the future world into the present world. The Desert Fathers therefore considered their going into the silence of the desert to be a first step into the future world. From that world their words could bear fruit because there they could be filled with the power of God's silence.
The Way of the Heart

Readings

4
God's Silence

Out of eternal silence God spoke the Word, and through this Word created and recreated the world. In the beginning God spoke the land, the sea, and the sky. God spoke the sun, the moon, and the stars. God spoke plants, birds, fish, animals wild and tame. Finally, God spoke man and woman. Then, in the fullness of time, God's Word, through whom all had been created, became flesh and gave power to all who believe to become the children of God. In all this, the Word of God does not break the silence of God, but rather unfolds the immeasurable richness of that silence....

A word with power is a word that comes out of silence. A word that bears fruit is a word that emerges from the silence and returns to it.
The Way of the Heart

Loneliness

One way to express the spiritual crisis of our time is to say that most of us have an address but cannot be found there.
Making All Things New

1

Loneliness is one of the most universal sources of human suffering today. Psychiatrists and clinical psychologists speak about it as the most frequently expressed complaint and the root not only of an increasing number of suicides but also of alcoholism, drug use, different psychosomatic symptoms—such as headaches and stomach and low-back pains—and of a large number of traffic accidents. Children, adolescents, adults, and old people are in growing degree exposed to the contagious disease of loneliness in a world in which a competitive individualism tries to reconcile itself with a culture that speaks about togetherness, unity and community as the ideals to strive for....

The roots of loneliness are very deep and cannot be touched by optimistic advertisement, substitute love images, or social togetherness. They find their food in the suspicion that there is no one who cares and offers love without conditions, and no place where we can be vulnerable without being used.
Reaching Out

2

But what then can we do with our essential aloneness which so often breaks into our consciousness as the experience of a desperate sense of loneliness? What does it mean to say that neither friendship nor love, neither marriage nor community can take that loneliness away? Sometimes illusions are more livable than realities, and why not follow our desire to cry out in loneliness and search for someone whom we can embrace and in whose arms our tense body and mind can find a moment of deep rest and enjoy the momentary experience of being understood and accepted? These are hard questions because they come forth out of our wounded hearts, but they have to be listened to even when they lead to a difficult road. This difficult road is the road of conversion, the conversion from loneliness into solitude. Instead of running away from our loneliness and trying to forget or deny it we have to protect it and turn in into a fruitful solitude. To live a spiritual life we must first find the courage to enter into the desert of our loneliness and to change it by gentle and persistent efforts into a garden of solitude. This requires not only courage but also a strong faith. As hard as it is to believe that the dry, desolate desert can yield endless varieties of flowers, it is equally hard to imagine that our loneliness is hiding unknown beauty. The movement from loneliness to solitude, however, is the beginning of any spiritual life because it is the movement from the restless senses to the restful spirit, from the outward-reaching cravings to the inward-reaching search, from the fearful clinging to the fearless play
Reaching Out

178 Embracing Life Series   Session 12

Readings

Solitude

1

Solitude begins with a time and place for God, and God alone. If we really believe not only that God exists but also that God is actively present in our lives—healing, teaching, and guiding—we need to set aside a time and space to give God our undivided attention. Jesus says, "Go to your private room and, when you have shut your door, pray to your Father who is in the secret place" (Matt. 6.6).

To bring some solitude into our lives is one of the most necessary but also most difficult disciplines. Even though we may have a deep desire for real solitude, we also experience a certain apprehension as we approach that solitary place and time. As soon as we are alone, without people to talk with, books to read, TV to watch, or phone calls to make, an inner chaos opens up in us. This chaos can be so disturbing and so confusing that we can hardly wait to get busy again. Entering a private room and shutting the door, therefore, does not mean that we immediately shut out all our inner doubts, anxieties, fears, bad memories, unresolved conflicts, angry feelings, and impulsive desires. On the contrary, when we have removed our outer distractions, we often find that our inner distractions manifest themselves to us in full force. We often use the outer distractions to shield ourselves from the interior noises. It is thus not surprising that we have a difficult time being alone. The confrontation with our inner conflicts can be too painful for us to endure.

This makes the discipline of solitude all the more important.
Making all Things New

2

Solitude is not a spontaneous response to an occupied and preoccupied life. There are too many reasons not to be alone. Therefore we must begin by carefully planning some solitude. Five or ten minutes a day may be all we can tolerate. Perhaps we are ready for an hour every day, an afternoon every week, a day every month, or a week every year. The amount of time will vary for each person according to temperament, age, job, life-style, and maturity. But we do not take the spiritual life seriously if we do not set aside some time to be with, and listen to, God. We may have to write it in black and white in our daily calendar so that nobody else can take away this period of time.
Making All Things New

3

Once we have committed ourselves to spending time in solitude, we develop an attentiveness to God's voice in us. In the beginning, during the first days, weeks, or even months, we may have the feeling that we are simply wasting our time. Time in solitude may at first seem little more than a time in which we are bombarded by thousands of thoughts and feelings that emerge from hidden areas of our mind. One of the early Christian writers describes the first stage of solitary prayer as the experience of someone who, after years of living with open doors, suddenly decides to shut them. Visitors who used to come and enter the home start pounding on the doors, wondering why they are not allowed to enter. Only when they realize that they are not welcome do they gradually stop coming. This is the experience of anyone who decides to enter into solitude after a life without much spiritual discipline. At first, the many distractions keep presenting themselves. Later, as they receive less and less attention, they slowly withdraw.
Making All Things New

4

When we are not afraid to enter into our own center and to concentrate on the stirrings of our own soul, we come to know that being alive means being loved. This experience tells us that we can love only because we are born out of love, that we can give only because our life is a gift, and that we can make others free only because we are set free by God whose heart is greater than ours. When we have found the anchor places for our lives in our own center, we can be free to let others enter in to the space created for them and allow them to dance their own dance, sing their own song, and speak their own language without fear. Then our presence is no longer threatening and demanding but inviting and liberating. *The Wounded Healer*

All articles used by permission.

Taking your place in the Body of Christ

Session 13

NOTES

> Now you are the body of Christ and each of you is a part of it.
> (1 Corinthians 12:27)
>
> It is by the grace of God that a congregation is permitted to gather visibly in this world to share God's Word and sacrament. Not all Christians receive this blessing. The imprisoned, the sick, the scattered lonely, the proclaimers of the Gospel in heathen lands stand alone. They know that visible fellowship is a blessing. (*Life Together*, Dietrich Bonhoeffer, p. 18)

We cultivate and nourish intimacy with Jesus through our inner devotional life, as we discussed in the last chapter. We looked at the foundational, inward disciplines (the study of Scripture and prayer) in that private life dedicated to becoming like Christ.

The present session focuses on a bigger picture, our public, corporate life together as members of Christ's body—the Church. We will examine the necessity of being knit into the body of Christ and explore how our individual relationship with Jesus flows outward in service. First, however, we will lay a foundation regarding what it means to be a part of the Church.

Session 13   Taking your place in the Body of Christ   **Embracing Life Series**   181

Session 13   Taking your place in the Body of Christ

NOTES

A spiritual reality: our membership

A life-altering condition does not change the fact that you are a vital part of the Body of Christ. God did not design the believer to exist detached from other believers. Whether we like it or not, we are intended to be a giving and receiving part of something much bigger than ourselves.

Being a part of the Body of Christ is not a choice for Christians or a *place* to visit seasonally. When we became Christians, we were instantly knit into the Body by His Holy Spirit making us members. We are Jesus' mouth, eyes, ears, hands, arms, legs and feet on this earth. The Church is the visible expression of Christ's love for and mercy to the world. Because you possess a free will, you choose to *take* your place in the Body or not. The Body suffers if you don't and operates below it's potential. We need one another to become all that God created us to be. We must stand and work together for the Kingdom of God to advance in this world. The Apostle Paul explained to the Ephesian believers:

> ...you are no longer foreigners and aliens, but fellow citizens with God's people and members of God's household, built on the foundation of the apostles and prophets, with Christ Jesus Himself as the chief cornerstone.
> In Him the whole building is joined together and rises to become a holy temple in the Lord. And in Him you too are being built together to become a dwelling in which God lives by His spirit.   (Ephesians 2:19-22)

A spiritual reality: our unity through Jesus

> For He Himself is our peace, who has made the two one and has destroyed the barrier, the dividing wall of hostility.... (Ephesians 2:14)

We are connected through Jesus. We are all joined with Him through the cross and the indwelling of his Holy Spirit. We share His Spirit and are a part of the same spiritual body.

We all arrive at the cross of Jesus in the same condition. We embrace there, not only in unity with the Father but also with each other. (There is always the potential for unity.) In addition to accomplishing our reconciliation with God, the cross made it possible for us to have true relationship with each other.

Taking your place in the Body of Christ   Session 13

The spiritual reality vs. our experience

We may hold expectations or fantasies of what our Christian community experience should look and feel like. Reality quickly teaches us that harmony may not come easily in our relationships with fellow believers. Past woundings by members of the Body, perhaps by a leader or a pastor, may leave us suspicious or wary of reaching out. Churches that say one thing and do another can be disillusioning. Sometimes our biggest obstacle to Christian community is our own ego or pride. Dietrich Bonhoeffer wrote that many come in search of some "extraordinary social experience" (*Life Together*, p. 26) Giving primary place to our own desire for connecting with people, while excluding Jesus, turns a church into a club that can never satisfy our deepest needs.

Although painful, the sooner these illusions are shattered and brought to the cross, the better for all. Bonhoeffer says of our attitude toward the Church, that we must come "...not as demanders but as thankful recipients." (*Life Together*, p. 28)

- Describe your church attendance and involvement, both past and present.

- Are there woundings or disappointments from your past or current involvements with Christians that are still unresolved?

- Describe how your church (leadership and members) has responded to your condition.

Our need for the Body of Christ

Regardless of the experience of some in the Church, God intended the Body of Christ to be a safe and healing place for those struggling with an infirmity or with its continual threat.

The Christian does not depend solely on his or her own resources any longer. There are things that the world cannot offer, money cannot buy, and only God can provide. As you have been discovering, He imparts His grace to you through other members of His Body. He delights in giving these things one-on-one within the fellowship of His Church.

Sustenance now comes from outside our own means, from the words of Christ that alone have the power to bring about true change. God puts his Word into our mouths in order to be spoken to another.

NOTES

Session 13 — Taking your place in the Body of Christ

NOTES

A sheep that separates from the flock is in danger of being devoured. The writer of Hebrews implies there is danger in being a lone ranger as times grow darker, exhorting believers to stay knit into a group so they may stay encouraged in the faith.

> Let us not give up meeting together as some are in the habit of doing, but let us encourage one another—and all the more as you see the day approaching. (Hebrews 10:24-25)

We are, in fact, a part of God's provision for each other. The Apostle Paul's letters are full of his longings for the company of other Christians. And Paul constantly expresses gratitude for the encouragement he has received from the various Christians who were with him.

Our need for healing prayer & the confession of sin

Believers are instructed to participate in two important practices that life in the Church makes possible: healing prayer and the confession of sins.

Praying for one another and hearing each other's confessions require two or more people. They are outward and corporate practices of our public devotional life, part of being in the family of God. They cannot be practiced alone.

> Is anyone among you sick? Let him call for the elders of the church and let them pray over him and anoint him with oil in the name of the Lord. And the prayer offered in faith will make the sick person well; and the Lord will raise him up. If he has sinned he will be forgiven.
>
> Therefore confess your sins to each other and pray for each other, so that you may be healed. The prayer of a righteous man is powerful and effective. (James 5:13-16)

Receiving prayer and the confession of sin are significant because they require making oneself known. James says that prayer for physical healing is initiated by the sick person.

The promise of restoration and healing motivates us to anoint one another with oil (a sign of the Holy Spirit) and pray in faith.

> Our brother stands before us as the sign of the truth and the grace of God. He has been given to us to help us. He hears the confession of our sins in Christ's name. He keeps the secret of our confession as God keeps it. When I go to my brother to confess I am going to God.
> (*Life Together*, Dietrich Bonhoeffer, p. 111-112)

Taking your place in the Body of Christ — Session 13

If sins have been committed, they will be forgiven. Sin is empowered in darkness and isolates one from the Body. Confessed sin loses its power to isolate. The believer reclaims the benefits of fellowship in the congregation as a sinner who lives by grace. Confession of sin is not a legalistic act, but God's provision for the sinners so they can *experience* the freedom of grace and mercy that is already theirs.

Consider the following questions in the group.

- Are you in relationships with Christians with whom you can confide and pray?
- What impact have these relationships—or the lack of them—had in your life?

Servanthood

> ...the Son of Man did not come to be served, but to serve, and give his life as a ransom for many. (Matthew 20:28)

The fullness of our redemption and healing must naturally extend beyond ourselves to include others. What we have received as individual sons and daughters of God is destined to be poured out in service. Service constitutes another outward and public act of devotion, and it requires a group in order to happen.

Service can be expressed in many ways. All the gifts of the Holy Spirit are modes of service (1 Corinthians 12:1-11; Romans 12:3-8).

In the process of caring for the unlovely, ministering to the dispossessed and clothing the outcasts, we act on the grace that is freely given us and share it with others. Only by this exchange can we know the fullness of God, exhibited by Jesus who gave "his life as a ransom for many" (Matthew 20:28). As James said, "Faith without deeds is useless" (James 2:20). The Christian who has no good works is like a stillborn child: so much promise of life, yet none to be seen.

True healing is relational by nature. We can never know who we were created to be until we have a relationship with God our Father. He holds all the answers to the questions about our "true self." Yet it is often in giving ourselves away, in serving others, that some of those answers are revealed and realized.

NOTES

Session 13 — Taking your place in the Body of Christ

NOTES

Personal healing is built upon both our internal reception of God's words of love and hope *and* service to others. Serving others is essential for strength and growth as children of God. In the fifty-eighth chapter of Isaiah, the Lord illustrates this foundational principle of healing. As we extend and invest ourselves in the lives of others in need, we are healed.

> Is this not the kind of fasting I have chosen: to loose the chains of injustice and untie the cords of the yoke to set the oppressed free and break every yoke?
>
> Is it not to share your food with the hungry and to provide the poor wanderer with shelter—when you see him naked to clothe him, and not to turn away from your own flesh and blood?
>
> Then your light will break forth like the dawn, and your healing will quickly appear; then your righteousness will go before you and the glory of the Lord will be your rear guard.
>
> …if you spend yourselves on behalf of the hungry and satisfy the needs of the oppressed, then your light will rise in the darkness, and your night will become like the noonday.
>
> The Lord will guide you always; He will satisfy your needs in a sun-scorched land and will strengthen your frame. You will be a well-watered garden whose springs never fail. (Isaiah 58:6-11)

Our own healing and restoration come as we are willingly involved in the healing and restoration of other people.

Proclamation

> I will sing of the Lord's great love forever; with my mouth will I make your faithfulness known through all generations. I will declare that your love stands firm forever, that you established your faithfulness in heaven itself. (Psalm 89:1-2)
>
> Let the redeemed of the Lord say so—those He redeemed from the hands of the adversary. (Psalm 107:2)

Public, outward devotion to Jesus requires proclamation; we all have a ministry of proclamation. The late Mike Hylton is an example of this. Mike was a husband and father to three and board member of the Southern California Hemophilia Foundation. He tested HIV positive in 1985. Mike said that his ministry was to "…promote an awakening and an awareness of God the Father, God the Son, and God the Holy Spirit within the church and the HIV-infected community" (*He Intends Victory,* p. 129). This may not seem unique or especially flashy. Yet, the contents of his life contained many

Taking your place in the Body of Christ   Session 13

instances of hope, life and redemptive news for the HIV-affected. His testimony, contained in the book, *He Intends Victory*, has now become a ministry tool that benefits many.

Those in *ELS* have valuable, life-giving stories to share. Our testimonies are a powerful means of touching people's hearts and calling spiritual and emotional prisoners out from their helplessness.

The culmination of our weeks together is the presentation of our testimonies. We anticipate the time we can share them with others who are looking for hope.

> They overcame him [Satan] by the blood of the Lamb and the word of their testimony; they did not love their lives so much as to shrink from death. (Revelation 12:11)

Consider for a moment the power of testimony in your life.

- Whose story of redemption deeply affected your own life when you heard it?

- What were the significant events or issues addressed that stirred you the most?

NOTES

Session 13
Taking your place in the Body of Christ

NOTES

SCRIPTURE READINGS

What do the following Scriptures tell us about being in and serving the Body of Christ?
Psalm 145:1-7; 133; Mark 5:1-20; John 4:28-29
Romans 12:4-8; 1 Corinthians 12; Ephesians 4:15-16;
Colossians 3:12-15; 2 Timothy 1:8; Hebrews 10:23-25

RECOMMENDED READING

Life Together by Dietrich Bonhoeffer

The Spirit of the Disciplines by Dallas Willard

He Intends Victory by Dan Wooding

THOUGHTS FOR JOURNALING

Has the church been an agent of healing and encouragement in your experience with a life-altering condition, or has it not? Describe your experience.

If you had the chance to address your church, how would you challenge them to minister to people with needs like your own?

Did the teaching, discussion and Scripture readings inspire you toward greater participation in the church?
How so?

Embracing Life Series: International Copyright © 1998 by Embracing Life Ministries. All Rights Reserved

Readings

From:

"Life Together"

by Dietrich Bonhoeffer

Excerpt from Chapter 5: Confession and Communion

"Confess your faults one to another" (Jas. 5:16). He who is alone with his sin is utterly alone. It may be that Christians, notwithstanding corporate worship, common prayer, and all their fellowship in service, may still be left to their loneliness. The final break-through to fellowship does not occur, because, though they have fellowship with one another as believers and as devout people, they do not have fellowship as the undevout, as sinners. The pious fellowship permits no one to be a sinner. So everybody must conceal his sin from himself and from the fellowship. We dare not be sinners. Many Christians are unthinkably horrified when a real sinner is suddenly discovered among the righteous. So we remain alone with our sin, living in lies and hypocrisy. The fact is that we *are* sinners!

But it is the grace of the Gospel, which is so hard for the pious to understand, that it confronts us with the truth and says: You are a sinner, a great, desperate sinner; now come, as the sinner that you are, to God who loves you. He wants you as you are; He does not want anything from you, a sacrifice, a work; He wants you alone. "My son, give me thine heart" (Prov. 23:26) God has come to you to save the sinner. Be glad! This message is liberation through truth. You can hide nothing from God. The mask you wear before men will do you no good before Him. He wants to see you as you are, He wants to be gracious to you. You do not have to go on lying to yourself and your brothers, as if you were without sin; you can dare to be a sinner. Thank God for that; He loves the sinner but He hates sin.

Christ became our Brother in the flesh in order that we might believe in him. In him the love of God came to the sinner. Through him men could be sinners and only so could they be helped. All sham was ended in the presence of Christ. The misery of the sinner and the mercy of God—this was the truth of the Gospel in Jesus Christ. It was in this truth that his Church was to live. Therefore, he gave his followers the authority to hear the confession of sin and to forgive sin in his name. "Whosoever sins ye remit, they are remitted unto them; and whosoever sins ye retain, they are retained" (John 20:23).

When he did that Christ made the Church, and in it our brother, a blessing to us. Now our brother stands in Christ's stead. Before him I need no longer to dissemble. Before him alone in the whole world I dare to be the sinner that I am; here the truth of Jesus Christ and his mercy rules. Christ became our Brother in order to help us. Through him our brother has become Christ for us in the power and authority of the commission Christ has given to him. Our brother stands before us as the sign of the truth and the grace of God. He has been given to us to help us. He hears the confession of our sins in Christ's stead and forgives our sins in Christ's name. He keeps the secret of our confession as God keeps it. When I go to my brother to confess, I am going to God.

So in the Christian community when the call to brotherly confession and forgiveness goes forth it is a call to the great grace of God in the Church.

Breaking Through to Community

In confession the break-through to community takes place. Sin demands to have a man by himself. It withdraws him from the community. The more isolated a person is, the more destructive will be the power of sin over him, and the more deeply he becomes involved in it, the more disastrous is his isolation. Sin wants to remain unknown. It shuns the light. In the darkness of the unexpressed it poisons the whole being of a person. This can happen even in the midst of a pious community. In confession the light of the Gospel breaks into the darkness and seclusion of the heart. The sin must be brought into the light. The unexpressed must be openly spoken and acknowledged. All that is secret and hidden is made manifest. It is a hard struggle until the sin is openly admitted. But God breaks gates of brass and bars of iron (Ps. 107:16).

Readings

Since the confession of sin is made in the presence of a Christian brother, the last stronghold of self-justification is abandoned. The sinner surrenders; he gives up all his evil. He gives his heart to God, and he finds the forgiveness of all his sin in the fellowship of Jesus Christ and his brother. The expressed, acknowledged sin has lost all its power. It has been revealed and judged as sin. It can no longer tear the fellowship asunder. Now the fellowship bears the sin of the brother. He is no longer alone with his evil for he has cast off his sin in confession and handed it over to God. It has been taken away from him. Now he stands in the fellowship of sinners who live by the grace of God in the Cross of Jesus Christ. Now he can be a sinner and still enjoy the grace of God. He can confess his sins and in this very act find fellowship for the first time. The sin concealed separated him from the fellowship, made all his apparent fellowship a sham; the sin confessed has helped him to find true fellowship with the brethren in Jesus Christ.

Moreover, what we have said applies solely to confession between two Christians. A confession of sin in the presence of all the members of the congregation is not required to restore one to fellowship with the whole congregation. I meet the whole congregation in the one brother to whom I confess my sins and who forgives my sins. In the fellowship I find with this one brother I have already found fellowship with the whole congregation. In this matter no one acts in his own name nor by his own authority, but by the commission of Jesus Christ. This commission is given to the whole congregation and the individual is called merely to exercise it for the congregation. If a Christian is in the fellowship of confession with a brother he will never be alone again, anywhere.

Breaking Through to the Cross

In confession occurs the break-through to the Cross. The root of all sin is pride, *superbia*. I want to be my own law, I have a right to my self, my hatred and my desires, my life and my death. The mind and flesh of man are set on fire by pride; for it is precisely in his wickedness that man wants to be as God. Confession in the presence of a brother is the profoundest kind of humiliation. It hurts, it cuts a man down, it is a dreadful blow to pride. To stand there before a brother as a sinner is an ignominy that is almost unbearable. In the confession of concrete sins the old man dies a painful, shameful death before the eyes of a brother. Because this humiliation is so hard we continually scheme to evade confessing to a brother. Our eyes are so blinded that they no longer see the promise and the glory in such abasement.

It was none other than Jesus Christ himself who suffered the scandalous, public death of a sinner in our stead. He was not ashamed to be crucified for us as an evildoer. It is nothing else but our fellowship with Jesus Christ that leads us to the ignominious dying that comes in confession, in order that we may in truth share in his Cross. The Cross of Jesus Christ destroys all pride. We cannot find the Cross of Jesus if we shrink from going to the place where it is to be found, namely, the public death of the sinner. And we refuse to bear the Cross when we are ashamed to take upon ourselves the shameful death of the sinner in confession. In confession we break through to the true fellowship of the Cross of Jesus Christ, in confession we affirm and accept our cross. In the deep mental and physical pain of humiliation before a brother— which means, before God—we experience the Cross of Jesus as our rescue and salvation. The old man dies, but it is God who has conquered him. Now we share in the resurrection of Christ and eternal life.

Breaking Through to New Life

In confession the break-through to new life occurs. Where sin is hated, admitted, and forgiven, there the break with the past is made. "Old things are passed away." But where there is a break with sin, there is conversion. Confession is conversion. "Behold, all things are become new" (2 Cor. 5,17). Christ has made a new beginning with us.

As the first disciples left all and followed when Jesus called, so in confession the Christian gives up all and follows. Confession is discipleship. Life with Jesus Christ and his community has begun. "He that covereth his sins shall not prosper: but whoso confesseth and forsaketh them shall have mercy" (Prov. 28:13). In confession the Christian begins to forsake his sins. Their dominion is broken. From now on the Christian wins victory after victory.

What happened to us in baptism is bestowed upon as anew in confession. We are delivered out of

Readings

darkness into the kingdom of Jesus Christ. That is joyful news. Confession is the renewal of the joy of baptism. "Weeping may endure for a night, but joy cometh in the morning" (Ps. 30:5).

Breaking Through to Certainty

In confession a man breaks through to certainty. Why is it that it is often easier for us to confess our sins to God than to a brother? God is holy and sinless, He is a just judge of evil and the enemy of all disobedience. But a brother is sinful as we are. He knows from his own experience the dark night of secret sin. Why should we not find it easier to go to a brother than to the holy God? But if we do, we must ask ourselves whether we have not often been deceiving ourselves with our confession of sin to God, whether we have not rather been confessing our sins to ourselves and also granting ourselves absolution. And is not the reason perhaps for our countless relapses and the feebleness of our Christian obedience to be found precisely in the fact that we are living on self-forgiveness and not a real forgiveness? Self-forgiveness can never lead to a breach with sin; this can be accomplished only by the judging and pardoning Word of God itself.

Who can give us the certainty that, in the confession and the forgiveness of our sins, we are not dealing with ourselves but with the living God? God gives us this certainty through our brother. Our brother breaks the circle of self-deception. A man who confesses his sins in the presence of a brother knows that he is no longer alone with himself; he experiences the presence of God in the reality of the other person. As long as I am by myself in the confession of my sins everything remains in the dark, but in the presence of a brother the sin has to be brought into the light. But since the sin must come to light some time, it is better that it happens today between me and my brother, rather than on the last day in the piercing light of the final judgment. It is a mercy that we can confess our sins to a brother. Such grace spares us the terrors of the last judgment.

Our brother has been given me that even here and now I may be made certain through him of the reality of God in His judgment and His grace. As the open confession of my sins to a brother insures me against self-deception, so, too, the assurance of forgiveness becomes fully certain to me only when it is spoken by a brother in the name of God. Mutual, brotherly confession is given to us by God in order that we may be sure of divine forgiveness.

But it is precisely for the sake of this certainty that confession should deal with *concrete* sins. People usually are satisfied when they make a general confession. But one experiences the utter perdition and corruption of human nature, in so far as this ever enters into experience at all, when one sees his own specific sins. Self-examination on the basis of all Ten Commandments will therefore be the right preparation for confession. Otherwise it might happen that one could still be a hypocrite even in confessing to a brother and thus miss the good of the confession. Jesus dealt with people whose sins were obvious, with publicans and harlots. They knew why they needed forgiveness, and they received it as forgiveness of their specific sins. Blind Bartimaeus was asked by Jesus: What do you want me to do for you? Before confession we must have a clear answer to this question. In confession we, too, receive the forgiveness of the particular sins which are here brought to light, and by this very token the forgiveness of all our sins, known and unknown.

Does all this mean that confession to a brother is a divine law? No, confession is not a law, it is an offer of divine help for the sinner. It is possible that a person may by God's grace break through to certainty, new life, the Cross, and fellowship without benefit of confession to a brother. It is possible that a person may never know what it is to doubt his own forgiveness and despair of his own confession of sin, that he may be given everything in his own private confession to God. We have spoken here for those who cannot make this assertion. Luther himself was one of those for whom the Christian life was unthinkable without mutual, brotherly confession. In the *Large Catechism* he said: "Therefore when I admonish you to confession I am admonishing you to be a Christian." Those who, despite all their seeking and trying, cannot find the great joy of fellowship, the Cross, the new life, and certainty should be shown the blessing that God offers us in mutual confession. Confession is within the liberty of the Christian. Who can refuse, without suffering loss, a help that God has deemed it necessary to offer?

Readings

To Whom Confess?

To whom shall we make confession? According to Jesus' promise, every Christian brother can hear the confession of another. But will he understand? May he not be so far above us in his Christian life that he would only turn away from us with no understanding of our personal sins?

Anybody who lives beneath the Cross and who has discerned in the Cross of Jesus the utter wickedness of all men and of his own heart will find that there is no sin that can ever be alien to him. Anybody who has once been horrified by the dreadfulness of his own sin that nailed Jesus to the Cross will no longer be horrified by even the rankest sins of a brother. Looking at the Cross of Jesus, he knows the human heart. He knows how utterly lost it is in sin and weakness, how it goes astray in the ways of sin, and he also knows that it is accepted in grace and mercy. Only the brother under the Cross can hear a confession.

It is not experience of life but experience of the Cross that makes one a worthy hearer of confessions. The most experienced psychologist or observer of human nature knows infinitely less of the human heart than the simplest Christian who lives beneath the Cross of Jesus. The greatest psychological insight, ability and experience cannot grasp this one thing: what sin is. Worldly wisdom knows what distress and weakness and failure are, but it does not know the godlessness of men. And so it also does not know that man is destroyed only by his sin and can be healed only by forgiveness. Only the Christian knows this. In the presence of a psychiatrist I can only be a sick man; in the presence of a Christian brother I can dare to be a sinner. The psychiatrist must first search my heart and yet he never plumbs its ultimate depth. The Christian brother knows when I come to him: here is a sinner like myself, a godless man who wants to confess and yearns for God's forgiveness. The psychiatrist views me as if there were no God. The brother views me as I am before the judging and merciful God in the Cross of Jesus Christ. It is not lack of psychological knowledge but lack of love for the crucified Jesus Christ that makes us so poor and inefficient in brotherly confession.

In daily, earnest living with the Cross of Christ the Christian loses the spirit of human censoriousness on the one hand and weak indulgence on the other, and he receives the spirit of divine severity and divine love. The death of the sinner before God and life that comes out of that death through grace become for him a daily reality. So he loves the brothers with the merciful love of God that leads the feath of the sinner to the life of the child of God. Who can hear our confession? He who himself lives beneath the Cross. Wherever the message concerning the Crucified is a vital, living thing, there brotherly confession will also avail.

Copyright 1954 by Harper & Brothers
renewed by Itelen S. Doberstein, p. 110-118.
Used by permission of HarperCollins
Publishers, Inc.

Readings

From:

"The Spirit of the Disciplines"

by Dallas Willard

pertinent sections excerpted from
Ch. 9: Some Main Disciplines for Spiritual Life:
The Disciplines of Engagement

> Arise, take up thy bed, and go thy way....
> (Mark 2:11)

Service

In service we engage our goods and strength in the active promotion of the good of others and the causes of God in our world. Here we recall an important distinction. Not every act that may be done as a discipline *need* be done as a discipline. I will often be able to serve another simply as an act of love and righteousness, without regard to how it may enhance my abilities to follow Christ. There certainly is nothing wrong with that, and it may, incidentally, strengthen me spiritually as well. But I may also serve another to train myself away from arrogance, possessiveness, envy, resentment, or covetousness. In that case, my service is undertaken as a discipline for the spiritual life.

Such discipline is very useful for those Christians who find themselves—as most of us by necessity must—in the "lower" position in society, at work, and in the church. It alone can train us in habits of loving service to others and free us from resentment, enabling us in faith to enjoy our position and work because of its exhalted meaning before God.

Paradoxically perhaps, service is the high road to freedom from bondage to other people. In it, as Paul realized, we cease to be "menpleasers" and "eyeservants," for we are acting unto God in our lowliest deeds: "Slaves, obey in everything those who are your earthly masters, not with eyeservice, as menpleasers, but in singleness of heart, fearing the Lord. Whatever your task, work heartily, as serving the Lord and not men, knowing that from the Lord you will receive the inheritance as your reward; you are serving the Lord Christ " (Col. 3:22-24, RSV).

Can this be applied by the mother of six who must leave her little children uncared for in a derelict neighborhood to support them by scrubbing office floors at night? Can it be applied by the refugee from Central America who pushes his ice cream cart around the neighborhood, ringing his bell as he goes? Yes it can be, if they have heard and received from the heart the gospel of the Kingdom of God—though this provides not the least shadow of an excuse for others failing to do all they reasonably can to help them. And, truly, it must be so applied by them. For they are where they are, and God has yet to bless anyone except where they are. Needless to say, only clear teaching and example, with much practice in the discipline of service, can make us strong here.

But I believe the discipline of service is even more important for Christians who find themselves in positions of influence, power, and leadership. To live as a servant while fulfilling socially important roles is one of the greatest challenges any disciple ever faces. It is made all the harder because the church does not give special training to persons engaged in these roles and foolishly follows the world by regarding such people as "having it made," possibly even considering them qualified to speak as authorities in the spiritual life because of their success in the world.

Some of the most important things Jesus had to say concerned the manner in which leaders were to live:

> Ye know that the princes of the Gentiles exercise dominion over them, and they that are great exercise authority upon them. But it shall not be so among you: but whosoever will be chief among you, let him be your servant. Even as the Son of man came not to be ministered unto, but to minister, and to give his life a ransom for many.
>
> (Matt. 20:25-28).

Readings

We misunderstand this passage if we read it merely as instructions on how to become great. It is, rather, a statement on how those who *are* great are to behave. To be "great" and to live as a servant is one of the most difficult of spiritual attainments. But it is also the pattern of life for which this bruised and aching world waits and without which it will never manage a decent existence. Those who would live this pattern must attain it through the discipline of service in the power of God, for that alone will train them to exercise great power without corrupting their souls. It is for this reason that Jesus told his disciples to wash one another's feet and set them an example (John 13:14). But where are our seminary courses that would teach leaders in all areas of life—even the church—how to do this and accustom them to it as the fine and easy thing to do?

Service to others in the spirit of Jesus allows us the freedom of a humility that carries no burdens of "appearance." It lets us be what we are—simply a particularly lively piece of clay who, as servant of God, happens to be here now with the ability to do this good and needful thing for that other bit of clay there. The experience of active love freed up and flowing by faith through us on such occasions will safeguard us from innumerable pitfalls of the spiritual life.

We must, then, strive to meet all persons who cross our path with openness to service for them—not, of course, in any anxious, obsequious, overly solicitous manner, but with ease and confidence born of our vision of our lives together in the hands of God.

Fellowship

In fellowship we engage in common activities of worship, study, prayer, celebration, and service with other disciples. This may involve assembling ourselves together in a large group or meeting with only a few. Personalities united can contain more of God and sustain the force of his greater presence much better than scattered individuals. The fire of God kindles higher as the brands are heaped together and each is warmed by the other's flame. The members of the body must be in con*tact* if they are to sustain and be sustained by each other. Christian redemption is not devised to be a solitary thing, though each individual of course has a unique and direct relationship with God, and God alone is his or her Lord and Judge. But The Life is one that requires some regular and profound conjunction with others who share it. It is greatly diminished when that is lacking.

The diverse gifts or graces of the Spirit—all of which are needed in some measure by each person from time to time—are distributed among the separate members of the body of Christ, the church. The unity of the body rightly functioning is thus guaranteed by the people reciprocating in needs and ministries. There are no "oughts" or "shoulds" or "won't-you-pleases" about this. It is just a matter of how things actually work in the new life:

> Each man is given his gift by the Spirit that he may use it for the common good. One man's gift by the Spirit is to speak with wisdom, another's to speak with knowledge. The same Spirit gives to another man faith, to another the ability to heal, to another the power to do great deeds. The same Spirit gives to another man the gift of preaching the word of God, to another the ability to discriminate in spiritual matters, to another speech in different tongues and to yet another the power to interpret the tongues. Behind all these gifts is the operation of the same Spirit, who distributes to each individual as he wills.

(1 Cor. 12:7-11, Phillips).

Because of this reciprocal nature within the corporate body of Christ, fellowship is required to allow realization of a joyous and sustained level of life in Christ that is normally impossible to attain by all our individual effort, no matter how vigorous and sustained. In it we receive the ministry of all the graces of the Spirit to the church.

Confession

Confession is a discipline that functions within fellowship. In it we let trusted others know our deepest weaknesses and failures. This will nourish our faith in God's provision for our needs through his people, our sense of being loved, and our humility before our brothers and sisters. Thus we let some friends in Christ know who we really are, not holding

194 **Embracing Life Series** Session 13

Readings

back anything important, but, ideally, allowing complete transparency. We lay down the burden of hiding and pretending, which normally takes up such a dreadful amount of human energy. We engage and are engaged by others in the most profound depths of the soul.

The New Testament church seems to have assumed that if a brother or sister had some sickness or other affliction, it might have been due to a sin that was separating that person from the full flow of redeeming life. So in the Letter of James we are told: "Confess your faults one to another, and pray one for another, that ye may be healed. The effectual fervent prayer of a righteous man availeth much" (5:16). We must accept the fact that unconfessed sin is a special kind of burden or obstruction in the psychological as well as the physical realities of the believer's life. The discipline of confession and absolution removes that burden.

But confession also helps us to avoid sin. The proverb tells us that "He that covereth his sins shall not prosper: but whoso confesseth and forsaketh them shall have mercy" (Prov. 28:13). The "confesseth" obviously is an aid to the "forsaketh," for persisting in sin within a close community—not to mention the fellowship of a transparent body of Christ—is unsupportable unless it is hidden. It is said confession is good for the soul but bad for the reputation, and a bad reputation makes life more difficult in relation to those close to us, we all know. But closeness and confession force out evildoing. Nothing is more supportive of right behavior than open truth.

And the baring of the soul to a mature friend in Christ or to a qualified minister enables such friends to pray for specific problems and to do those things that may be most helpful and redemptive to the one confessing. Confession alone makes *deep* fellowship possible, and the lack of it explains much of the superficial quality so commonly found in our church associations. What, though, makes confession bearable? Fellowship. There is an essential reciprocity between these two disciplines.

Where there is confession within a close community, *restitution* cannot be omitted and it too serves as a powerful discipline. It is difficult not to rectify wrong done once it is confessed and known widely. Of course not all sin calls for restitution. But it is unthinkable that I should sincerely confess to my brother or sister that I have stolen a purse or harmed a reputation and then blithely go my way without trying to make some restoration for the loss.

In general, our own innate integrity, a force within our personality, *requires* such restitution. This often is not a pleasant experience, but it actually strengthens us in our will to do the right thing. Confession then is one of the most powerful of the disciplines for the spiritual life. But it may be easily abused, and for its effective use it requires considerable experience and maturity, both in the individual concerned and in the leadership of the group—which leads us to our final discipline.

Submission

The highest level of fellowship—involving humility, complete honesty, transparency, and at times confession and restitution—is sustained by the discipline of submission.

In the letter to the Hebrews we read: "Obey them that have the rule over you, and submit yourselves: for they watch for your souls, as they that must give account, that they may do it with joy and not with grief" (13:7). In 1 Peter those older in The Way are told to take the oversight of the flock of God, not by being forced to do so and not as lords over God's heritage, but as examples to the flock (5:2-3). The younger are then told to submit themselves to this gentle oversight by the elders, and all are caught up together as a community of mutual servants in mutual submission: "Yea, all of you be subject one to another, and be clothed with humility: for God resisteth the proud and giveth grace to the humble" (5:5; see also Eph. 5:21).

The order in the redemptive community here implied obviously is not a matter of an iron hierarchy in which unwilling souls are crushed and driven. Instead, it functions in the power of truth and mercy inhabiting mature personalities, being the expression of a kingdom not of this world (John 18:36) —but truly a kingdom nonetheless. Otherwise the church would revert to the model of purely human government. Unfortunately, we see this actually happening in certain misguided attempts at Christian community. The Way of Jesus knows no submission outside the context of mutual

Readings

submission of all to all (Eph. 5:21, Phil. 2:3)

Submission, though, is a call for help to those recognized as able to give it because of their depth of experience and Christlikeness—because they truly are "elder" in The Way. In submission we engage the experience of those in our fellowship who are qualified to direct our efforts in growth and who then add the weight of their wise authority on the side of our willing spirit to help us do the things we would like to do and refrain from the things we don't want to do. They oversee the godly order in our souls as well as in our fellowship and in the surrounding body of Christ.

But these "wise" people will not be looking at themselves as "leaders" actually. Their being examples we submit to is but one aspect of their submission to servanthood. It is a case of true leadership, not of the drivership that so often prevails in secular society and in some church groups where those "in control" do not know of an alternative. How truly blessed is this free "order that is in beatitude." Here are the beginnings of that kingdom "cut out without hands" (Dan. 2:34), which will in time fill the earth and make the kingdoms of this world into the kingdom of our God and of his Christ!

Copyright 1989, p. 182-191.
Used by permission of HarperCollins Publishers, Inc.

Readings

Testimony of Jonathan Hunter

"God sets the lonely in families..."

Psalm 68:6

Recalling the early, formative years of my life brings back a flood of memories awash with the loneliness that pervaded our home. My father, mother and brother (for a short time) were present though family cohesion was not. We all were lonely at heart, but for different reasons. The Lord changed my heart and filled it with hope at age 29 when I became one of His own through His Spirit of adoption. Finally I found the unconditional love and sense of belonging I had always longed for—in the family of Christ.

My parents tried hard to keep things together when I was growing up but everything always seemed to come unravelled in our home. As for God, well, there were sporadic occasions when we attended a local Episcopal church, but those visits ended by the time I reached my teens.

My father's alcoholism was obvious early on; I knew he was out of control by the time I was six or seven. Night after night, into the early morning hours, my parents would argue with each other about their discontent. During those sleepless nights of confusion, I would make vows never to be like my father, never to get married, never to have kids and put them through what I experienced. I longed for a stable family life but feared it just the same.

My mother did her best to make up for my father's sorry state and unemployment. It was clear, however, that she was neither comfortable with, nor capable of taking up his slack. In time, being the sole bread winner took its toll on her health. At the age of 46, resigned to the ravages of cancer throughout her body, she just gave up and died, leaving behind a mere shell of a husband and father.

The lack of bonding with my father and an emotionally conflicted mother helped produce a lot of the insecurity I felt about my gender identity. By the time I got to high school I was experiencing a tumult of confusion inside. I experimented sexually with girls—mimicking what the other guys were doing—all the while trying to quell the growing homosexual feelings which were demanding attention; their increasing insistence frightened me.

After graduating, I set off for a university in Florida—as different a place as I could think of from the staid Philadelphia suburbs I had grown up in. At last, I thought, I can get a whole new start.

In my freshman year, I developed my first male crush which threw me into even greater confusion. By my second year (1969) I was into "recreational drugs." Drugs were to become the means by which I abandoned any sexual inhibitions. By summer of that year I had my first real homosexual encounter with a friend while we were high on drugs. We swore to secrecy—a promise he could keep for only a few short weeks.

After my sophomore year, I moved to New York to pursue acting. I soon got a job in a play which eventually toured overseas and which led me to move to Paris to get into the film business. Two intense years of drugs, sexual chaos and not much work, brought me back to the states—Hollywood—to further my career.

L.A. offered lots of things—stardom wasn't one of them! I delved into heavier drugs and immersed myself in the gay lifestlye. It wasn't long before I bought the prevailing idea that I must have been born gay, though I never felt terribly comfortable with the label. The all-male social events I went to reeked of artificiality and narcissism. The prevailing attitude seemed to be: "We can't get acceptance in the heterosexual world, so let's create one of our own where we can do whatever we want." The sexual idolatry in that environment was powerful and intimidating. In truth, I was unfaithful as the next one, always looking over someone's shoulder hoping to spot that non-existent "perfect" guy. Relationships, some lasting a month, some a year or more, always left me more dissatisfied and lonelier than before. I partied hard and heavy, sometimes staying up on drugs two days at a time. The stardom I strived for as an actor had devolved to waiting on tables just to earn money to buy drugs for the weekend. I was desperate and clearly out of control.

Readings

Finally, everything came crashing down on December 14, 1979 when I had an accidental overdose. Days later, out of the hospital, I realized God had given me a second chance to live. I became determined to find out who this God was who had rescued me from the precipice of death.

Gratefully, my brother and his wife—both Christians—were only too willing to take me with them to church. Their obvious concern and compassion for my well being—in spite of my ravings about homophobic Christians—convinced me that there were Christians that really cared. In short, they loved me into the Kingdom. Exactly a year to the day of my overdose, I was baptized in the Pacific Ocean, a new member of the Body of Christ.

Leaving drugs behind wasn't difficult for me as a Christian, but homosexuality was another thing altogether. Though I had read in my church bulletin about an ex-gay group called Desert Stream, I blew them off thinking they were probably just a bunch of pious losers. Not in my remotest thoughts could I have imagined that five years later I would be on their staff!

I travelled a lot over the next few years, acting and modeling. I had one six-month relationship with a man that finally ended in frustration. In 1981 I made the decision to remain abstinent, to give myself time to get to know *the* new man in my life, Jesus Christ.

Over the next three years, two things happened that became catalysts for healing: receiving Colin Cook's tape series, *Steps Out of Homosexuality* and meeting Andy Comiskey at the Vineyard Christian Fellowship. Through those tapes I came to understand that I was a heterosexual who struggled homosexually. Through my relationship with Andy, God brought me a mentor and friend who encouraged, guided and challenged me on to wholeness in Christ.

In the fall of 1984, I went through *Living Waters*, the sexual and relational healing program offered by Desert Stream Ministries. Reveling in the new-found vision I had for gender wholeness, I was irrepressible when it came to sharing my discovery with gay friends. One of them ended up being the brother of a former partner of mine. He had AIDS.

Though I knew next to nothing about the disease, I was able to share with him my friendship with Jesus, introducing him to the hope I already knew. After months of prayer, he received Jesus Christ as his Lord and Savior just weeks before he died. Our shared experience convinced me that Jesus was the anecdote to the hopelessness surrounding people with AIDS. It was also the beginning of what soon became the AIDS Resource Ministry and eventually, Embracing Life.

In 1985, free and anonymous AIDS testing became available. I had been abstinent and healthy for four years, so, when I went to get tested I was sure that I was free from infection. However, I was still quite ignorant about how the virus worked. When the results came back as sero-positive, I was shocked. The stark realities of life—the consequences of my promiscuous past and my naive concept of God—leveled me with disappointment and disillusionment.

Thankfully, Christian friends were present for me that day. Their unflagging faith and prayers would continue to buoy me up and give me the lifeline I needed to stay emotionally afloat after getting that depressing news. The hopelessness of AIDS never had a chance to take hold because of their steadfast spirit. They stood with me on the promises of God, demonstrating His love for me by their presence.

My faith continued to grow as the Lord delivered me from countless circumstances—spiritually and emotionally—that could have driven me to despair. When I read Paul's words in 2 Corinthians 1, I totally related to them: "Indeed in our hearts we felt the sentence of death. But this happened that we might not rely on ourselves but on God, who raises the dead. He has delivered us from such a deadly peril, and he will deliver us" (vs.9,10). Certainly my trials were never as severe as Paul's, but my deliverance from the dread of death was just as real.

Over the intervening years, I have shared my testimony in hundreds of churches, schools and meetings all around the world. To this day, I remain living proof of God's sustaining love and that becoming HIV positive is not a death sentence. My prayer is that this offers hope to those dealing with all kinds of life-altering conditions. Only Jesus Christ can deliver us from the spirit of death and give us abundant life in return. In John 10:10 Jesus says: "I came that they might have life and have it to the full." The ministry of Embracing Life is the product of

Readings

God's faithfulness and generosity in fulfilling his word.

I have encountered many affected by emotional and physical conditions who have amazing testimonies of the healing, restorative power of Jesus Christ. And our stories are not yet over. As C.S. Lewis puts it: "We are not metaphorically but in very truth, a Divine work of art, something that God is making and therefore something with which He will not be satisfied until it has a certain character." That character, of course, is Christ-likeness–becoming true image-bearers of God.

The "author and finisher of our faith" has more in store, more life to reveal, much of it through brothers and sisters in Christ who are right in our midst. He has placed us in a family of "art" restorers who have the skills necessary to restore us—prayer. What Paul writes is true indeed:

"He has delivered us from such a deadly peril, and he will deliver us. On him we have set our hope that he will continue to deliver us, as you help us by your prayers. Then many will give thanks on our behalf for the gracious favor granted us in answer to the prayers of many" (2 Corinthians 1:10,11).

What a friend and family we can have in Jesus Christ our Lord!

Bibliography

David Atkinson, *Jesus Lamb of God*, London, UK: Society for Promoting Christian Knowledge, 1996.

Mike Bickle, *Passion for Jesus*, Lake Mary, FL: Creation House, 1993.

Donald Bloesch, *The Evangelical Dictionary of Theology*, Walter Ewell, ed. Grand Rapids, MI: Baker Book House Company, 1984.

Dietrich Bonhoeffer, *Life Together*, New York, NY: HarperSanFrancisco, 1954.

John Bradshaw, *Healing the Shame that Binds You*, Deerfield Beach, FL: Health Communications, Inc., 1988.

Paul Brand and Philip Yancey, *Fearfully and Wonderfully Made*, Grand Rapids, MI: Zondervan Publishing House, 1980.

Paul Brand and Philip Yancey, *In His Image*, Grand Rapids, MI: Zondervan Publishing House, 1984.

Brother Lawrence and Frank Laubach, *Practicing the Presence of God*, Sargent, GA: The SeedSowers Publishing Company, 1978.

Oswald Chambers, *My Utmost for His Highest*, Uhrichsville, OH: Barbour Publishing Inc., 1935.

Andrew Comiskey, *Living Waters Guidebook*, Anaheim, CA: Desert Stream Ministries, 1996, previous edition, 1988.

Debra Jarvis, *HIV Positive: Living with AIDS*, Batavia, IL: Lion Publishing, 1990.

Thomas Keating, *Intimacy with God*, New York, NY: The Crossroad Publishing Company, 1996.

C.S. Lewis, *Miracles*, New York, NY: Macmillian, 1947.

C.S. Lewis, *The Problem of Pain*, New York, NY: Macmillian, 1966.

C.S. Lewis, *The Screwtape Letters*, New York, NY: Macmillian, 1982 revised edition.

Bibliography

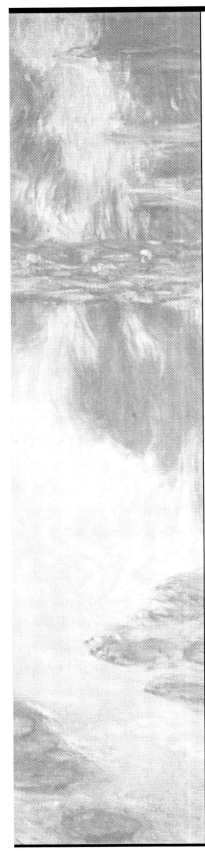

Craig Lockwood, *SALT (Sex Addicts Learning Trust) Program* unpublished notes, Anaheim Vineyard Christian Fellowship, CA: 1997.

Marcy Fenton, Jefferey Bowman, *Making Meds Easier to Take*, Positive Living, Aids Project Los Angeles, CA Issue: Sept 1996.

Francis Frangipane, *The Three Battlegrounds*, Cedar Rapids, IA: Arrow Publications, 1989.

Gerald G. May, MD, *Addiction and Grace*, New York, NY: HarperSanFrancisco, 1988.

Robert McGee, *The Search for Significance*, Houston, TX: Rapha Publishing, 1987.

Henri J.M. Nouwen, *Making All Things New*, New York, NY: HarperCollins, 1981.

Henri J.M. Nouwen, *Seeds of Hope: A Henri Nouwen Reader*, edited by Robert Durback, New York, NY: Bantam Books, 1989.

Henri J.M. Nouwen, *Reaching Out*, New York: Bantam Doubleday Dell Publishing Group, Inc., 1975.

Henri J.M. Nouwen, *The Inner Voice of Love*, New York, NY: Doubleday, 1996.

Henri J.M. Nouwen, *The Road to Daybreak*, New York, NY: Image Books, 1988.

Henri J.M. Nouwen, *The Way of the Heart*, New York, NY: HarperCollins, 1981.

Henri J.M. Nouwen, *The Wounded Healer*, New York, NY: Bantam Doubleday Dell Publishing Group, Inc., 1972.

Dave and Linda Olson, *Listening Prayer, My Sheep Hear My Voice*, El Cajon, CA: Listening Prayer Ministries, 1996.

Leanne Payne, *Listening Prayer*, Grand Rapids, MI: Baker Books, 1994.

Leanne Payne, *Restoring the Christian Soul*, Grand Rapids: MI, Baker Book House Company, 1991.

Agnes Sanford, *The Healing Light*, Minneapolis: MN, Macalester Park Publishing Company, 1947.

Bibliography

David A. Seamands, *Putting Away Childish Things*, Wheaton, IL: Scripture Press, 1982.

Lewis B. Smedes, *Forgive and Forget*, San Francisco, CA: Harper & Row, Publishers, 1984.

John Stott, *The Cross of Christ*, Downers Grove, IL, InterVarsity Press, 1986.

The Book of Common Prayer, according to the use of The Episcopal Church, Seabury Press, 1979.

A.W. Tozer, *The Knowledge of the Holy*, New York, NY: Harper & Row Publishers, 1961.

David Watson, *Fear No Evil*, Wheaton, IL: Harold Shaw Publishers, 1984.

Dallas Willard, *The Spirit of the Disciplines: Understanding How God Changes Lives*, New York, NY: HarperCollins Publishers, 1988.

Dan Wooding, *He Intends Victory*, Irvine, CA: Village Books Publishing, 1994.

About Embracing Life Ministries

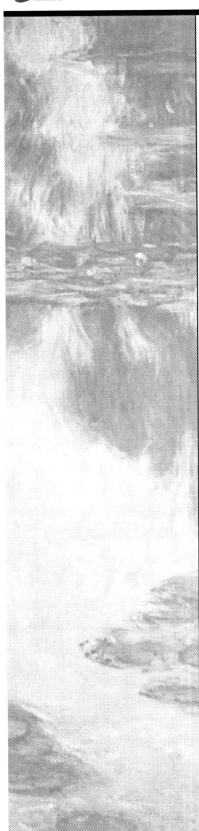

Mission Statement

Embracing Life Ministries extends encouragement, healing and Christian discipleship for those with life-altering conditions. Through equipping seminars, leadership trainings and small groups, Embracing Life prepares the Body of Christ to effectively minister transforming life and healing to others.

For more information
and other resources
contact Embracing Life Ministries:

www.embracinglife.us

Pasadena, California USA

CPSIA information can be obtained at www.ICGtesting.com
Printed in the USA
LVOW051606120112

263602LV00004B/17/A